China Turning Inward

HARVARD EAST ASIAN MONOGRAPHS
132

兩宋之際

文化內向

半賓

CHINA TURNING INWARD

Intellectual-Political Changes
in the
Early Twelfth Century

JAMES T. C. LIU

Published by COUNCIL ON EAST ASIAN STUDIES, HARVARD UNIVERSITY, and distributed by HARVARD UNIVERSITY PRESS, Cambridge (Massachusetts) and London   *1988*

Printed in the United States of America

Chapter Seven is a revised version of the author's article, "How Did a Neo-Confucian School Become the Orthodoxy?" and is reprinted with permission from *Philosophy East and West* Vol. 23, no. 4 (1973).

The Council on East Asian Studies at Harvard University publishes a monograph series and, through the John King Fairbank Center for East Asian Research and the Edwin O. Reischauer Institute of Japanese Studies, administers research projects designed to further scholarly understanding of China, Japan, Vietman, Inner Asia, and adjacent areas.

Library of Congress Cataloging-in-Publication Data

Liu, James T. C., 1919–
    China turning inward : intellectual-political changes in the early
twelfth century / James T. C. Liu.
       p. cm. – (Harvard East Asian monographs : 132)
      Bibliography: p.
      Includes index.
      ISBN 0-674-11725-5 :
      1. China–History–Sung dynasty. 960–1279.   2. China–Intellectual
life–960–1644.   3. Neo-Confucianism.   I. Title.   II. Series.
DS751.L56   1988
951'.02–dc19   88-3579
                                      CIP

Contents

Preface

A fascinating turn occurred in China's long history during the eleventh and twelfth centuries. With much dynamism, it seems that the on-going cultural transformation might have pushed on further toward more outreaching changes. Yet the opposite took place. The cultural pattern settled into a stable, internally reinforcing and therefore rigid one. In fact, this pattern permeated the whole country and persisted till the beginning of the twentieth century. What happened? The problem concerns not only Chinese history but represents an important case in world history.

Some textbooks describe this period, Sung China, as "early modern." Impressive were the rise of enormous cities, the flourishing of urbanism, the technological progress in handicraft industries, the expansion of trade, and the amazing use of paper currency which was hardly conceivable in other cultures. These and other economic developments were accompanied by a mature civil service system, civilian supremacy in the government, respect for law, the spread of education, manifold achievements in arts and literature, and last, but by no means least, the Neo-Confucian reconstruction of the ancient heritage. Sung China thus looks quite similar in development to modern Europe, except that it occurred much earlier.

The present research holds a different view. It rests on the hypothesis that different cultures do not conform to a universal model, because they do not evolve along a single track through the same sequence of definite stages. On the contrary, the center of gravity often varies in one culture as opposed to another.

Historians in Asia as well as the West who see Sung China as an "early modern" period have understandably used European history as a yardstick in the interest of comparative history or global history.

Likewise, they put much emphasis on economic factors. But such factors, no matter how important, did not necessarily constitute the center of gravity in the pre-modern Chinese culture. In the case of Sung China, it seems, politics in close relation to intellectual trends, occupied the central stage. They were not the full or direct reflections of economic interests.

One may describe Sung China as having an absolutist head, a bureaucratic body, and many plebeian hands and feet. By and large, the bureaucratic ruling class imposed regulations on and took advantage of the economic progress. It would not allow merchants or merchant interests to have a strong voice in determining policies. While some descendants of merchants through the vertical social mobility of the examination system did join the ruling class, they were by then assimilated into the scholar-official subculture, thereby ceasing to represent their family economic background.

Sung China cannot be described as "early modern," for there was no late modern afterwards, not even with the coming of the modern West. In the Chinese path of evolution, the Sung pattern was a most developed and advanced bureaucratic society. Only some of its achievements superficially resemble what is known later as modern in the European sense of the term.

If this is so, how did the Sung ruling class, developing and advancing in many ways, stop short of becoming outreaching? How did it on the contrary tend to turn inward? This is the focal question the present book seeks to explore.

To many, the author has been much indebted: to my wife, Dr. Hui-chen Wang Liu, for her sustaining forbearance and forgiveness; to the late Professor William Hung (Hung Yeh) of Yenching University in China and Harvard-Yenching Institute in this country, for his various demonstrations of scholarship; to the late Professor Leland D. Baldwin and Professor George B. Fowler at the University of Pittsburgh, my alma mater, for their stress on balanced views; to Professor Emeritus Lien-sheng Yang of Harvard University, for his encyclopedic knowledge and generous advice during my visits to Cambridge through the years; to the late Professor Anatole Mazour and also Professor Albert E. Dien, for encouraging me in my years at Stanford; to Professor Tu Wei-ming, for constantly stimulating me during our joint efforts of course work and book editing when he was at Princeton before going on to the University of California at Berkeley and then back to Harvard; and to Professor Willard J. Peterson of Princeton, who joined me in a seminar and kindly remains interested in my research.

While errors in this volume are exclusively my own, I have also benefited from numerous exchanges with a number of scholars overseas: Professor Sung Shee and Professor Wang Teh-yi among others in Taipei; Professors Teng Kuang-ming (Deng Guangming), Wang Tseng-yü (Zengyu), and Ch'en Chih-ch'ao (Zhichao) in Beijing, to mention but a few; the late Professor Aoyama Sadao and particularly professor Shiba Yoshinobu in Tokyo; and last, but by no means the least, Professors Miyazaki Ichisada, Saeki Tomi, Chukusa Masaaki, Umehara Kaoru, and Kinugawa Tsuyoshi in Kyoto.

Finally, thanks are due to Dr. Katherine Keenum of the Council on East Asian Studies Publications, Harvard University, a most helpful and patient editor who put this manuscript in good shape. Dr. James Geiss, my colleague in the Department of East Asian Studies, Princeton University, has also given me numerous suggestions on writing.

China Turning Inward

Prologue

The Southern Sung dynasty (1127–1276) was born of war and calamity, yet the political and intellectual developments of its first tumultuous decades were to shape China for centuries. In some ways, the precipitating crisis—conquest by an alien, pastoralist people—fits the broad outline of a pattern in Chinese history. Therefore, just as the men and events to be studied closely here illuminate what was to come, so a brief glance back helps delineate the special character of the twelfth century.

The remote background of the period to be discussed was T'ang China, from the seventh to the ninth centuries. Its cosmopolitan, cultural splendor spread from the Pacific coast to Central Asia. The highest civilization of its time, it enjoyed loose contacts with Persia and India. Europe was totally unknown, hidden, distant, backward. At the turn of the tenth century, however, T'ang China plunged into misery as regional military usurpers or warlords set up separate kingdoms. To internal disorder were added invasions by aggressive groups of northern nomads, who swept down the line of the legendary Great Wall into parts of North China. To the native Han Chinese on the farming plains, they were alien conquerors; yet many of them absorbed an assortment of T'ang cultural elements, mixing these with their own.

Chronic disorder and invasions notwithstanding, Han China, by virtue of a large population, wide geographic base, and long tradition, held its own. In fact, vigorous economic growth sprang up in parts of the Yangtze River valley and farther south. As soon as peace returned, Han culture flourished once again with new and greater strength under the Sung (960–1276).

Sung China reunified most of the T'ang farming regions, though not all parts of the empire. Peace was bought from its aggressive new neighbor in the north, the Khitan empire, through tribute, a practice common throughout Asia when a sedentary country was confronted by a horseback adversary. Then a century and a half later came more conquerors of pastoralist origin, the Jurchens. At first, in alliance with the Sung, they helped destroy the Khitan empire. But then they moved on to take the whole Yellow River valley, the cradle of Chinese civilization, lovingly revered by the Han people as the central plain. Calling themselves the Chin or "Golden" Empire, the Jurchens asserted their superiority and demanded a much higher annual tribute than had been paid the Khitan. No irredentist attempt by Sung China ever got the north back. Central and south China, however, almost two-thirds of the original empire, survived under the restored court, which was afterwards known as the Southern Sung.

The story of these contending empires—one in the north and the other in the south—was drawn to a close in the thirteenth century by yet another people, the nomadic Mongols. These world conquerors, like whirlwinds, overran the vast Eurasian landmass from the Yellow Sea to the gates of Vienna. Inside China, their dynasty went by the name of Yuan (1279–1368); and gradually like the tribesmen who had superseded the T'ang, they adopted Han ways. When the age of exploration in the West began the expansion of Europe, the course of world history was altered; but the Chinese continued evolving their own separate culture in their own separate way. The most characteristic features of Han Chinese life in the Sung remained recognizable in China until the twentieth century.

The major pattern of conquest by outsiders, then, is balanced by the persistence of Han culture. Nevertheless, although it was long-enduring, that culture was not static. The broad outlines tell one set of truths; but to understand the full picture, it is necessary to look closely at the smaller strokes to see what set the patterns. Despite similarities, each dynasty had its own characteristics. In the case of Sung China, it is important to see what shaped the Southern Sung as a period distinct from the Northern Sung (960–1126) in order to understand why, in subsequent centuries, cherished traditions evolved in the ways that they did. This book begins, therefore, with a focus on contrasts that will lead to a study of the ways that politics and intellectual developments affected each other in twelfth-century China.

Part One
From the Northern to the Southern Sung

ONE

A Focus on Contrasts

Like traditional Chinese sources, modern historians tend to divide Chinese history by dynasties. Treating the Sung—the Northern and the Southern—as one time period, however, can be a trap. True enough, after the fall of the northern capital at K'ai-feng and the revered central plain to the Jurchens, the imperial house and government that survived in the south considered themselves to be the legitimate continuation of the Sung dynasty. China, nevertheless, underwent significant changes. Even before the fall of the north, the economic center of gravity had been shifting to the Yangtze delta, where the Southern Sung made its capital at Lin-an (modern Hang-chou).[1] There were, moreover, intellectual and political changes. These are the subject of the present study. A critical point of transformation occurred at the beginning of the Southern Sung. Not only was the second half of the dynasty quite different from the first, but the changes that affected it also shaped subsequent centuries.

Although modern historians often overlook the differences between the two parts of the Sung dynasty, they are readier to see a great divide between the T'ang and early Sung, a division that separates ancient China from later times. More than that, some of them see in the Sung a great forward movement in world history because many features of Sung life appear to be similar to developments that occurred in modern Europe centuries later.[2]

In government, for instance, the Sung adopted and developed the T'ang form of bureaucratic administration.[3] Under the emperor was an enormous centralized administration that consisted of scholar-officials, most of whom had entered the civil service by way of impartial, written examinations and come up through the ranks by seniority, merit ratings, and recommendations. They conducted governmental affairs in accord with specific laws, codes, regulations, rules, and collected precedents. Because these bureaucrats were not an hereditary aristocracy with far-off, feudal domains, they took up permanent abode in the cities. Sung China had as many as two dozen cities with a population of over one hundred thousand people. When Venice and Paris were cities of a hundred thousand,[4] the Northern Sung capital of K'ai-feng was a city of a million and the metropolitan area of the Southern Sung capital at Lin-an encompassed a million and a half. These and other large cities, furthermore, were cosmopolitan.[5] Trade, artisans' crafts, and entertainments flourished in them. Confucian, Taoist, and Buddhist practices and festivals coexisted. Paper currency was used,[6] and the printing press (though not yet movable type) made books readily available and relatively cheap. The comfortable scholar-officials lived in neighborhoods adjoining the working classes, and each saw the other daily. Officials, merchants, pilgrims, and roving performers carried urban culture through the countryside as they traveled between cities; and laborers returned to rural homes for celebrations, bringing the latest with them. Although there were national markets for only a few goods, many-stepped channels of distribution organized regional and local trade in such goods as rice, tea, and silk.

Important as urban life was to the life of the country, the economy rested on agriculture, and on an agriculture that was the most productive and technologically advanced in the world.[7] The introduction of early-ripening rice made two crops a year on a single piece of land feasible while Europe lagged behind with the two-field or three-field systems that left a half or a third of all arable land fallow each year. Productivity continued to rise in China as a result of such innovations as sealed waterpipes for irrigation and water-driven machinery for pumping, draining, threshing, and milling; and approximately two acres per person were under cultivation, making Sung China the richest agricultural country of its time. Manufacturing also made advances in the production of such quality goods as porcelain; and many processes were carried out in factories that employed as many as five hundred workers operating on a system of division of labor.[8]

Because all these aspects of life in the Sung sound modern, the period is sometimes labeled as the early modern period in China.[9] There is, however, a flaw in this view: Sung China was not followed by continued modernization nor by late modern developments. Paradoxically, along with its modern-looking dimensions, it evolved a tenacious heritage. Whatever may be described as early modern features were frozen inside a rigid cultural pattern; they continued to grow, not by reaching out to new ideas and technologies but by modifying those within. Despite the rise in commercialism and an expanding economy, for instance, scholar-officials continued to look down on commerce and manufacture, preferring to pursue a classical education and government careers. Next to the government as an institution, the bureaucrats as individuals were the primary consumers of commercial goods; but they did not otherwise contribute to trade developments. Nor, after the Reform of Wang An-shih in the mid-eleventh century, did they show much interest in economic planning by the state. In times of uncertainty, they stressed thrift instead and reiterated the Confucian emphasis on patrilineal kinship groups as the source of mutual aid.[10] The rituals of ancestor worship and the practical responsibilities of the Confucian family were emphasized in books of instruction for much the same reasons that they were first enunciated centuries before in an aristocratic culture that sought security through a system of personal bonds.[11] In these and many other ways, Sung China and especially the Southern Sung looked backward and inward. What would explain this rather strange turn of events? Something must have happened to turn many broad sweeps of outward-reaching advance into an intricate weaving of inward refinement and reinforcement.

It would probably be less confusing if we did not try to relate the changes in Sung China to those in modern Europe, their superficial similarities notwithstanding.[12] The forces and conditions that produced changes in Sung China were entirely different from those that eventually caused Europe to develop in the modern era. Sung China saw innovations as well as renovation of accepted ways, the opening up of new dimensions and the reconstruction of inherited approaches to life; but the paths taken were uniquely Chinese. The period from the Sung on may be called neo-traditional to signify that in redeveloping China's culture, the new changes were based on the old foundation and accepted as part of the lasting tradition. This tradition was not a stagnant constant but an organism frequently undergoing modification, renewal, enrichment, and reinforcement.

To use an analogy, Sung China looks like an old, luxuriant tree surprisingly vigorous as it grows taller and larger than before, with new branches and fresh leaves spreading all over it. Old roots sprawl beneath the trunk. Then a stormy season somehow saps the vigor of its internal chemistry. The vitality that remains is turned to protective functions. The tree manages to keep on growing quite sturdily, but it remains the same size and shape. What was the critical change, then, of its internal chemistry?

Looking closely at both early- and late-Sung China, historians are often more impressed by the multifarious advances of the eleventh century or mid-Northern Sung than by their further transformation during the twelfth century or the Southern Sung. An even closer scrutiny, however, sharpens the perspectives. Among the seemingly continuing trends of the twelfth century, qualitative changes have occurred.

A quick way to grasp the qualitative differences between these two centuries is to accentuate their arresting contrasts. Methodologically this is permissible so long as it is clearly understood that the contrasts are not full representations of the facts. They are the pictures we perceive from our way of looking at them, much like what we capture through a magnifying glass under specific lights.

The eleventh century was a time when culture among the elite expanded. It pioneered in new directions and blazed promising trails. With optimism it emphasized prospects. In contrast, the twelfth century saw elite culture paying more attention to consolidating and extending its values throughout society. Turning more retrospective and introspective than before, it became tempered by a circumspect and sometimes pessimistic tone. In short, while the Northern Sung characteristically reached outward, the Southern Sung essentially looked inward.

A tendency to continue, synthesize, and refine does not mean that the elite culture of the twelfth century turned conservative. The facile word *conservative* hardly does justice to it; for, in fact, it did not stop growing. On the contrary, it pushed on to greater depth and intensity, and on occasion greater height, than in earlier times. Its values permeated all levels of society and, above all, became ingrained in Chinese life across the land. This was especially due to the efforts of new variety of Confucian philosopher, often referred to as Neo-Confucians, who devoted themselves to educational and social reconstruction. No other group among Chinese intellectuals had ever done so much for so many people.[13] Their efforts, however, were largely directed toward pursuits along defined channels with few attempts made in searching for new ones. In short, the elite culture developed; but stayed *within* accepted categories. Its creativity was contained. In this sense, the present study takes the view that, on the whole, Chinese culture from the twelfth century on turned *inward*. The question, of course, remains, why?

THE CLUES AND THE APPROACH

Historians tend to emphasize one of the two Sung periods, depending on what attracts their attention. For instance, there are many works on the government affairs of the Northern Sung, but relatively few on those of the Southern Sung. The opposite is true in economic history and art history. In the history of philosophy, much scholarship is devoted to the dominant Southern Sung figure of Chu Hsi (1130–1200), the synthesizer and founder of the Neo-Confucian orthodoxy, who has sometimes been compared to Thomas Aquinas. Yet these otherwise satisfactory books take little explicit notice of the changes that took place between the eleventh and the twelfth centuries. Nevertheless, on the problem of why such changes did occur, the standard books offer a few suggestions that do not go far enough, but provide some useful clues to the answer we seek.[14]

The first suggestion is geo-political: When the Southern Sung empire was reduced in size and demoted to second-class rank in relation with the Jurchens, its scholar-officials tended to lower their sights and narrow their perspectives. This theory, though plausible, is not quite adequate. The Northern Sung scholar-officials had belonged to an empire much smaller than the previous T'ang without suffering a comparable sense of limitation. Nor should one underestimate the geographical size of the Southern Sung. The southwest extended as an interior frontier, while improved means of transportation nearly everywhere made the far reaches of the country more accessible. The scholar-officials could, if they chose, travel to broaden their perspectives; yet few of them did. Likewise, while more sea routes opened up, only a handful of scholar-officials were among those who traded with, visited, and settled down in Vietnam and Thailand. In any case, regardless of the comparative military and diplomatic weaknesses of the Southern Sung, nothing challenged the supremacy of its culture or its awareness of that supremacy.

The second suggestion is related to the first: Huge military expenditures occasioned by external threats and wasteful administration left insufficient resources for cultural development. It is true that the military drained resources. Yet how decisive a role in cultural development was played by resource availability, a relative factor, is doubtful. Furthermore, there is another question: Did the scholar-officials try hard to marshal more than what they had from the state and various local groups for what they aspired to do culturally?

The third suggestion reflects conventional Marxist thinking. Wealth concentrated in the hands of landlords or the landowning class led to their indulgence in comfort, pleasure, and luxuries. They neither reinvested for economic expansion nor supported cultural growth. But the landed class as an economic group and the scholar-officials overlapped to a great extent as the ruling class and as the cultural elite. This line of reasoning in effect merely alleges that in the economic and cultural domains, the interests of the ruling class were against those of the ruled, even of the society at large. While this may be so, what would explain the splendid cultural progress achieved earlier by the Northern Sung whose social structure had been the same?

The fourth suggestion is a standard one in traditional Chinese historiography. The emperors failed to listen to good Confucian advice and made bad decisions. When they reigned but did not rule personally, things got worse. The surrogates to whom they delegated power misruled and ruined the empire. This is true insofar as it goes; but it does not quite answer our question. No doubt surrogates shaped policies and politics. But how did bad policies and politics affect the cultural outlook of the intellectuals? Is there not a missing link somewhere?

These suggestions should not be dismissed out of hand. They are helpful clues leading to an answer. For example, the scholar-officials in the Southern Sung do seem to have been geographically limited in their outlook, not because the empire was smaller than before, but because they themselves stayed too close together. On account of their interest in politics, they preferred to stay as long as possible in the capital area around Lin-an. For private residences and land properties, they chose to buy in a region near it, on either side of the Hang-chou bay, either in the Yangtze delta or in eastern Chekiang. Lin-an was, as a matter of fact, far more beautiful and more pleasant in climate than the old capital at K'ai-feng.[15] The Yangtze delta and the Lake Tai area of Chekiang, moreover, were long the centers of culture in China, as can be seen, for example, in the history of Chinese painting. When Kai-feng ceased to be the capital, the bureaucrats, who were the most important element in most Chinese cities, left. And when the bureaucrats left, the city dwindled to provincial insignificance. In contrast, even after Lin-an ceased to be the political capital, its natural endowments, its commercial advantages as a port city, and its position at the juncture of two cultural corridors caused it to continue to flourish. The narrow perspective of the Southern Sung scholar-officials may, paradoxically, have been partly the result of not needing to look very far from their own doorsteps.

In response to the suggestions that funds were diverted to the military or to landowners' luxuries, one may turn to the variety within Confucianism. Under the New Policies of Wang An-shih, the Northern Sung had seen drastic attempts to introduce administrative reforms, to seek the development of economic resources, to curb the abuses and defects in the tax system, and to introduce significant changes in various institutions.[16] To discontinue such efforts was not merely an economic matter. It was a political decision that concerned the whole ruling class with land property, as Marxist and other economic interpretations of history generally claim. The policy decision, however, also depended upon the prevailing intellectual orientation or what kind of bureaucratic leadership was in power.

This leads to the fourth or traditional explanation. Besides determining the merits or demerits of emperors or surrogates, modern political science would seek further explanation: how much power they had and how much they shared with others. This would entail an examination of the variations in the power structure. When the court and the bureaucracy effectively controlled the armies and the local government units, we say that the central control was strong. When an emperor or his surrogate personally or institutionally exercised this control with little more than routine assistance of the bureaucracy, we call it concentration of power at court. When either of them or both made irreversible decisions with little bureaucratic participation or input, we call it autocracy, a distinct mode by which the monarchial structure functioned.

Under an autocracy, the bureaucracy shared the administrative power but had little share in making policy. When an autocrat or an extraordinary official elevated to be an autocratic surrogate disallowed or even suppressed competing views from other officials as well as from intellectuals no longer in the bureaucracy and private scholars who expressed strong beliefs, autocracy escalated into absolutism, yet another mode in the functioning of the monarchial structure. The essence of absolutism was not only the disappearance of any shared policy-making power but also the negation of the authority of an ideology, such as Confucianism, independent of its state-approved formulation. But it was not despotic. For it set the laws and functioned in an orderly manner. These designations—central control, concentration of power, autocracy, and absolutism—merely serve us as reference points. In reality, the power structure functioned in overlapping ways.

Under the Sung emperors and their surrogates, the ordinary bureaucrats at the next echelon had their administrative jurisdiction. They could play their political role by expressing their individual opinions either officially or privately. The Chinese referred to these elements in the ruling class as scholar-officials (*shih ta-fu*). It is interesting that Marxist-influenced scholars denounce them, just as both traditional and other modern Chinese scholars tend to criticize them, without in either case undertaking much analysis of their political role and, not too far removed from politics, their intellectual role. To ignore these active elements would be to miss a great deal of history or reality.

Who were the Sung scholar-officials? Sometimes referred to as the "gentry," they were individuals who had a Confucian education in the classics and related knowledge. Upon recommendation or through success in state examinations they became permanent members of the civil service or career bureaucrats. As such, they constituted the ruling class.

They owned land; but in the value scale of the Chinese social structure, their ownership of land properties carried far less weight than their access to power, the status of their rank, and the prestige of their learning, normally in that order. Since they were both scholars and officials, the inquiry here will accordingly examine how the intellectual and political dimensions in their activities intertwined.

By Sung times, as prosperity and education spread, more books were printed, and the civil service examinations became greatly attractive, the rank of aspiring scholars and successful scholar-officials swelled. We will not, however, study most of them, but focus on the small number of top intellectuals among them.

What is meant here by an intellectual? It is not synonymous with such broad terms as scholar, writer, man of learning, academician, teacher, nor even knowledgeable official or wise statesman. An intellectual was an outstanding scholar with an elite status who by his recognized achievement in learning, usually in combination with an official position or previous government experience, was able to share his concern for universal values of the state and the society with others and through such communication influence or try to influence broad trends in thought and public affairs. This definition excludes most of the ordinary literati, who were socially lower than the elite and who were referred to as "the plain-clothed" (*pu-i*) because they were not permitted to wear silk, an elite status symbol reserved only for those who had an official degree or rank. It was true that a few who remained "plain-clothed" stood out as private scholars on account of their renowned learning, which earned them the respect or patronage of some leading scholar-officials. But such private scholars were not the social equals of the elite and generally lacked power, though they might be prominent in local education or in other community activities. Strictly speaking, however, we cannot regard them as intellectuals unless they had some influence on the broad intellectual-political trends of the time. The same standard holds with respect to degree-holders and scholar-officials; some of them were more learned than others or more respected by their peers for their outstanding knowledge or other accomplishments. They were high on the social scale, but they were not necessarily intellectuals.

The universal values cherished by the Sung intellectuals usually concerned two major areas: state affairs and general welfare of the society.[17] He studied such values in a search for true knowledge or what was called among some Confucians the *tao* or "the way," usually beyond the narrow confines of particular academic specialties.[18] Although in most cases he took the examinations to become an official, his prime motivation was greater than desire for a bureaucratic career.[19] As a bureaucrat, he did not confine himself to the routine matters of his office but continued to express a general interest in state policies, in moral standards, in the conduct of the elite, in philosophical orientations, in social welfare, in education—in short, in the ideal Confucian way of life. When in opposition to the current state policies, though still serving in the government, or after leaving the bureaucracy as a result of dismissal or resignation, he became a part of the adversarial elite with the same concern as before. Thus in all circumstances, he had an urge to communicate with others. He knew that to realize these values, isolated actions would not suffice. He would need to persuade others to go in the same direction. In short, the intellectuals were the leading actors on the political-intellectual stage.

This definition of the intellectuals is by no means peculiar to Sung China. A concern for national affairs and recognition of the need for active communication were common to intellectuals of other cultures, such as those on the eve of the French Revolution (when the word *intellectual* first came into circulation) and the intelligentsia of the Russian Revolution. Only the modern context of revolution is irrelevant to the Sung period, for the Chinese intellectuals' belief in Confucianism had nothing to do with changing the social order by violent means.[20]

THE DATA AND THE HYPOTHESIS

To analyze the changes between the Northern and the Southern Sung, it is natural to focus on the time interval from the Jurchen invasion through the time of the restoring emperor, Kao-tsung (r. 1127–1162), who succeeded in reviving the regime in the south. Not only is this literally the period of changeover, but a chain of key events at this time had long-range political and intellectual consequences. Yet, strange as it may seem, past studies have concentrated only on war heroes and the humiliating peace accepted by the southern court. There is, nevertheless, ample information available on the court politics and intellectual atmosphere of the time. The standard sources include the *Sung Dynastic History* (*Sung-shih; SS*), a partially extant collection of selected government documents (*Sung Hui-yao chi kao; SHY*), encyclopedias such as the *Comprehensive Studies of Documentary Evidence* (*Wen-hsien t'ung-k'ao; WHTK*), other collections and compilations, a fair number of collected works by scholar-officials, and miscellaneous informal writings.[21]

Since this was a period of crisis for the empire, two perceptive historians devoted their attention to it soon afterwards and each left an invaluable work. The first is a compilation called *Sources on the Jurchen Relations under the Three Sung Reigns* (*San-ch'ao pei-meng hui-pien; PMHP*).[22] While the selected sources are attached to the major events in chronological order, the connections between what is said in one piece and what comes up later are often not clear. The compiler tried neither to organize the information nor to evaluate it, but we are grateful to him for gathering the information from 196 prime sources, in addition to other scattered writings of scholar-officials.

The second work by Li Hsin-ch'uan, a renowned historian, is a model compilation. The title is *Chien-yen i-lai hsi-nien yao-lu* (*HNYL*).[23] As Chien-yen was the initial reign title of the restoring emperor, this work may be called *The Essential Annals from the Beginning of the Southern Sung*. It is generally agreed that Li's scholarship ranks with the best in transmitting with minimal bias a maximal amount of information. Neither of these two qualities was easily attainable in dealing with a time of trouble. When, around 1800, traditional Chinese historiography reached the zenith of emphasis on evidential research, a monumental work—the *Sequel to the Comprehensive Mirror in Aid of Government* (*Hsu tzu-chih t'ung-chien; HTC*), compiled with the help of several eminent historians—invariably cited the *HNYL*. Only in a very few instances did they find minor errors in it.[24]

Yet after the Sung, during the period of the Mongols, the *HNYL* was somehow missing from government and leading libraries. Much to our surprise and regret, the official editors of the *SS* never saw it. Fortunately this work was found later on in the early Ming and quietly incorporated into the multitude of collections in the immense encyclopedia of the early fifteenth century known as the *Yung-lo ta-tien* without coming to the attention of historians. Only as late as 1773 was it "rediscovered" and restored as a separate book. This puts us in a favorable position over previous studies that have relied mainly on the standard history. In fact, most data in this study come from the *HNYL*.

A careful examination of this work suggests that within the transitional period there were three overlapping phases, each of which had a theme. In phase one, the Jurchen invasion and the tragic fall of the Northern Sung caused both unexpected shocks and humiliation. Most shocking to the intellectuals were the many acts of infamous misconduct by scholar-officials whom they either knew or had heard of. Apparently the existing Confucianism, despite its variety and richness of content, had not helped to prevent shocking wrongdoings. This rude awakening prompted disillusioned intellectuals to make a fresh start. They believed that the Confucian heritage was in urgent need of reconstruction and reinforcement. The first theme, then, is shock and response.

The theme of the second phase, which lasted roughly from the selection of Hang-chou as the court's temporary location in 1132 until its formal designation as the capital in 1138, is the shift of emphasis from institutional to moral concerns. Many intellectuals in the early Southern Sung rightly or wrongly regarded and even condemned the assertive Reform of 1069–1085 and its revival in 1093–1125 as the cause of degeneration that led to the fall of the empire. The restoring emperor agreed with them. The door was thereupon closed to reform in general or any kind of institutional change. Moreover, the very concept of dynastic restoration was nostalgic and implied a conservative outlook, a wish to go back to the glorious days of the founding emperors or at least the good old days before the Reform. Some of the intellectuals, aroused by indignation against the Reform and its aftermath, not only supported conservatism but did so from a perspective that stressed morality in the interpretation of the Confucian heritage. They believed that the moral way is the *only way.* Both the state and society must be persuaded to follow. Hence, we refer to these intellectuals as moralistic conservatives.

The third phase lasted a long time, from the beginning of peace negotiations with the Jurchens in 1139 until 1162 when the restoration emperor chose to abdicate. It witnessed the defeat of the Confucian concerns or ideals of the moralistic conservatives by the reality of power politics. Contrary to their expectations, these intellectuals found the court had become autocratic and sometimes even absolutist. The demands of the war years had made the emperor eager to gather more power in his own hands for the sake of both external and internal security. It was considered necessary both to make the Jurchens stop their invasions and to strip military power from the generals who were thought to be not loyal or obedient enough. On the paramount issue of war or peace, the emperor chose to make the decision by himself alone. He decided to accept peace in 1141 at the cost of humiliating terms and to delegate power to a surrogate in order to silence those who opposed. A chain reaction followed. The objecting intellectuals, mostly conservatives who argued on moral grounds, persisted in voicing their criticism through means outside the government. The surrogate, Ch'in Kuei (1090–1155), with the apparent approval of the emperor, broadened the punishment of critics of the peace terms into a general policy of discouraging intellectual dissent.[25] The effectiveness of this suppression escalated autocracy to absolutism. Although the surrogate died in 1155, the suffocating atmosphere hung on. While the emperor modified some of its severity, he did not abandon it, let alone reverse it.

Throughout this critical process of intricate transitions, intellectual diversity had little chance to survive or revive. Vigor vanished first from politics and then from intellectual life. A subdued and cautious mood gradually spread into other areas of the elite culture. When the intellectuals changed, other scholar-officials watched and then followed. When the elite went that way, the ruling class as a whole leaned toward the same direction. The ripple effect affected the entire society. The pattern of traditional Chinese culture changed forever.

The three phases of transition were over when the reign of the restoring emperor ended. Thereafter, the intellectual-political atmosphere markedly improved, allowing the voicing of criticism and dissenting opinions. This openness lasted for some thirty years into the 1190s. In the last decade of the twelfth century, however, an acute crisis occurred in the imperial succession. The outcome was the rise of another surrogate, Han T'o-chou (1152–1207), under the fourth emperor, Ning-tsung (r. 1195–1224), who reigned but hardly ruled. In order to remove and silence his critics, this aggressive but insecure surrogate formally banned the Neo-Confucians, who were the heirs of the moralistic conservatives and followers of Chu Hsi.

The persecution of Neo-Confucians darkened the political and intellectual atmosphere. Only after an ill-advised war against the Jurchens that ended in defeat and the ensuing assassination of the surrogate Han T'o-chou did the situation improve slowly. While some Neo-Confucian followers came to be prominent at court afterwards, they could neither break the conformity, nor widen the intellectual horizons. They championed their beliefs as the orthodox tradition of Confucianism in the hope of rubbing the rough absolutist edges off autocracy. They won in a nominal sense, for the state ultimately recognized the doctrines they advocated as the state orthodoxy or ideology. Yet it turned out to be a pyrrhic victory, for the autocracy was never sincere in translating Neo-Confucian values into concrete policies. In intellectual terms, the newly established orthodoxy for its part paradoxically added another measure of conformity at the expense of dynamic growth and outreaching diversity.

For better or worse, Neo-Confucianism permeated the whole society and endured. Not until 1898, with the impact of the West and the victory of Japan in war, was the desperate need for modern reform driven home. While successive generations of concerned intellectuals debated changes, traditional China was disintegrating.

To sum up, in order to see the picture in context as well as in depth, it helps to change lenses and look from different angles. After a view of the varieties of Confucians in general and those of moral and conservative persuasion in particular, the lens is changed to show how the conservatives fared, depending on the relationship between the autocratic emperor and the councilors he chose. To examine that relationship in depth, a case study takes a microscopic look at the career of one chief councilor. This is followed by a look at the aftermath, the emergence of state orthodoxy, through a macroscopic lens. Finally, changing the lens again, the relevancy to the present day is seen by a telescopic sighting.

TWO

Sung Learning

To understand what happened politically in the Southern Sung, one must understand the intellectual climate as well as the impact of war, economics, and the ambitions of individual leaders. For in traditional China, scholar-officials were by training and culture men for whom intellectual pursuits were a way of life. To view them simply as politicians or bureaucrats interested only in the acquisition and exercise of power is to overlook major elements of their thought, motivation, interests, and environment. The major path to government was through the state examination system, which tested a man's literary ability and understanding of the classics. As a result, by the time they joined the bureaucracy, usually in their thirties, most scholar-officials had acquired literary tastes and opinions on intellectual issues; and many had acquired a deep commitment to what in modern terms would be called an ideology. This was particularly true of the best among them who served at court. Their habits and beliefs influenced their actions, and the quality of learning that prevailed at any given time shaped those habits and beliefs.

This chapter, therefore, examines three of the four traditional branches of Chinese learning—literature, classical studies, and historical writing. The fourth, philosophy in the form of Confucianism, is discussed in the next chapter. Together, these two chapters provide an integrated yet succinct overview of Sung learning, something that is not often available elsewhere. There have been a number of books devoted exclusively to Sung philosophy, others to Sung literature. For classical studies and historical writing, however, discussions of Sung contributions are available only within broad surveys of all periods or in narrowly specialized articles. And rarely has there heretofore been a coherent examination of the four branches together. These two chapters fill that need. In line with the focus of the previous chapter, moreover, the contrast between the eleventh and twelfth centuries is specially examined in each case for clues to why the Southern Sung changed so markedly from the Northern Sung. Furthermore, the next chapter makes clear why Confucianism was all-embracing, influencing the other branches of learning and politics alike.

LITERATURE

In traditional China, literacy for scholar-officials and other educated men meant more than being able to handle routine written documents. In their world, to be well-educated was to compose literary works; and high value was placed on creative pieces in an elegant style. The literati wrote not only as a pleasure, as a means of expression and communication, and as a vehicle of personal advancement, but also to enrich their culture and to shape its growth. Because literary composition was so important to them, they took seriously questions of style and critical theory that in the modern West seldom concern anyone besides the professionals and those who wish to be.

The two leading forms of Chinese literature, regulated verse poetry and literary prose, were the necessary accomplishments of a gentleman as well as the required subjects of state examinations. Others—such as short essays, informal narratives, miscellaneous notes, conventional writings on social occasions, recorded tales, songs, and the like—carried far less weight. Regulated verse poetry was regarded as the highest art form. Historically it occupied the first place of honor, although from the Sung period on prose acquired greater utilitarian value as the principal instrument of effective communication.

While T'ang poetry has won universal acclaim as the finest product of a golden period, Sung poetry of the eleventh century was its worthy successor. It reached maturity of form and content, in many ways different from the T'ang style and yet as splendid. In fact, the T'ang and Sung form a pair of twin peaks.[1] In subsequent periods, only a small number of individual poets ever climbed to such heights again.

One characteristic of Sung poetry was a thrust toward popularity in vocabulary, expression, setting, and theme. Breaking through the limitations of classical vocabulary, poets began to incorporate colloquial expressions and images of daily life into their verses. Their emphasis turned from self-expression to communication directed at other people, if only at other educated people like themselves. A well-known theory in the poetics of this century goes as follows:

> Poets like to follow inspirations. The difficulty they encounter is in finding the right expressions. One does well when he can skillfully express new ideas, setting forth what has never been said by anyone else before. But to qualify as one of the best, he must be able to portray a scene rather hard to describe, to make it come alive, as if it stood right before the eyes, and moreover to convey beyond the explicit words endless implicit meanings.[2]

By the turn of the century, however, numerous poets were pushed by the pressure of intense competition toward complicated tropes, such as packing several layers of metaphors, allegories, and associations in one verse and linking them up with other parts of the poem. Poems, it was said, should be condensed (*ning*) as much as possible and refined by being gone over again and again, like smelting (*lien*) metal in a furnace. This development reflected growth beyond maturity into over-ripeness. Some of these poems show a contrived refinement at the expense of true feelings, while others are difficult to comprehend.

After the general current of T'ang and Northern Sung poetry had run its course by the twelfth century, various streams of specialization went off in diverse directions.[3] Some poets picked up things at hand, even such a minute object as a drop of dew on a fallen leaf or a tiny insect seemingly lost under the moonlight, in order to project their deep feelings in a highly concentrated and abstract form. Other poets focused upon their deep-down feeling of individuality (*hsing*) or moments of lucid inspiration (*ling*). Others aimed at being neither merely skillful nor clever, but skillfully clever (*ch'iao*) in their verbal constructions; or being not just sharp, but pointedly sharp (*chien*). Yet other poets, who did not care so much for such sophisticated and intricate poetic constructions, stressed instead their emotions, sentiments, and feelings by expressing them in great subtlety, minute discrimination, or fine shades of meaning.

By the time these diverse poetic styles reached a point of saturation, a different growth in poetry—the poetic-songs (*tz'u*)—had already taken over the main arena of competition. It had begun with the eleventh-century poets who were stimulated by and borrowed from professional entertainers. The singers were highly accomplished in popular songs, but these poets initiated a new genre, a song not necessarily accompanied by music.[4] At first a minor poetic form, it became in the twelfth century a major one, widely appreciated for its lyrical quality. Even though such poetry was freed from the original musical accompaniment, it always abided by musical rules by transcribing tunes into phonetic patterns with lines of varying length. As a form, it was far more flexible than regulated poetry. Normally, a poetic-song would be longer than a regulated-verse poem, making twists and turns and shifting from one mood to another at different speeds. Mixing colloquial vocabulary and elegant phrases allowed a wider range of lively, vivid, and creative expressions to pinpoint fine shades of meaning as well as a multitude of feelings. In short, the Sung poetic-songs were as supreme a genre in their own right as the T'ang poems.

There was something next to poetry. Verse and prose are in Western usage, dichotomous; nothing exists in between. But in the case of traditional Chinese literature, something did. The genre of *fu*, respected in almost the same way as poetry, stood by its very nature on the borderline between verse and prose. In its original, classical form, a *fu* may be described as a "prose-poem," a kind of wide-ranging poem with much elaboration. From the Northern Sung on, however, a new form emerged. Pulled by the rising prestige of prose, it changed its character into "poetic prose," or prose with highly poetic qualities.

We can hardly afford here to get into the technical intricacies of this genre; perhaps a simplified explanation will be sufficient to illustrate its evolving change. Originally, the *fu* adhered to rigid requirements of parallel or paired sentences that rhyme. The civil service examination, for example, set strict rules on rhyming. As to parallel sentences, they were a pair, one soon after the other, with exactly the same number of words in the same or similar semantic and syntactic order, with each word matched, compounded, contrasted, or otherwise related to the meaning of the corresponding word in the other sentence.

The mid-eleventh century added a new form when several bold and brilliant pioneers made a breakthrough. While they brushed aside the strict technical requirements for both rhymes and sentence patterns, thus gaining a freedom of expression, they still in a natural way made some sentences rhyme here and others pair there. This is, of course, much closer to prose in the Western sense of the word. Yet the Chinese have never regarded such composition as ordinary prose at all. Because it retains or reflects the kind of high poetic qualities as the classic *fu*, it was honored as a new variety and respected as much as the old. In this sense it may be called "poetic prose." This change did not stem from the poetry side; it was stimulated by the powerful rise of prose during the Northern Sung, to which we shall now turn.

Prose had ranked after peotry and *fu* in the value scale of the literati since ancient times. During the T'ang period, the most prestigious form of prose was parallel prose (*p'ien-wen*). In fact, this form had been much influenced by the *fu*. For example, much of it followed a pattern of parallel sentences, usually in the sequences of 4-6-4-6 words in the set of sentences. Hence its informal name was "four-six composition." Despite the prestige of parallel prose, a few nonconformists arose. Freeing themselves from all patterns and restrictions on formal and rhetorical devices, they wrote and advocated a kind of essay that may be described as loose-style prose (*san-wen*).

Prominent among the dissenters was Han Yü (786–824). Upholding ancient Confucian tradition in an attack on both Buddhism and Taoism, he declared, "Literature [*wen*] is to be used to carry the Confucian way." In other words, the proper purpose of prose was to transmit correct ideas. Obviously, neither parallel prose nor a formalistic style was the best means to this end, for they often prevented authors from saying what they wanted to. To practice what he preached, Han Yü championed loose-style prose by developing it along the lines of ancient models. His later admirers claimed that his "ancient style" (or "pseudo-ancient," to describe it objectively) had rectified a mode that had become more decorative than meaningful over the course of centuries.

Early in the eleventh century, a small number of young talents discovered the trail blazed by Han Yü and his contemporary, Liu Tsung-yuan (773–819). When they promoted the cause of Confucianism, they proudly called the mode in which they wrote *ancient-style*. At the pioneering stage, their writings were faulted for being crude and diffuse, sometimes abrupt and awkward; but through continuing efforts, they improved in vocabulary, expression, syntax, sentence construction, composition, and other rhetorical techniques. Although the style reflected not so much a return to the archaic as an advance to new excellence, its champions insisted on the name *ancient-style* because they believed it was the best means of expression to revive the spirit of the ancient Confucian teachings.[5]

A political breakthrough came after hard struggle. Leading this movement was the prominent statesman Ou-yang Hsiu (1007–1072), who made ancient-style prose into a supreme literary form in which ordinary words by artful composition came out in stirring sentences, concise expressions, and elegant pieces that could convey a delicate feeling or profound thought, a grand spectacle or striking notion. In a memorial, Ou-yang Hsiu urged the court to discourage parallel prose and encourage this style in civil service examinations because it offered the best means to express ideas freely in statecraft and philosophy. As the presiding official at one of the examinations, he himself carried out what he had recommended. This had an immediate effect upon aspiring literati in the country, and ancient-style prose rose in popularity. Many did object to the shift in emphasis away from parallel prose on the grounds that parallel prose demonstrated the height of a writer's skill and could be judged with fair objectivity without reference to political opinions; that its use in the examination system had worked well for decades; and that those who opposed it had, in fact, come up through that very system using it. Yet ancient-style prose was destined to be the wave of the future. Once its artistic standing became established, it functioned so admirably well as the principal means of communication among the elite that it continued as the leading mode in Chinese writing until the early twentieth century.

Ou-yang Hsiu played the pivotal role not only in shaping a whole era but in influencing succeeding generations. The centuries from the Southern Sung on honored most the eight masters of ancient-style prose. They were the two T'ang forerunners, Han Yü and Liu Tsung-yuan; Ou-yang Hsiu; his disciple Tseng Kung (1019–1083); his erstwhile protégé and eventual political adversary Wang An-shih (1021–1086), the famous reformer; and Ou-yang's three friends of the same Su family who were best known as Su Shih (Tung-p'o; 1036–1101), his younger brother, Su Ch'e (1039–1112) and their father, Su Hsun (1009–1066).

After the turn of the century, the literary genres specially associated with ancient-style prose slid from the peak. Their quality never equaled that of works written in the Northern Sung. The literati of the Southern Sung did maintain the same lofty stylistic standards and even elaborated on them in theories; but they themselves did not produce masterpieces that would be greatly honored by succeeding generations. One of them compiled a much respected anthology entitled *The Mirror of Sung Prose* (*Sung wen chien*).[6] He made selections only from model authors of the Northern Sung, without including anything of the early Southern Sung closer to his own time. Perhaps it was realized that no recent literary writers were as good as their predecessors of a century ago. Perhaps there was another reason: By this time creative energy no longer went so much into literature. Philosophy came to be greatly emphasized instead, and its transcendental dimensions made it far more challenging than belles-lettres. Philosophy in the form of Confucianism, however, was not a totally isolated, separated branch of learning. It rested on the classics.

STUDIES OF THE CLASSICS

The ancient Chinese classics, though secular in nature, were revered as almost sacred, the work of sages. The Sung Confucians were even more indefatigable than their predecessors in writing numerous commentaries on these authoritative books, which they used as the basis from which to develop theories of their own. Generally speaking, quite a large number of Northern Sung studies on the classics were refreshing, challenging, and original. In the Southern Sung period, the quality of the exegeses began to decline; they became disputatious, minutely attentive to technicalities, and narrowly specialized. They became more diffuse than diverse, and less creative intellectually.

A brief analysis will illuminate the intellectual atmosphere from the eleventh to the twelfth century. On the study of the *Book of Changes* or *Book of Divination* (*I ching*), the main difference in the eleventh century was between those who took the forms and the numbers in the book to be of divine or supernatural origin and those who interpreted it by rational principles. Yet in the twelfth century other approaches were used: Some added historical illustrations to their commentaries; some linked their interpretations to the naturalistic philosophy of Lao-tzu; yet others combined theirs with Ch'an (Zen) Buddhist teachings. The prevailing trend, however, was a compromise between the typological-numerological and a rational approach. Chu Hsi, for instance, did more in synthesizing earlier interpretations than in contributing new ones.[7] The thrust was no longer an outreaching one.

The *Book of Documents* (*Shu ching* or *Shang shu*) suffered from controversies over the authentication of its text, which came down from Han times and contained many words and phrases of dubious and authenticity. Interpretations in the eleventh century varied widely. Wang An-shih wrote a new explanation of it, emphasizing the functions of governmental institutions, just as he did with the *Rituals of Chou*, which he used as the anchor of his reform program. But Su Shih wrote one of the best commentaries, stressing the human side. The vigor of competition declined during the twelfth century. Chu Hsi, critical of Su Shih otherwise, praised his work on this classic; but the Neo-Confucian school after Chu Hsi chose to ignore it because Su had sarcastically attacked Ch'eng I (1033–1107), a pioneer of the school.

The study of the *Book of Songs* or *Book of Poetry* (*Shih ching*) may seem to be an exception to our generalization; for the eleventh century had only a few interpretations and gentle debates, while in contrast, many twelfth century scholars found this classic important and wrote a great deal on it. Their interest was due to the growth of poetry and poetic-songs. As the earliest anthology of Chinese poetry, this classic provided indispensable references. There was a sign of decline in quality, however, amid the apparent expansion. Most studies of this classic, including the one by Chu Hsi, tended to be less than authoritative.[8]

The word *rituals* in the ancient classics did not refer only to ceremonies. It included various aspects of social custom, conventions, economy, and government. To put it in modern terms, it meant formal activities governed by the rules of propriety. Among the three classics on rituals, two were of relatively little importance in the Sung period; but the third, the *Rituals of Chou,* became the object of a great controversy. Before Wang An-shih, there had been a fair diversity among its varying commentaries, characteristic of early-eleventh-century scholarship. Then Wang found in it the model of his Reform. Thereafter, while he and later his followers in the next generation were in power until the end of the Northern Sung in 1127, the majority of scholars followed his commentaries voluntarily or under the pressure of the reform system. Not diversity but conformity prevailed.[9]

When the opposing conservatives briefly returned to power from 1085 to 1093, they tended to downplay the three classics on rituals. This inadvertently narrowed the intellectual horizon still further. For their part, the conservatives advanced a chronological classic, *The Spring and Autumn Annals* (*Ch'un-ch'iu*). Since the wording in this historical record emphasized proper status and moral concerns, as reputedly edited by Confucius himself, the conservatives relied on it to distinguish justifiable from improper behavior. They argued along with an earlier scholar, Sun Fu (992–1057), that the *Annals* fosters great respect and loyalty to the sovereign. But they would not follow another scholar, Liu Ch'ang (1019–1068), who had boldly pointed out textual errors in the *Annals* that would make emendation necessary. Nor did they value new interpretations by Liu or anyone else. In the meantime, the followers of Wang An-shih resisted this classic, for Wang had characterized it as a compilation made up of "torn and worn court bulletins" (*tuan lan ch'ao pao*). Diversity suffered from the factional dispute.

Under the conservatives' influence, the *Annals* regained prominence in the Southern Sung, but without much intellectual growth in the commentaries. Some intellectuals used it to comment on current events and developed from it their art of disputation. Both were popular approaches, but neither produced much high-quality scholarship.

There was, however, one very important result of the Northern Sung conservative interest in the *Annals.* Ssu-ma Kung (1019–1086) took it as a model and compiled a monumental sequel to it, going from where the *Annals* ends (481 B.C.) to the eve of the Sung (959 A.D.). Its effect on the writing of other histories will be discussed in the next section. What is

of interest here is an indirect consequence of this sequel for the intellectual climate of the Southern Sung. Chu Hsi had one of his disciples
write an outline of the sequel, which he then published under his own
name. Ssu-ma's original ranks as a great work because of its honest and
objective craftsmanship. It contains moralistic pronouncements, which
may involve subjective judgment; but they are appended separately to
the narrative. In contrast, what was purported to be Chu Hsi's work
often overgeneralizes or oversimplifies history. Although intended merely as a quick reference, it became the standard, authoritative guide to
history for the candidates in state examinations. It hurt intellectual
growth.[10]

Studied intensely from the late Southern Sung on, even more so than
the classics, was a set of standard readings called the Four Books: the
Great Learning (*Ta hsueh*), the *Analects* of Confucius (*Lun yü*), *Mencius*
(*Meng-tzu*) and the *Centrality and Commonality* (*Chung yung*, conventionally known by a rather misleading translation as the *Doctrine of the
Mean*). During the eleventh century, opinions on these books varied. For
example, Li Kou (1009–1059) criticized *Mencius* severely; Ssu-ma Kuang
had his reservations; and Wang An-shih praised the work. It was, however, Ch'eng I and his elder brother who wrote commentaries on all four
books. Inspired by the Chengs, Chu Hsi designated the Four Books,
along with selected commentaries including his own, as the fundamental
reading of Confucianism as a whole. In time, Chu Hsi's interpretation of
the Four Books became the only official one in the state examinations
and hence for all literati. The price for this triumph of orthodoxy over
diversity was intellectual constraint.[11]

Finally, during the Sung, there appeared many other books on self-
improvement and on education—books on the proper volition and
aspirations of scholars, on children's education, on family instruction
and discipline, on kinship relations and their organizational regulations,
on daily and annual schedules of progress for studying Confucian teachings, on running local administration or how to be a good magistrate, on
tutoring the prince, and on serving the emperor in his imperial studies.
While Confucianism always stressed education of one's self as well as of
others, the Neo-Confucian school gave particularly strong emphasis to
self-cultivation, or, in modern terms, internalized discipline. The number

of such publications increased appreciably with the affirmation of state orthodoxy. Most of them, however, lacked originality or creativity. Repeating or citing one another, they were conventional guidebooks that molded thought rather than stimulated it.[12]

To conclude, the Sung period as a whole made a tremendous headway in classical learning. Because its achievements surpassed those of preceding times by a great margin, Confucians and many other Chinese in later ages were proud of the Sung era. What this brief analysis has sought to amend is the failure to distinguish changes over time. The intellectual advance made in the eleventh century was in large measure from plurality through diversity to maturity. By the twelfth century, despite such an exceptionally erudite scholar as Chu Hsi, a great deal of learning suffered in relative terms from narrowness, adherence to orthodoxy, insufficient originality, and other similar limitations. Intellectual growth began to slow down.

HISTORICAL WRITINGS

Quantitatively and qualitatively, the Sung exceeded all previous ages in producing historical writings. Quantitatively, it was facilitated by improvements in printing technology; qualitatively, it was marked by the output of excellent works and the development of new genres. A majority of the authors were scholar-officials who were interested in such work or had been commissioned by the government; a small number of them chose to do it as professionals.

In the mid-eleventh century, two standard or dynastic histories were rewritten as improvements, though the old versions still stood as well. The first one was the new T'ang history, produced by imperial order. The second was on the Five Dynasties, the period immediately preceding the Sung. Although it was written privately by Ou-yang Hsiu, the court unprecedentedly granted it the status of an official compilation.[13]

Eleventh-century historians stimulated the rise of historiographical criticism. Ssu-ma Kuang's chronological history contained research notes and interpretative commentary. Both its method of weighing sources illustrated by the notes and its interpretative approach to history led many a historian to aspire to the same high standards. After factual information had been ascertained by evidential proof, moral principles, as Confucianism required, became the ultimate consideration in authors' discussions of the past. Both past events and earlier histories were assessed with new acuity. After Ou-Yang Hsiu had found errors in the old history of the Five Dynasties, other scholars discovered mistakes in his new version. Various minor monographs began to bear such titles as "Correction of Errors" (*chiu-miu* or *cheng-wu*).[14] Also helpful were advances in archaeology and bibliography, the branches of learning in which Ou-yang Hsiu had also pioneered.[15]

As its title implies, the chronological history by Ssu-ma Kuang, the *Comprehensive Mirror for Aid in Government* (*Tzu-chih t'ung-chien*), was written so that the lessons of history could be drawn and applied to contemporary events by rulers. It rested on the Confucian belief that moral actions assure good order and deviations lead to disaster. Ssu-ma's approach in gathering factual information, however, was fairly objective in selection and quite rigorous in testing accuracy. His writing reflects this approach. Whenever he could not resolve a conflict in the sources, he inserted a research note to so explain. These merits made his monumental work a model that inspired, among many others, two distinguished historians of the twelfth century to work likewise: Li T'ao (1115–1184) covered the entire length of the Northern Sung, and Li Hsin-ch'uan (1166–1243) dealt with the beginning years of the Southern Sung in the *HNYL* that provides a wealth of information for the present study.[16]

Indeed, the twelfth century surpassed the eleventh century in historical writing. For one thing, there appeared a new genre of history, the narrative summary, which pulled together into focused chapters the essential information on important events that was usually scattered among accounts of imperial reigns, biographies of leading individuals, and separate monographs on various government functions. Each major event became the topic of a chapter. While the new, consolidated arrangement did not add new information, it provided different perspectives. From then on, formal Chinese historical accounts had three standard genres: dynastic histories written from the standpoint of the state, general chronologies arranged according to time sequence, and narrative or topical summaries of events.[17]

The many other advances made during the twelfth century are too numerous to discuss in detail here, but a summation of general trends will suffice. First the shift from official histories toward a growing number of private historical accounts gained momentum.[18] Second, formal histories became outnumbered by informal accounts, narratives, and notes.[19] Third, smaller, more manageable topics came to be preferred to broad surveys. Fourth, attention was given to the study of a specific geographical area instead of the whole empire,[20] notably in local gazetteers and unprecedentedly descriptive accounts of urban activities.[21] Fifth, specific aspects of a general category were singled out for intensive study. (For example, following a book on the famous gardens in Lo-yang came another work that traced the history of peonies there.) Sixth, efforts were made to supplement historical information by research on obscure but significant subjects. Seventh, twelfth-century historians were aware that the discipline of history had to utilize the knowledge of other branches of learning, such as military science, historical geography, art history, studies of architecture, medical books, and so on.

The advance made by later Sung historians over their predecessors can be illustrated by a major area of historical writing, the encyclopedic compilation. In the early Northern Sung, the court ordered two enormous works to be edited: the *Prime Indicators of Government Files* (*Ts'e-fu yuan-kuei*) and the *Imperial Reader for Peaceful Reign* (*T'ai-p'ing yu-lan*). Such compilations merely put under various headings relevant excerpts from extant documents without criticism or annotations. In the Southern Sung, some private scholars began to edit encyclopedias on their own and subjected the information to critical examination. There had been a T'ang period model entitled *Comprehensive Compendium* (*T'ung-tien*); but in the twelfth and early thirteenth centuries historians improved on it by devising more detailed and systematic classifications, gathering information with care, citing sources when desirable, and adding research comments to clarify doubtful or complicated points. The two leading Sung compilations were *Comprehensive Records* (*T'ung-chih*) and *Comprehensive Studies of Documentary Evidence* (*Wen-hsien t'ung-k'ao*), the last title being a true reflection of the book's sophisticated scholarship. The T'ang model and these two works came to be known as the set of "three comprehensives" (*san-t'ung*).[22]

Some present-day scholars are of the opinion that these encyclopedias and similar reference works are not histories in the Western or modern sense of the term. To Westerners they appear to be reference tools useful to bureaucrats in their administrative functions. Such scholars have not quite understood the elite culture of traditional China. Few bureaucrats had the occasion or the need to use these works. The real users of these encyclopedias, local gazetteers, and the like were private scholars in pursuit of historical information.

Of greater interest to the bureaucrats in their official capacity was another category of books that the historians produced. They were explicitly labeled as "administrative books" (*cheng-shu*). Some were anthologies of memorials, summaries of institutions, case books on jurisprudence, and so on. Some of them have such titles as *Compendium on Agricultural Administration* (*Nung-cheng ch'uan-shu*) and *Compendium on Relief Administration* (*Huang-cheng ch'uan-shu*). Others have vivid titles, such as *Book on Famine Relief and Life-saving* (*Chiu-huan huo-ming shu*).[23]

The advance in historical writings was not without a darker side. Among the expanding quantity of historical writings were some works of dubious quality in two categories. First were the books of historical comments (*shih-p'ing*) that claimed to offer analyses of historical cases but were usually colored by subjective evaluation. They tended to be argumentative, speculative, or lacking in substantive research—in a sense a-historical—for many Sung Confucians, the Neo-Confucians among them, put their moral concerns ahead of historical facts in oversimplified versions to make a moral point. Such habits were formed early in their careers when they prepared for the state examinations.

The second category comprised self-serving compositions. To defend or whitewash themselves or their friends, a small number of scholar-officials wrote memoirs, while many inserted their versions of recent events under the genre of miscellaneous notes. The opposite also took place. Attacks were made on political adversaries or literary enemies by publishing biased or partisan accounts based on prejudice, gossip, distortion, and falsehoods. These writings merely made life miserable for professional historians thereafter. They reflect a narrow contentiousness that crept into the intellectual climate of the Southern Sung.

To sum up, it can be said of learning in the Southern Sung that while literature and scholarship of high quality continued to be produced, the direction changed. Even at its best, learning in the twelfth century moved toward refining, improving, elaborating, or specializing. When compared to the learning of the previous century, it seems limited in its intellectual horizon. This generalization certainly admits of exceptions. Chu Hsi, for example, systematized the broadest range of knowledge then available and made original contributions in many fields. Such outstanding individuals, however, were exceptional, few, and far between. They did not change the general picture. Practically all of Chu Hsi's own followers were relatively lacking in breadth, depth, originality, or creativity. On the whole, the eleventh century may be known for its pioneering expansions in intellectual growth, while the twelfth century must be credited primarily for achievements in consolidation.

This observation may be further illustrated by comparing developments in history and classical studies. Although the eleventh century had produced such great historians as Ou-yang Hsiu and Ssu-ma Kuang, the twelfth century produced a decidedly larger quantity of historical writings. This does not appear to be true for classical studies. A crucial question arises: How did it happen that one field continued to develop while the other did not?

Our explanation has two parts. To begin with, history and classical studies were inherently different; they also played different roles in politics. Classical studies grew by inspiration and the stimulation of ideas. They thrived in diversity. Diversity, however, always faces three dangers: First, it can degenerate into divisiveness, especially when compounded by political or factional strife. Second, diversity can arouse opposition that may escalate to outright suppression. Third, diversity may decline under a towering orthodoxy and spreading conformity. All these dangers beset Sung classical studies.

In contrast, the growth of historical writing owed much to the accumulation of information. Increases in available information resulted in multiplicity, but not necessarily in diversity. Although there were some divisiveness, controversies, and restrictions that came with political suppression or the establishment of an orthodoxy, they did not hurt history as much as classical studies. Historical writing had its last line of self-defense resting upon indisputable factual information.

The second part of the explanation was the dual role of the scholar-official. In studying the classics as sources of ideology, scholars found it difficult to avoid the issues of ideological authority or correctness. In the Confucian state, ideology shaped power. It was equally hard for them as officials to ignore the questions of political power that were interwoven with ideological considerations. Their road was bound to be a bumpy one, and the study of the classics declined when scholar-officials had to proceed at their own risk.

The field of history was in a sense a semi-retiring and secluded undertaking, distant from the stage of ideological-political struggle at court. The scholar-officials who engaged themselves in historical writings usually worked in private. Those who remained concurrently in government service did not hold executive, critical-advisory, or other sensitive positions. Ssu-ma Kuang is an outstanding illustration. After strenuous objections to the reform policies, he asked for leave to retire to his home in Lo-yang, where he spent seventeen quiet years working on his chronicle history. During these years, he avoided dealing with questions of ideological authority or political power that usually came up in classical studies. By the time the emperor summoned him back to head the anti-reform administration, he had completed his monumental work.

Learning in any culture has many dimensions whose importance varies. In Sung China, neither historical nor literary works shone the brightest among the literati. They were more like the light illuminating the gentle slopes of a hillside. They do not reflect the silhouette of the whole mountain. It was classical studies and the Confucian ideological theories based on them that stood like the summit and peaks at the top.[24] When flames were set ablaze there, their light was cast over the entire landscape. When the flames were quenched, a long shadow fell, either of divisiveness or of conformity.

THREE

Sung Confucianism

Of all the areas of Sung learning, philosophy in the form of Confucianism had the greatest direct impact on politics, on behavior, and on other areas of thought. Although Buddhism and Taoism still played a role in Chinese life during the Sung dynasty, the thought and scholarship of the educated elite were centered on Confucianism. For them, it had the authority of an established ideology. This vast complex of thought and institutions had been originally, and remained basically, a moral philosophy; but for the elite, it had come to dominate the value system and way of life. From the Sung period on, they upheld it generally as an inviolate body of secular truth and revered it with an attitude approaching religious faith. Under their influence, it was accepted and internalized in varying degrees by the rest of society later on and shaped the general social and ethical values that prevailed in China. It offered guidance for conducting governmental affairs, regulating the society at large, and the family, and cultivating individual lives. This chapter, therefore, examines the general nature of Confucianism and its role as an ideology in the political structures of Sung China before discussing various specific schools of Sung Confucian thought.

CONFUCIAN IDEOLOGY AND INSTITUTIONS

A modern word like *ideology*, of course, did not exist in traditional China; but a classical expression that comes close is *cheng-chiao*, or "governing and educating." The word *governing* (*cheng*) refers to society as well as the state.[1] It means not just governmental administration but rectifying thought and regulating conduct, in everyone from the emperor himself to the common people. And the word *educating* (*chiao*) refers to more than just teaching and schooling; it means instilling and perpetuating a moral standard of social order. To this concept of educating, a related compound *chiao-hua* adds the idea of "transforming" (*hua*). The ideal of Confucianism as it evolved through the centuries was to fulfill all these functions—governing, educating, improving, and transforming individuals, society, and rulers. Belief in the value and power of this ideal may be called the Confucian ideology.

While it rested on a foundation of moral values that were upheld to govern proper conduct and appropriate actions, Confucianism had an exceedingly long and complex evolution. The Confucian ideology that played a decisive role in the political events and intellectual developments of the Sung dynasty was itself somewhat elastic; that is, more than one interpretation of it was possible. Furthermore, over the centuries, Confucianism had acquired a host of eclectic components. Some Confucians, partially influenced by the Taoist philosophy of Lao Tzu and Chuang Tzu, adopted an emphasis on nature. Other Confucians who synthesized their philosophical precepts with such ancient beliefs as *yin*, *yang*, and the five agents (metal, wood, water, fire, and earth) added a universal dimension that unifies the human world and the natural order. When Buddhism from India penetrated Chinese culture, its influence, too, introduced yet another eclectic ingredient within the complex body of Confucianism.

By the Sung dynasty, however, although the *Tripitika* or Buddhist canon was reprinted under state auspices early in the eleventh century with additional texts, Buddhism in China was in a sense losing some of its vitality. It lacked strong religious leadership in the Sung; abbots in the monasteries tended to stress discipline or their preferred sectarian doctrines rather than to produce new vigor. Even the Ch'an (or Zen) sect, though prominent especially among the educated, did not have many fresh dimensions to offer. As printing made books cheaper and more widely available and as private schools came into existence, the large, old Buddhist libraries with their precious scrolls and the quiet of the monastery environment had less to offer the Confucian students who had previously studied there. These students had formed friendships that served the Buddhists well when they went on to become scholar-officials, but now fewer and fewer bureaucrats knew the monks or their teachings well. Similarly, Buddhist artisans and financial services, which had previously filled important roles in the daily life of villages and towns, were superseded as the Sung economy expanded and developed; and the monasteries lost local power.[2]

Some Confucian purists, moreover, had always reacted against Buddhism's otherworldly, unverifiable theology. Likewise, they objected to the superstitious folk practices of Taoism, which remained largely an unsophisticated, polytheistic religion of the uneducated, who sought practices to promote health and long life and relief from daily anxieties. The purists devoted themselves to searching for the truth according to the original Confucian heritage of ethical thought; to teaching, learning, scholastic pursuits, and education in general; and to self-cultivation and personal morality. To them, moral ideals were the ultimate test by which to judge not only their own lives, but the state, its policies, and the conduct of the bureaucracy and even the emperor himself.

The extreme purists, who were never more than a small number at any time, believed that all the eclectic components of non-Confucian origin were peripheral, unnecesary, or, worse than that, misguided and undesirable. The majority among other Confucians, however, found it practical, acceptable, reasonable, and even advisable to combine some of these eclectic dimensions with the basic Confucian moral concern. It was such syntheses that became the mainstream or conventional Confucianism throughout the centuries. Politically conventional Confucians tended to be conservative. They did not see much wisdom in initiating institutional changes, making new laws, introducing innovative policies, or implementing reforms. They always claimed that moral leadership to exercise proper influences and upright officials to administer just laws honestly would be all that was necessary to put the country in good order. They would criticize the status quo when they felt that it was not moving toward the ideal of a moral transformation.

For practical reasons, many Confucians who served as officials had to adopt, to a certain extent, the Legalist philosophy and the theories of the so-called strategiests that had originated in the Warring States period

(475–221 B.C.). In fact, this produced an eclectic *realpolitik* practice in conventional Confucianism. Likewise, on the basis of government experience, many officials espoused utilitarian approaches. Although such pragmatic ways were actually followed by officials, they did not necessarily hang together in Confucian theory but strayed from basic Confucian tenets. Dissatisfaction with such practices eventually led to the search for a revisionist solution. It was institutional reform.

According to the theories of those Confucians who stressed the importance of institutions, the ancient classics had provided the models. The institutions described there were believed not to have been mere ideals or utopian systems; allegedly they had been implemented. Since these teachings held the truth, it was reasoned, how could they possibly be impracticable or unrealizable? Only repeated failures to find ways of applying them had pushed them aside as theories to be honored but not to be used. In order to save the situation, certain Northern Sung reformists argued that it was desirable, indeed necessary, to ascertain the underlying principles in the ancient classics and then to adapt them to existing conditions. Their objective was to devise political, economic, social, and educational institutions that would promote moral values which, they believed, were really at one with utilitarian ends. In other words, good institutions should be both uplifting and practical. In this light these Confucians may be regarded as institutional reformers.

Wang An-shih, mentioned earlier, was the paramount exponent of reform. Under his New Policies or reform system, the government became assertive: it engaged in trade and made loans to farmers at the beginning of the sowing season to get them started. The premise of the platform was an active, circulating, in effect inflationary and expanding economy. This would increase income both for the government and for the working or economically active people. The government abolished requisitioned labor service by having the people pay a tax for the government to use flexibly in hiring laborers to perform needed services. The government also organized peasants into self-policing units. It assigned some households to breed horses to aid defense. Wang An-shih then reorganized the state examination system by having candidates trained and tested at the Advanced Institute (Tai-hsueh, often rendered as "National University"), where the study of statecraft problems was stressed. He also instituted a separate degree program for those who studied law. To the moralistic conservatives and other critics of the Reform, this was more like Legalism than Confucianism. In rebuttal, Wang cited passages in the ancient classics to buttress his position that moral values could not be divorced from either the well-being of the state or the welfare of the people.

Whether Wang was a true or a misguided Confucian and whether his institutional emphasis was a proper one in Confucianism are intricate questions that need not burden the discussion here. Suffice it to mention that in the aftermath of his Reform, disaster struck. After the phase of the initial Reform in 1069–1085, the conservatives took over and turned the clock back. From 1093 to 1125, however, the eve before the fall of the Northern Sung, the conservatives lost power and most of the reform measures were put back into effect. This was the phase of the Restored Reform, sometimes called the Postreform. It gathered notoriety from the lack of Wang An-shih's original idealism, the vanishing of the reform spirit, the absence of moral scruples, the prevalence of corruption and abuses, the refusal to rectify defects in the reform system, the unjustifiable and unprecedented persecution of the conservatives who continued to oppose it, the self-congratulatory complacency of the emperor and his extravagant indulgences, and general demoralization. The end came when the government recklessly undertook dangerous expeditions beyond the borders that ultimately brought about the Jurchen invasion and the destruction of the dynasty.

The Southern Sung court established itself in mid-year 1127 in an ambivalent political climate. The reform program, and with it the institutional approach, were bankrupt and discredited. No one openly advocated them any more. Most officials, however, were career men from the old days. Accustomed to the ways of the reform system, they did not particularly welcome contrary opinions from other branches of Confucianism. But the original conservative opposition, other surviving critics, and their followers in the next generation, especially a group that may be called the moralistic conservatives, demanded to be heard. They criticized and condemned the various reform measures, calling them unworthy, unseemly, unscrupulous, and undesirable. In their unalterable view, while the immediate cause of the dynastic disaster lay with the phase of the Restored Reform, the underlying trouble had come from the original Reform itself. By putting alleged utilitarian values ahead of moral values and by wrongly believing that the state comes before society, Wang An-shih had put the cart before the horse. What was urgently needed, the conservatives pleaded, was precisely a proper emphasis on the moral principles of true Confucianism.

During the early decades of the Southern Sung, however, the conservative side did not gain power for a variety of reasons. The resistance of entrenched bureaucrats was one among many factors. The ambivalence of the emperor was another. Moreover, the conservatives had their own weaknesses. First, they had few concrete programs of alternative policies to offer. Second, not many of them happened to be talented, skillful, or experienced administrators who could cope with the numerous exigencies and difficulties facing the struggling dynasty. Third, there were times during periods of trouble when political compromises appeared necessary, if only temporarily; yet many conservatives often considered such compromises to be morally wrong, inadvisable, and unacceptable. Last, but by no means least, was the conservatives' own divisiveness.

There were three probable causes for the divisions among them. First many conservatives seem to have been intellectually narrow or inflexible. Attached to their own interpretations of Confucian principles, they did not often arrive at a consensus among themselves. Second, at court they were divided into cliquish geographic or provincial groups: the Lo group (from the lower bend of the Yellow River), the Shuo group (from the highland region along the upper Yellow River reaches), and the Shu group (from the self-contained Szechwan basin of the upper Yangtze). Provincial mentalities, combined with intellectual rigidity, led to considerable friction and disagreement. Third, there were simple personality conflicts among some conservative leaders. It is only fair to say that the conservative cause sorely lacked political leadership.

Generally, the political philosophy of the conservatives, varied as they were, was not creative, profound, or striking. Not until the twelfth century did a new tide of thinker unprecedentedly swell the mainstream. They not only provided a cosmological and metaphysical dimension to raise Confucian philosophy to an unsurpassed height, but more significantly integrated the entire Confucian heritage into a most comprehensive system.[3]

VARIETIES OF NEO-TRADITIONAL THOUGHT

Sung Confucianism developed energetically in many directions; but because its vigorous intellectual contributions were additions to an ancient heritage, it may generally be described as neo-traditional. Although many of its leaders were concerned with ethics and metaphysics, it was not confined to philosophy; nor was its philosophical output limited to one dominant school. An overview of Sung Confucian thought on government and education (*cheng-chiao*) should correct the mistaken impression that only one branch made contributions. Unfortunately, a host of both premodern sources and twentieth-century scholars—Chinese, Japanese, and Western—have conventionally given overwhelming and sometimes even exclusive attention to its prominent philosophical dimensions, particularly to the renowned Neo-Confucian school.

The term *Neo-Confucianism* was originally used in Western literature to designate the Chu Hsi school of thought. Since the middle of the present century, it has also been loosely applied to other Sung Confucians, in the broad sense that they were different from those of earlier periods. This has led to some confusion and needs to be clarified. Recent scholarship prefers to revert to the original, narrow usage.[13] Neo-Confucianism refers exclusively to the Chu Hsi school or Li-hsueh, the School of Principles, and no one else. The present study identifies the moralistic conservatives, especially those who followed the teachings of Ch'eng I (1033–1107), as the forerunners of the Neo-Confucians. It characterizes the Neo-Confucians themselves as transcendental moralists, in recognition of their profound metaphysical system.

The special emphasis on Neo-Confucianism, which began with important historical sources, is not without reason; for Neo-Confucianism eventually became the state orthodoxy. The Sung dynastic history creates a special category for the "biographies of the True Way masters" (*Tao-hsueh chuan*), that is, biographies of the leading thinkers of the school. (Tao-hsueh, or the True Way school, was the name collectively applied to the forerunners of Neo-Confucianism, Chu Hsi himself, and his followers.) After the fall of the Ming empire, an apparently painful failure of the Confucian way, the loyalist Huang Tsung-hsi (1610–1695) started to compile a monumental work to uphold the intellectual contributions of the Sung Confucians. Entitled *Sung Yuan hsueh-an,* it is often translated as *Sung and Yuan Intellectual History.* Its literal translation is *Sung and Yuan Schools of Learning;* but a more informative rendering would be *The Sung and Yuan Confucian Schools of Learning,* for it virtually equated formal intellectual activity with Confucian learning. It did not include any Buddhists, literary figures, or intellectuals, working outside Confucianism. Instead, its author took Neo-Confucianism to be the mainstream of intellectual life and traced one school after another, listing masters and disciples, companions and friends, often with cross-references to show the collateral affiliations between one school and another. He relegated other thinkers and Confucian schools to brief summations at the very end of the book because by Ming times they were considered heterodox. Among these were Wang An-shih the reformer and Su Shih (1036–1101) from the Northern Sung; the School of the Mind (Hsin-hsueh), which was the chief rival of Neo-Confucianism; and a few intellectuals in the northern, Jurchen empire, who were beyond the pale of Sung society. Huang did not finish this work, but its completion by an editor in the eighteenth century and its voluminous nineteenth-century supplement complied by two adherents kept strictly to the original approach.

A number of modern works on Sung thought continue to follow the same approach, limiting themselves to the mainstream, Neo-Confucian philosophy and paying much attention to the five masters of the Northern Sung whom the Neo-Confucians honored: Chou Tun-i (1017–1073), Shao Yung (1011–1077), Chang Tsai (1020–1077), Ch'eng Hao (1032–1085), and his brother Ch'eng I. Other works in this field, however, especially in the history of political thought, have revised the approach, considering it necessaary to deal with many other thinkers, such as Sun Fu (992–1057) and Fan Chung-yen (989–1052), who both taught before the five Northern Sung masters; Ssu-Ma Kuang, a great historian-statesman; Lu Hsiang-shan (1139–1192), the founder of the School of the Mind and adversary of Chu Hsi; Ch'en Liang (1143–1194), a hawkish utilitarian theorist who argued against Chu Hsi; and Yeh Shih (1150–1223) who excelled in utilitarian studies of key institutions. The picture so revised in these books of modern scholars already indicates the rich variety of neo-traditional Confucianism other than Neo-Confucianism.[4]

These revised views, however, have not really redressed the balance. They retain an emphasis on Neo-Confucianism and simply add material that should not be omitted. Furthermore, they fall short of suggesting themes or devising schemes of analysis that would order the whole intellectual array. Without any pattern, the picture looks confused: the Neo-Confucians–plus–others does not hang together. The remedy is to place the various Sung thinkers and schools in an organized or meaningful pattern.

The suggested classification that follows is but one such possible pattern. Historical realities are so very complex that they do not lend themselves to a single classification system or reduction to one and only one way of looking at them. On the contrary, a fully adequate treatment would be pluralistic. It would proceed to analyze reality from one viewpoint after another, shedding more light at each turn. A simple analogy is the way to look at a finely cut diamond: One does not look at it from a fixed angle only, but keeps turning it over and over again to see its shifting facets.

To accomplish a particular purpose, however, a single system has the advantage of clarity. The classification offered here is designed for the specific purpose of looking at various Sung ideas and developments in government and education, both of which were central to Confucianism. The intellectuals and schools of thought to be analyzed are those that played a part in the evolution of Sung Confucianism. When intellectuals are here separated into groups, the group labels are broad. They by no means specify exactly the characteristics of each individual in the group; they represent only clusters or trends. Nor are such groupings watertight or mutually exclusive; they merely help define the positions each group held in relation to others of their own time and to similar trends of thought across time.

The point of departure for this classification scheme is the received Confucian tradition that prevailed throughout the Sung dynasty. Although this was the beginning of neo-traditional China, it must be emphasized that there was hardly much *neo* about the majority of scholar-officials. They were conventional Confucians who abided by the long-established value system with relatively little thought of changing it. Their writings were legion but received scanty attention from later generations, for they contributed few original or creative ideas. This is to be expected. Like bureaucrats and members of the elite in other cultures, many Sung scholar-officials tended to be conservative and opposed to innovation. Nevertheless, a small but highly significant number of intellectuals, rising like sparkling tips above the submerged icebergs, refused to remain conventional. What they advocated were what they believed to be much needed changes in the establishment. And they justified their opinions by their innovative interpretations of the ancient classics.

Of course, these neo-traditional Confucians did not necessarily agree among themselves about what should be changed or how to make the changes. A simple yardstick that would clarify the diversity is the relative degree to which the intellectuals were critical of the established Confucian ways that prevailed in thought, government, and society. Some wanted to infuse them with new, idealistic enthusiasm in order to revitalize or re-energize them, but not necessarily to change them otherwise. Others wished to introduce some selective changes within the current system. Yet others with much stronger convictions, would go so far as to demand fundamental and even sweeping changes of the establishment. From this particular standpoint, the Neo-Confucian school, while they claimed to be orthodox and not innovative, and seemed conservative with reference to the eleventh-century Reform that had failed, were in a very real sense also reformers insofar as they desired to change on-going practices and the value system. No Neo-Confucian would ever admit that, for the word *reform* had a bad reputation in the Southern Sung. Nevertheless, from the standpoint of our classification, it is evident that both the earlier reformers and the Neo-Confucians shared something significant. Both groups wanted fundamental improvements. Both groups aimed to reconstruct existing ways in some thorough manner. They differed categorically and clashed diametrically mainly about what was to be reconstructed, in which direction, and how.

To describe briefly these groups, clusters, or trends along with their respective exponents, a tabular presentation would save a great deal of verbiage. Table 1 is a panorama in miniature of the whole Sung Confucian landscape.

Explanation of this table can be quite brief, for information on these thinkers is amply available in all of the standard works. The advocates of

TABLE 1 Advocates of Change in Sung Confucianism

	Re-energize Ideals Only	*Renovate Selectively*	*Improve Fundamentally*

Northern Sung Intellectuals	Sun Fu
	Ssu-Ma Kuang
	Su Shih
		Fan Chung-yen
		  1043–1044 Minor Reform
		
		Ou-yang Hsiu
		  essay style and
		  state examinations
		
		Ch'eng I
		  philosophy
			Wang An-shih

Southern Sung Intellectuals	Yang Shih	Ch'en Liang
		  military
		
		Ch'en Fu-liang
		  state institutions
		
		Yeh Shih
		  state institutions
		
		Lu Chiu-yuan
		  education
			Chu Hsi

re-energizing ideals put emphasis on relatively simple principles, without elaborate theories. Sun Fu, for example, issued a "Confucian manifesto," attacking Buddhism and Taoism for ideas and practices that violated the precepts of Confucian society. Ssu-ma Kuang stressed personal conduct and values in social groups beginning with the family. History shows, he reasoned, that moral standards in government are of decisive importance. As the leading opponent of Wang An-shih's New Policies, he directed his basic objection to their deviations from traditional principles and to their demoralizing effects. Although he is invariably labeled as a conservative and did oppose the Reform and drastic changes, in fact, he himself sought *gradual* changes to improve the administrative quality of the government through the selection of upright officials. Su Shih, the multifarious genius, upheld the hope of promoting refined culture, without indoctrination, as the way to raise the level of enlightenment among scholar-officials and through their influence that of society in general.

As time went on, a fair number of neo-traditional intellectuals followed this line of thinking without necessarily making outstanding or very distinguished contributions. This was true of a forerunner in the Neo-Confucian school, Yang Shih (1053–1135), a disciple of both Ch'eng brothers, who was credited with being the key transmitter of their teaching to the Southern Sung. Lecturing briefly at the court of the restoring emperor Kao-tsung, he, too, gave more emphasis to uplifting moral standards and conduct than to philosophical formulations. In short, those who advocated re-energizing ideals tended to produce few elaborate theories or platforms.

The second cluster or trend consisted of the selective renovators, who believed in developing both theory and a feasible platform designed to make the old system work better. They tried to introduce significant changes, but not on a grand scale, so as not to upset the current situation. This approach applied to the diverse categories they engaged themselves in: state affairs, education, literature, study of the classics, and metaphysics. Fan Chung-yen expressed what may be called "the scholar's declaration of dedication," a statement still used today, that "a scholar should be the first to be concerned with the worries of the world and the last to enjoy its happiness." He was the leader of a short-lived Minor Reform of administrative affairs in 1043–1044. Ou-yang Hsiu, though an important participant in this Minor Reform, did not push hard for it. His greatest contribution was in developing a clear prose style and new interpretations in classical studies. Surprising though it may seem, the Ch'eng brothers and other philosophers, who were later honored as pioneering masters by the Neo-Confucian school, did not advocate in their time a thoroughgoing transformation of either the government or society. The significant changes they produced were in philosophy, their specialty and select area of emphasis. Theirs was a reform of ideas that developed profound dimensions in metaphysics and cosmology.

In a time of peace and prosperity, these Neo-Confucian forerunners could afford the luxury of philosophical speculation in quietness. Yet, sensing signs of possible troubles ahead, they went to the root of the matter and raised ultimate questions about life, the universe, and their meaning. These questions pertained to a field that had been previously dominated by Buddhism, though not quite monopolized by it. Now, the

Confucian philosophers took them up and formulated refreshing, absorbing, and invigorating concepts, such as supreme principle, great ultimate, great harmony, human nature, and humanity. Even to those not convinced, these formulations appeared to be impressive, deep, and challenging. At least in metaphysics they did no less than build a strong, new foundation for Confucianism, making it much more profound than it had ever been. Nonetheless, they were not interested in an immediate social reconstruction.

The selective renovators, on the other hand, eagerly searched for and identified certain key elements in Confucianism that would, they believed, lead to the way of a stronger state and a better society. This approach reverberated in the Southern Sung. Ch'en Liang, the best known utilitarian "hawk," advocated in the mid twelfth century needed improvements in government affairs, with an insistent stress on his proposed reforms in the military system. His hope was to recover the North China plain from the Jurchen enemies. Ch'en Fu-liang (1137–1203), another utilitarian thinker, realized the inseparable relationship between the military system and other parts of the government. He studied how to improve and change certain key institutions in a practical way. Later on, while citing the classics and simultaneously observing current conditions acutely, Yeh Shih proposed a number of excellent, original ideas to improve specific institutions.

Lu Chiu-yuan (better known as Hsiang-shan) was the founder of the School of the Mind, much admired at the same time but more so in subsequent centuries as the worthy adversary of the great philosopher Chu Hsi. Instead of concentrating on such areas as the military or institutions, he chose philosophy and developed deep dimensions of psychology. In place of the standard Confucian emphasis on conduct or morality, he focused on the concept of mind. Only better mind, he explained, would make better individuals and hence a better society. In this respect, he paralleled but did not agree with the Northern Sung Confucian forerunners.

The third major group, the advocates of fundamental improvements, wanted nothing less than to set the whole system right once and for all. With comprehensive and high-minded ideas, they tended to be insistent, uncompromising, and aggressive. The reformer Wang An-shih was like that; he overflowed with self-confidence. But he was not alone. The great founder of Neo-Confucianism, Chu Hsi himself, and his followers as well also had the boldness to call for a thorough reshaping of government and society. It may seem preposterous to group Chu Hsi and Wang An-shih together, yet it is often the case that adversaries at opposite poles tend to share characteristics. Wang wanted to make drastic institutional changes in intellectual, economic, and political areas, while the Neo-Confucians led by Chu demanded an equally thorough transformation of society through philosophical, moral, intellectual, and ultimately social and political improvements. In short, the Neo-Confucians aimed not only at a state orthodoxy but at the reorientation of everything. Although they claimed that their teaching constituted what had been the true way since antiquity, in reality it represented no less than a new way of thinking about the whole of society.

Wang An-shih and the Neo-Confucians differed not only in approach—institutional change versus philosophical orientation—but also in ideals. Wang valued and sought an effectively regulating government; the Neo-Confucians aspired to a society morally uplifting in itself. The two sides nonetheless shared a similar outlook rooted in protest. Acording to them both, the existing Confucian practice had fallen into disrepair. No piecemeal remedies could possibly suffice, for its defects stemmed from many fundamental errors. Hence, Confucianism had to be thoroughly reconstructed on a new foundation.

The issue of what constituted the Confucian orthodoxy had an interesting historical and geographical background. In the Northern Sung, Wang An-shih believed that government and education should uphold one set of virtues (*i tao-te*), one uniform value system. This was why he wanted his interpretation of the classical text, the *Rituals of Chou* (*Chou li*) and his work on etymology (*Tzu-shuo*) to be the standard references for state examinations. Although he did not go beyond that and his School of New Learning (*Hsin-hsueh)† was never considered to be the Confucian orthodoxy, his policy partially raised the issue of what it should be. The conservatives who opposed him, continued to follow

---

†In this book, the romanization *Hsin-hsueh is used for the school of New Learning to distinguish it from Hsin-hsueh, the School of the Mind. The characters for each are provided in the glossary.

the old practice of the Yellow River regions in the North. Rather than "deciding on one" (*ting-yü-i*) interpretation, they chose to let various theories "co-exist" (*chien-ts'un*). The five Northern Sung masters honored by the Neo-Confucians were all northerners. Self-righteous as they were, they did not go to the extremity of rejecting other interpretations. But the Neo-Confucians who came after them in the Southern Sung, despite a general respect for earlier thinkers, did not esteem theories at variance with their own school of thought. Paradoxically, they were as extreme as Wang An-shih had been in self-righteousness, or even more so with their claim of exclusive orthodoxy. Interestingly, both Wang and the Neo-Confucians were from the southern coastal regions and the Yangtze Valley in what is today central China. In Sung times, these regions were, culturally speaking, frontier areas. The outspoken intellectuals there, in efforts to gain leading roles for themselves and their theories, tended to be more aggressive than others.[5]

For the transcendental moralists, the establishment of Neo-Confucianism as state orthodoxy in the thirteeth century was the ultimate reward for that vigor and aggressiveness. Before its acceptance, however, they and their forerunners, the moralistic conservatives, had to endure the frustration of ridicule and exclusion from political power.

Part Two
The Twelfth Century

FOUR

The Moralistic Conservatives

In the insecure, early years of Emperor Kao-tsung's reign, the idea of institutional reform was a dead issue. The Reform of Wang An-shih was discredited; Chu Hsi's vision of a transformed society still lay in the future. Nevertheless, although Wang's idealism was gone and even lip service to his policies was unfashionable, the daily workings of the government were still in the hands of bureaucrats who were accustomed to them. These experienced civil servants, moreover, tended to prefer a flexible pragmatism to any dogmatism in handling practical affairs. They were the conventional Confucians who were comfortable with the established ways of the last half century. The entrenched power of the incumbents, the emperor's ambivalence, and their own weaknesses kept the moralistic conservatives out of office.

THE SHOCK OF SHAME

Although frustrated in their attempts to regain power, the conservatives refused to be silenced. Their anger was not directed against followers of the Reform alone. Something else aroused their moral indignation even more: The fall of the Northern Sung had inflicted cultural humiliation on the whole empire.

Of course, the military defeat was shocking in itself; but the old measures taken by the Sung emperors in the fear of an internal coup was a major cause that led to it. The best troops had for centuries been posted around the capital instead of along the borders. Military administration was habitually poor. Standing armies of impressed soldiers were small, inadequately trained, poorly led, and frequently rotated among garrisons so that loyalty was not built up between officers and men. On the borders, it is true, were armies led by profesional soldiers from military families in command of soldiers who were bound to them in a fictive father-son relationship. They formed a kind of Maginot line. But once this thin line was penetrated, the whole defense broke up; and in the dreadful year 1127, no stand could be made anywhere. At one point the emperor was even forced briefly to take refuge at sea.

To many observers at the time, however, what was most deeply distressing was the disgraceful weakness exposed in the scholar-official class. Many scholar-officials, nominally Confucians, had surrendered or defected to the enemy. Many others had put their selfish interest in survival ahead of official duties or personal integrity. This intolerable misconduct came as a tremendous shock. The conservatives could not help crying out, Shame!

The Jurchen conquerors ruled just as harshly in their conquered areas as did their Manchu descendants centuries later. They ordered the subjugated people to stop wearing the Han style of dress and to adopt the Jurchen hair-style or face the death penalty. Affecting personal appearance and one's own sense of dignity, such rules were painful to accept. At first, the orders were not strictly enforced. A dozen years later, when the Jurchen occupation was perpetuated by the peace of 1139, wearing Jurchen clothing and hair-style became largely voluntary, especially among those elite who served as officials under the conquerors. In 1150 the Jurchen government finally regarded dress and hair-style to be optional.[1] This afforded little comfort to the Confucians in the south who heard about it. To them, the disdain for the Han Chinese way of life implied by the order was unforgettable. More than upsetting, it was, in their words, "the crisis that turned the relationship between the Han Chinese and uncivilized barbarians upside down" (*Hua Jung chih pien*).[2] In previous periods of pastoral-nomadic penetration—for example, during the Northern-Southern dynasties (420–589)—cultural humiliations had not been so patently shameful.

The unspeakable humiliation suffered by the imperial clan members in captivity and years of exile was another source of great dismay. The captives included Kao-tsung's father (Hui-tsung, r. 1101–1125) and his empress; Kao-tsung's eldest brother (Ch'in-tsung, r. 1126–1127) and his young empress; Kao-tsung's mother and his wife; other princes and princesses; scores of ladies and female palace attendants; and some nine hundred imperial clansmen and their families.[3] Two reports circulating at the time were particularly shocking. One alleged that Kao-tsung's mother had become a concubine of a Jurchen prince, popularly known as the "Sky-shielding Lord," who was one of the generals in charge of the Sung prisoners.[4] The other story went further by asserting that she had a child by him.[5]

Traditional Confucian values held family relations inviolable and that of the imperial family particularly so. Such loss of chastity under duress as these accounts reported was, if true, an insufferable personal insult to Emperor Kao-tsung. Most historians in the past chose either to ignore these two accounts or dismiss them as dirty stories. Their reliability remained a vexing historiographical problem through the centuries until some rare sources resurfaced in the early twentieth century that prove them to be deliberate fabrications.* The two accounts were actually circulated after a Jurchen defeat south of the Yangtze by some of their generals as slanderous propaganda to insult and weaken the Southern Sung court.[6] While many Sung palace ladies were in fact mistreated in various

---

*According to the sources recently discovered, a large number of Sung palace ladies were either married to Jurchen nobility or violated by them. A few of them committed or attempted suicide. The wife of Emperor Kao-tsung tried to kill herself without succeeding. But Lady Wei, Kao-tsung's mother (later honored as the empress-dowager after her return) was not among these. She, thirty-eight years old at the time of her capture, and eighteen other palace ladies were classified as "women of good families," which was a protective designation. On the other hand, these fabricated stories were not entirely groundless. The "Sky-shielding Lord" was a Jurchen general in charge of transporting captured palace ladies, Lady Wei among them. He wanted to have Kao-tsung's wife, not his mother. When he left this group of prisoners after twenty-four days, Lady Wei remained with the rest. Subsequently he took a Sung princess as his concubine, but she died young. A decade later, in 1140, he was one of the envoys who escorted Lady Wei, by then the empress-dowager, to Lin-an, the Southern Sung capital. Because he had been a familiar as well as prominent figure in the experience of the captives, to exaggerate his role would lend the fabrications some credence.

ways while in captivity, the mother of Emperor Kao-tsung along with a few dozen other noble ladies, was spared serious humiliation. In subsequent peace negotiations, Kao-tsung pleaded with the enemy to return her in dignity and told his own ministers that to get her back was an act of filial piety that made peace imperative.

Still, even if these accounts had not a grain of truth, they must have been known as gossip to many people in the Southern Sung, though no one would talk openly about the unspeakable humiliations.[7] Furthermore, aside from such rumors, the terrible fate of hundreds of palace ladies in Jurchen hands was an undisputed fact known to the public. How painful and shocking it was to the Confucian intellectuals!

For the Southern Sung to sustain military defeats was understandable. But to the conservatives, for the court after indecisive battles to set aside its dignity and to beg for peace, as if such self-inflicted shame meant nothing, was unforgivable from the standpoint of both love of country and old Confucian doctrines. These doctrines valued status as well as morality. It was ignominious for the emperor who had the mandate of heaven (*tien-ming*) to yield to a barbarian court. It was impious for him to give up the land held by his imperial ancestors and the subjects there who had been loyal to him. Impiety was made worse by the failure to avenge, for his father and his eldest brothers—the previous emperors—had been captives in enemy hands. The cumulative effects of an ignominious as well as impious policy could call into question the very legitimacy of the dynasty.

Despite these strenuous objections, however, soon after Kao-tsung became emperor, he made peace overtures by sending envoys to the enemy, ostensibly to send greetings to his captured parents, brother, wife, and relatives. Chu Pien (?–1144), an early envoy, was a conservative who volunteered to go on this precarious mission out of a sense of loyalty to the two former emperors in Jurchen hands.[8] Other envoys, though often under suspicion of political treachery as seen by conservatives, proved to be loyal. These peace overtures went on intermittently, despite the fact that the enemy in a triumphant and arrogant mood rejected the Sung envoys and never let them travel beyond the Jurchen army headquarters to the Jurchen court. In 1129, during the third year of his reign, Kao-tsung wrote to the Jurchen vice commander-in-chief in the field, begging for terms of peace. His words were exceedingly humble:

At present, there is a lack of manpower for our defense . . . just as there is no place for us to run to . . . It is hoped that Your Excellency will pity us . . . As indicated previously in several communications from us, we are willing to eliminate our old title [of emperor]. This means that all places between heaven and earth would become parts of the great Chin [i.e. Jurchen empire].[9]

At this time, Liu Yü (1079–1143), a ranking scholar-official, had surrendered to the Jurchens. Instead of being denounced, this turncoat was asked by the Sung court to be an intermediary in forwarding a similar message to his new master. When Liu was installed as the head of a bogus regime under Jurchen patronage, the Sung politely referred to this puppet government by its dynastic designation as the Great Chi, just as it referred to the Jurchen empire as the Great Chin. Not until much later, when Liu's forces began to take part in Jurchen-led invasions did the Sung denounce him in derogatory terms.[10]

Although Kao-tsung found his peace overtures rebuffed, he voluntarily assumed a humble status in his communications with the Jurchens and addressed them as superiors. In 1131, for example, the emissary he sent had the title of "the envoy bearing 'deposition' and concurrently the envoy bearing greetings to the front line."[11] A 'deposition' (*piao*) was conventionally a declaration of allegiance submitted by a subordinate to affirm or acknowledge his humble status. In 1133, the Sung envoys for the first time were permitted to present themselves as messengers at the Jurchen court. At the first peace in 1139, the Jurchens sent the Sung court a proclamation and required Kao-tsung to receive it in person by standing up from his throne. Though a simple formality, this was the symbolic equivalent of an investiture ritual. An uproar took place at the Sung court. Through vexing negotiations with the Jurchen envoy, who agreed on a compromise in order to accomplish his mission, the formality was abbreviated. Still Kao-tsung had to submit a response to the Jurchens in which he referred to himself as a subordinate or servant without mention of his title of emperor.[12]

Negotiations for the second peace of 1141 started with a letter from Kao-tsung, which said, "Having been granted the endless benefaction of peace by the Emperor of the superior state, we have been keeping His Majesty in our thoughts day and night without knowing as yet how to repay his great kindness."[13] When the second peace was concluded, the envoy sent to the Jurchen court used the title of "conveying gratitude and submitting the sworn deposition."[14] When the Jurchens returned Kao-tsung's mother from captivity, he announced to the Sung people that it was the compassion (*jen*) of the superior state that had enabled him to fulfil his filial duties (*hsiao*).[15]

Of course, Kao-tsung did not intend to remain so humble forever. Having stabilized his position through humiliating terms, he hoped to improve it by bargaining later on. In 1151, he asked the Jurchen court to grant him the permission to call himself emperor. For a long time, though, this and similar efforts met with no success.[16] It was not until after he had abdicated in 1162 with the title of Sovereign Emeritus with full honors and his adopted heir, Emperor Hsiao-tsung (r. 1163–1189), had initiated another war with the Jurchens in 1163, that the Jurchens finally recognized the Sung ruler as emperor when peace was resumed in the following year.

The diplomatic language cited above did not, of course, convey genuine feelings. But it occurred in formal documents that raised public questions of status and moral principle in a society that always placed high value on propriety. An outspoken critic, Hu Yin (1098–1156), remarked that the court "ignored enmity, went against moral principle, submitted like inferiors to the northern enemies as if they were the superiors . . . and regarded the great humiliation as a great benefaction."[17]

Many so-called Confucian scholar-officials disgraced themselves. An early edict issued by Kao-tsung reprimanded them for their lack of loyalty at the time of crisis. Although the court was not strong enough to repeat the reprimand or to condemn them further, many intellectuals found their shocking misconduct hard to forgive. As Chu Hsi reflected decades later, "Upon the fall of the northern court, extreme were the disasters all over the country. Among the high as well as the low officials, few would take up their duties resolutely without thinking about their personal safety."[18] When the Northern Sung capital was besieged, a number of high officials collaborated with the Jurchens. Certain notorious ones even pressured the two emperors to visit the Jurchen headquarters outside the city where they soon became captives. They never returned. These disloyal officials helped to hasten the end of the dynasty and to install Chang Pang-ch'ang as the first puppet ruler in the old capital.

They were, however, only the early defectors; many others followed suit or acquiesced. Most of them stayed on to work for Liu Yü, the second puppet emperor, who ruled a sizeable portion of North China.[19]

Once these shameful precedents had been set, shocking defections were no longer confined to the north; they became common when the Jurchen army went southward. The manner in which the so-called Confucians demeaned themselves was particularly obnoxious. They fled from their official posts before anyone else, greeted the enemy with deep bows, and volunteered their services either to the enemy or to the puppet ruler. A few traitors went so far as to present to the enemy strategic plans for further conquest and, in one extraordinary case, a plan to massacre the civilian population of a fallen city. Even more astonishing to principled Confucians were those scholar-officials who, without any sense of honor, excused their misconduct by claiming that they, like the literati of the ancient Warring States period, were free to leave the service of one state for that of another.[20] As the war between the Jurchens and the Southern Sung reached a stalemate, some Sung officials near the battlefront chose to be opportunistic, rather than patently disloyal. They kept in touch with both sides, while retaining a measure of autonomous power in the local area.[21]

At one point a memorial was in circulation, advocating centralized control over the generals and attacking military men categorically for their disloyalty and unreliability. Some infuriated officers got a scholar to write a satirical rebuttal. It alleged that "the civilians today are the ones who default on their duties . . . Ordered to assume local command, they surrender to the enemy. Told to defend a city, they abandon it and flee. It is they who advocate peace negotiations . . . It is they who are in favor of giving up territories to the enemy . . . Even worse, Chang Pang-ch'ang set up the first bogus regime and Liu Yü the second. Had they not been civilian officials? How else could they have done it?"[22] Though a satire, its factual basis was irrefutable.

The court, insecure itself, dared not take a strong stand on the principle of moral integrity. On the contrary, it was willing to overlook defectors without punishing either them or their family members in the south, hoping that magnanimity might induce them to switch back. In terms of *realpolitik*, the more scholar-officials and their families the court could keep on its side, the better, regardless of what they might have done. According to a prevailing observation, this was the time for the government "to accept dirt and filth." The calculation was not mistaken. In fact, many officials, military officers, and bandit leaders committed double defections: Having surrendered to the Jurchens or their puppet, they returned at a later date to the Sung fold.[23] After the Jurchens abolished the bogus regime of Liu Yü and then concluded the first peace with the Southern Sung, a fair number of bureaucrats in the north once again became Sung officials.

Many military men behaved far worse. Repeated defections from one side to the other happened frequently. From the Sung side, they moved over to join Liu Yü; then they either betrayed him to be with the Sung again or became bandits. Sometimes the pattern was in reverse: from banditry to armed forces on either side. The intellectuals never criticized these opportunistic military men or bandits severely. The degeneration of the army under distrustful Sung emperors had led the scholar-officials to ignore military theory and day-to-day operations. Young men who failed to get a degree in the civil service examinations might go through the much easier test to get a military degree instead, with the intention of requesting a transfer into the civil service;[24] but even military officers who had the privilege of periodically requesting a military appointment for a dependent often did not want family members to follow in their footsteps.[25] At the time of the Jurchen conquest, therefore, intellectuals took it for granted that uneducated military men could not be expected to live up to the high moral standards of Confucians.

But the scholar-officials were different; they ought to know better. Besides, they always had the option of leaving government service altogether, retiring from active life, or choosing eremitism.[26] The fact that so many of them were so shamelessly opportunistic cast grave doubts: Was Confucian education efficacious enough? What was the moral worth of the scholar-official class? And what should be done to save the situation?

The scholar-officials revealed other demoralizing traits. Of the many complaints about the deteriorating "literati lifestyle" (*shih feng*), two complaints are specially worth paraphrasing. The first satirically outlined what a scholar-official should do at successive points of his career: First, assume a good posture while waiting for appointment; aim at a

good commission, and try to add a concurrent appointment. If not satisfied, ask for a transfer. If found guilty of misconduct, request rehabilitation or, at least, try to get a retirement pension under a sinecure title.
If successful, move up to an office near the court. While serving at court,
try to get a good promotion out of turn. Finally, get close to a minister
whose petition by memorial would lead to a special assignment to work
directly under him.[27] This was a caricature of insatiable greed devoid of
moral scruples. The other complaint was relatively mild. It allowed that
"everyone has the desire to get ahead, but it is hard to understand why
most scholar-officials are afraid of appointments to be local magistrates
or sub-prefects."[28] In spite of a shortage of positions in an overcrowded
bureaucracy, few candidates were eager to take local government posts,
especially in distant, impoverished places. Although Confucianism
valued duty, many scholar-officials did not give it high priority.

The severe shocks of misconduct, compounded at many levels, aroused
the incessant moral indignation of principled intellectuals. To help save
the country, they were convinced that military defense, while necessary,
would not be sufficient. To begin with, the society had to be worth
saving; then it would save itself. The only hope in their opinion was a
moral reconstruction.

THE REFORM AVENUE CLOSED

The shocks aroused demands for change. But exactly what sort of change
should it be? Was not some kind of reform badly need? In the minds of
many scholar-officials at this time, the very idea of reform or institutional
change was associated, rightly or wrongly, with the fall of the Northern
Sung. In the early Southern Sung, those who had sided with Wang An-
shih's institutional approach and his reform system usually kept quiet.
Those who spoke up at court often expressed nostalgic admiration for the
Yuan-yu era of 1085–1093 when the reform measures had been repealed by
the conservaties then in power. In 1129, Chao Ting (1085–1147), though
only a junior official at the time, boldly accused the Northern Sung chief
councilor Ts'ai Ching (1046–1126) of having caused the fall of the dynasty
by enforcing the reform system.[29] A few years later Emperor Kao-tsung
himself went further, blaming Wang An-shih more than Ts'ai Ching. He

commented that while people merely knew the crimes of Ts'ai and his associates, "trouble in the empire had really begun with Wang."[30] This echoed the opinion of another conservative, Ch'en Yuan (?–1145) who asserted that "unless the Wang school of learning becomes extinct, the good government of the founding fathers will not return . . . and the present restoration cannot succeed."[31]

As a result of such hostile opinion, the court removed the honorific table for Wang An-shih from the temple of the former emperor, Shen-tsung (r. 1068–1085). Shortly thereafter, it rescinded his posthumous title of Prince Shu and purged the original order of his investiture from the record as if it had never happened. By then Wang had become fair game for denunciation. His attackers, however, did not concentrate so much on his New Policy programs as on his Confucian theories. In fact, the severe critics denied that Wang was a Confucian. They alleged that he had borrowed the ways of the ancient Legalists and hegemons and caused a number of Confucian gentlemen (meaning the conservatives) to be dismissed from court. They even charged that some of his famous poetry betrayed deviant sentiments. Kao-tsung agreed with these criticisms, remarking that Wang had a "wrong frame of mind," neither proper, nor orthodox.[37] All such attacks amounted to a virtual "excommunication." Henceforth any suggestion that smacked of reform or any kind of institutional change might be suspected of being not quite Confucian.

It was easy to criticize but hard to undo the reform measures one by one. Haphazard dismantling was not without practical difficulties or complications, nor did it always produce good results. The first reform program to go was the unpopular farming loans, the so-called young-shoots or green-shoots money on credit, that was allotted to peasants at sowing time, to be repaid with interest at harvest time. There was no dispute on its abolition, for administering it had involved many abuses. Local government clerks forced the loans on unwilling peasants, and local magistrates insisted on meeting the quota of the allotted sum. The next reform measure to go was the guild-exemption tax. Its payment had exempted the guilds from their compulsory contribution of various supplies to local government. Its abolition, however, led to complaints from many local troops who had neither sufficient supplies on hand nor funds to buy them. Under such circumstances they had to make extra demands on various trade guilds. A few years later this reform measure was restored. A lesson was learned from the process of instituting and then abolishing a system: What had been there for a long time could not be changed suddenly without causing trouble.[33] Wang An-shih had made the mistake of changing the system in a hurry. Those who wanted to get rid of his system after it had been in place for thirty to fifty years were equally at fault.

Service to the local government was always a troublesome problem. Conventional bureaucrats and conservative Confucians preferred to rely on the requisitioned service of selected households, usually the wealthy upper-grade households because these people were thought to be relatively trustworthy.[34] The reformers under Wang An-shih insisted on letting the magistrates replace the requisitioned service by organizing an extension under the bureaucracy that hired clerical staff and miscellaneous helpers. While their number would be large, the reformers believed that it would be more efficient, because unsatisfactory hired hands could be fired or severely punished.[35] In 1129, in the course of repealing various reform measures, the court decided to restore the old requisitioned service. Yet in many places local government officials reported that they could not implement the directive, for there were many difficulties: the lack of enough households that could afford to render the service, the need for experienced personnel, and the fact that people were accustomed to paying the tax in lieu of performing services. As late as 1147, it was found that the tax regulations for the hired service system, supposedly defunct after the directive of 1129, had remained in the law codes. Ultimately it was recognized that the requisitioned service and the hired service each had their respective merits and demerits, whereupon the court granted the local government the option of using either one as local conditions warranted.[36] After all, Sung China was a large empire and local conditions did vary considerably. Could the empire have been spared this great controversy over the service system (*i-fa*), its attendant heated debates, and widespread confusion, had the statesmen of one kind or another recognized early on the wisdom of being flexible? No one in the Southern Sung would know the answer. In fact, Confucianism was already turning inward to study specialized problems in established fields. No one even raised such a question!

The "ever-normal" granaries (*ch'ang-p'ing ts'ang*) that the local governments held in reserve for relief, price stabilization, and emergencies, had
been in operation long before the reform system, but the Reform increased their numbers and extended their functions in many ways. Using
their reserve resources far more actively and flexibly than before, they
got in and out of the grain market as well as other commodity markets
to keep government supplies in balance, provide disaster relief for the
people, and stabilize market prices.[37] From the outset, the Southern
Sung government wanted to change this system. In order to curtail the
operations of the granaries, it abolished the offices in charge of them and
put some of their functions under the jurisdiction of other revenue
offices. Then, it issued another order contravening the first one and keeping the ever-normal granaries fully staffed for the time being. Finally,
came a third edict to disregard the second order and proceed with the
abolition of the supervisory offices. These somersaults in policy occurred
within a short time interval, between 1127 and 1128. Another reduction
came in 1135 when the remaining functions of the ever-normal granaries were combined with the duties of the revenue officials in charge of
tea and salt monopolies. Only much later was it realized that these low-
level officials had no way to prevent the governors and others who out-
ranked them from borrowing the various commodities in the granaries.
Consequently, the granaries fell into disarray.[38]

The criticisms against the reform measures and the efforts to get rid
of them reinforced the general opinion in favor of conservatism as well
as an over-generalized prejudice against any kind of reform. "A system
that has lasted for a long time must not be trifled with," so generalized
Emperor Kao-tsung, quoting a injunction from ancient Han period that
"unless there should be a hundred advantages, do not change the law."
On another occasion, he invoked the authority of his ancestors by observing: "Many who give us advice urge us to reform, but we think the
old ways of our ancestors have been good enough. How can we tamper
with such?" Ch'in Kuei, his scheming surrogate, promptly assured him:
"The empire basically has no trouble. It would be good to follow the
established institutions." Greatly pleased by this remark Kao-tsung added another comment: "Only petty persons would like to make changes
in the laws."[39] With the gate of reform closed, it was the conservative

influence that shaped the outlook of most young scholars. For instance, Yü Yün-wen, a talented man in both civilian and military affairs who later on won a great victory over the Jurchens, won high praise as a young official for an essay written in 1158 outlining three ways of government common to good emperors: to revere heaven in awe, to calm the people, and to emulate the ways of ancestors.[40] He said nothing about reform or change of policy, for the political-intellectual atmosphere was set against such.

Change always involves practical difficulties. As several councilors explained, officials who made new proposals were not necessarily familiar with either the background of a policy or current conditions. In discussing a possible change of state policy, some would cite old regulations, while others would argue on the basis of recent practices. Some policies proved successful in particular regions but were of questionable applicability to other parts of the country.[41] It was difficult to alter established ways: Their inertia was great and conservatism was often the name of following routine. Someone once asked Emperor Kao-tsung to do something about the defects in the system of licensed wineshops. Kao-tsung responded helplessly, perhaps wryly: "If it were possible to reform it, would it be like what it is today?"[42]

The conservative aversion to reform often found expression in the medical analogies that Confucians had used since ancient times. A person seriously ill for a long time, it was said, should not be given a potent drug, for in his weakened condition he might not get over its adverse reactions. The safest and therefore the best treatment was good rest and mild medicines for a slow recovery. Several councilors of varying persuasions shared the conservative view that the Southern Sung state's condition called for similar treatment. The emperor eventually came around to the same point of view.[43]

The gate to the avenue of reform was firmly shut. For a regime always under threat from the Jurchens, even in the decades of peace, it was hardly time for a drastic change.

THE CONSERVATIVE CLAIM TO ORTHODOXY

How to strengthen the early Southern Sung was basically a problem of direction. What could be safer than a new emphasis on the proven values of the good old days? Instead of attempting institutional changes, the regime looked to build a new image on high moral standards in the belief that morally sound officials would naturally bring about improvements. While the leading advocates of this approach were what we call the moralistic conservatives—a minority among court officials plus a few others who were summoned to court as imperial lecturers—conservatives of various other persuasions and even conventional Confucians generally favored it as well; for it was much closer to the traditional Confucian outlook than were reform ideas.

Emperor Kao-tsung, a well-educated prince and an accomplished calligrapher, was early on much impressed by the late Su Shih, whose versatile achievements in calligraphy, theory of painting, poetry, prose, essays on statecraft, classical learning, philosophical ideas, humor—indeed, the whole range of elite culture—best represented the spirit of Northern Sung diversity. He restored to Su Shih posthumously the titular rank of academician.[44] Soon he developed an admiration for Ssu-ma Kuang, the veteran conservative leader against the Reform and renowned historian of impeccable character.[45] At the imperial lectures, Ssu-ma's *Comprehensive Mirror for Aid in Government* was prominently featured. *The Comprehensive Mirror* itself, of course, was explicitly intended to serve as a guide to the lessons of history, especially to their moral implications. Studying it, Kao-tsung agreed, would help one understand the basic causes behind order and chaos (*chih* and *luan*). He liked the book so much that in 1134 he sent a copy as a gift to a Jurchen commander, his enemy and would-be conqueror.[46] It was probably the ill-advised gesture of a young sovereign who was not yet politically mature.

The avenue to good order, the conservative theory of Ssu-ma Kuang repeatedly expounded, lay in the "rectification of names" (*cheng ming*) or, in modern terms, the voluntary affirmation of one's proper status and mutual recognition of the relationships that govern one's role and duties (*ming-fen*). Kao-tsung also appreciated Ssu-ma Kuang's view that the key to propriety was the practice of "rectifying the mind and making the thoughts sincere" (*cheng hsin ch'eng i*), as taught by the ancient classic, *The Great Learning*. This expression later became a slogan in Chu Hsi's Neo-Confucian school. In calligraphy, Kao-tsung praised Ssu-ma Kuang's style of archaic script for being like the work of Han period artists; but more than anything else, he admired what Ssu-ma Kuang had written on self-cultivation and the regulation of family life. The emperor went so far as to say that he wished some way could be found for the civil service examination to evaluate self-cultivating and family virtues.[47] Apparently a cornerstone of moralistic conservatism had already been set down in his mind fairly early in the reign.

How would the state implement such ideas as Ssu-ma Kuang had proposed? The moralistic conservatives, generally speaking, had few concrete measures to suggest. What they excelled in was mainly theoretical philosophy. While they held definite views about history and held strong opinions on current affairs, they were neither professional historians like Ssu-ma Kuang nor experienced in government. At one point, Ssu-ma had proposed a new office for general auditing, but this was never implemented. The same suggestion was made twice at the southern court, but the bureaucracy rejected it as impractical. The only institutional improvement that Ssu-ma had been known for was separating officials into ten functional categories according to their talents, but even this system was never fully put into practice. When Kao-tsung wished to institute the same system, opinions among the established bureaucrats at court differed on its efficiency. The court did approve a revised proposal listing only six categories; but the revised version was soon abandoned, for it did not fit in with the rest of the established civil service system.[48]

Kao-tsung sought out the intellectual heirs of Ssu-ma Kuang or scholars of kindred persuasion and made them imperial lecturers or readers at court so that they would give him proper orientation. A number of these happened to be near his new capital at Lin-an because the Jurchen conquest of the north and penetrations of the south had forced a remarkable convergence of Sung political, economic, and intellectual centers at the coast. By the end of the eleventh century, the vigor of the conservatives who had gathered in Lo-yang in the Yellow River region was beginning to diminish and their schools definitely declined in the first quarter of the twelfth. Nevertheless, their thought was carried out from the region and gathered momentum as it went south. Particularly significant was the phenomenal growth in Fukien, where Yang Shih, who had studied with both Ch'eng Hao and Ch'eng I, attracted considerable fame as their leading disciple and the first master to establish the Ch'eng school in the south. When the Yellow River region was occupied by the Jurchens, most of the school's remaining strength scattered. Some went to Shansi, Szechuan, or the mid-Yangtze region. In Chekiang near the lower Yangtze and in coastal Fukien, several of the more influential conservative groups were established. Thus, although the moralistic conservatives were in a decided minority at court, their leading intellectuals could keep a close watch on events and were at hand when the emperor wished to hear them.

The first conservative intellectual summoned to Kao-tsung's court was Ch'iao Ting (dates unknown), who had studied under Ch'eng I. When he arrived, no one seemed particularly impressed. He himself realized that his views would hardly be acceptable to the court and most of its officials. When the court considered moving away from a threatening military situation, he asked for leave to return to Szechwan. A plain citizen thereafter, he was never heard from again.[49]

The second intellectual adviser summoned to court was Yang Shih. Though already seventy-five years old, he had high prestige for having studied under both Ch'eng brothers. He also knew the ways of the government for he had held office briefly at the end of the Northern Sung. The only step of symbolic consequence he took was his proposal to strip Wang An-shih, the reformer, of all his posthumous official and ritual honors. His admiring followers compared it to a surgeon's knife cutting right into the heart of the matter, a laudatory observation few others shared. Otherwise, Yang confined himself to lectures on purely academic matters. After a short time he resigned on account of old age.[50]

Hu An-kuo (1074–1138), the third intellectual summoned to court, was a disciple of the first one and nearly as famous as the second. He served for about six years, longer than either of his predecessors. By this time Kao-tsung's interest in history had gone beyond the period covered by Ssu-ma's famous chronicle to remote antiquity. Hu An-kuo was therefore asked to lecture on the *Spring and Autumn Annals* and the accounts in the *Tradition of Tso* (*Tso chuan*); but Kao-tsung later remarked that he had learned ancient history less from Hu than from another, younger conservative named Chang Chiu-ch'eng (1092–1159). Hu succeeded neither in getting the emperor interested in studying other classics nor in making a strong impression with his opinions on current affairs. In frustration, he confided to his son: "I have written twenty essays on current affairs. They may not have covered enough ground, but even if Chu-ke Liang [of the third century; reputedly the most brilliant strategist-statesman in Chinese history] were alive, he could hardly improve on these." However, according to the compiler of the *SYHA*, his essays consisted mostly of platitudes.[51]

While his predecessors stayed away from court politics, Hu became involved. At the time, Chu Sheng-fei (1082–1144), a moderate councilor, was criticized for practicing favoritism in personal matters, for being in favor of making peace overtures, and for not doing enough to strengthen defense. Hu made an open attack on him that contributed to his dismissal. On the other hand, Hu was friendly toward Ch'in Kuei, unaware that this manipulative councilor was secretly promoting peace negotiations with the Jurchens. Apparently the eminent scholar, naive in politics, lacked good judgment. In the end, the majority opinion at court, which had been polite but never warm, turned markedly cool toward the conservative side. Ch'en Kung-fu (1076–1141), who seemed to have been a friend at first, seized an opportunity to attack Hu An-kuo and the Ch'eng school in general for advocating strange theories and attempting a factional monopoly of Confucian interpretations. The attack caused Hu to be dismissed from court, though subsequently what he wrote in retirement on the *Spring and Autumn Annals* won him delayed court recognition.[52]

The fourth intellectual adviser at court was Yin Ch'un (1011–1132). A native of the Lo-yang area like the Ch'eng brothers, he had stayed behind under Jurchen occupation but later managed to escape to the south. Fan Ch'ung (1067–1141), a nephew of Hu An-kuo, recommended Yin Ch'un highly, saying that his views were superb. Other high officials also praised him, but the emperor felt that his lectures and discussions offered little beyond the philosophy of the Ch'eng brothers. As Ch'eng I had done at the Northern Sung court, Yin Ch'un criticized some inconsequential personal tastes of the emperor. For example, he objected to Kao-tsung's reading the poems of the renowned Huang T'ing-chien (1045–1105): "What good purpose can be served by reading the poetry of that fellow?"[53] When Yin Ch'un found himself at odds with what was going on at court, he complained that many officials who were not learned enough regarded his scholarship as "impractical and irrelevant." In his conviction moral philosophy was the necessary foundation for defense and the emperor's moral frame of mind was the very essence of state policies. In a memorial objecting to the peace negotiations as well as in a personal letter to Ch'in Kuei, he insisted on principle that he must resign from the court post. Later, Chu Hsi and his school paid high tribute to Yin Ch'un. Following their line, the original compiler of the *SYHA* overpraised him, but its editor questioned this evaluation. He asked, For all that Yin Ch'un had studied throughout his life, how much did he contribute to state affairs?[54]

None of these moralistic conservatives who served as imperial lecturers fared very well. One reason was their own failure to develop new theoretical dimensions beyond the known teachings of the eleventh-century masters. They were in a sense compounded conservatives: not only politically conservative in opposing institutional change but also intellectually conservative in confining themselves to their own frame of mind. They turned inward in the sense that they worked hard only within the perimeters that had been set by their mentors.

Nor did they write a great deal. Perhaps in the trough between one intellectual wave and the next they could not help being relatively unproductive, especially considering the trouble and dislocation of war time. Nor were they favored by the political environment, in which most active scholar-officials were politically realistic and calculating, rather than philosophically inclined.

The emperor wanted to have a few moralistic conservatives at court in part to satisfy his own intellectual curiosity, in part as a political gesture within the bureaucracy to show that his policy orientation was different from that of the dark days that had preceded his reign, and in part as window dressing that would help his public image in the country at large. He never intended to rely on them for political advice. Nonetheless, these seemingly impractical scholars did leave their mark on history. By standing on principle, they lent support to those in opposition to the current policies and kept alive hope for the outlook of moral reconstruction. They inspired some young scholars of the next generation to keep on struggling and in the end to form a new school, that of the transcendental moralists.

The ineffectiveness of these conservative intellectuals notwithstanding, Kao-tsung shared their nostalgic admiration for the conservative Yuan-yu reign that followed the Reform.[55] Since its leaders had been persecuted as the Yuan-yu faction in the late Northern Sung, with a notorious tablet listing their names erected in many parts of the country, Kao-tsung ordered a rehabilitation. All of them were to be given posthumous honors "to attract the attention of the eyes and ears of people everywhere."[56] The honor roll, however, had omissions; for the condemnatory tablets had mostly been destroyed at the end of the Northern Sung, and written records were also incomplete. But soon some remote local government discovered a rubbing of the persecution tablet; the complete list was then announced by a repeated court order. The sons and grandsons of these Yuan-yu worthies were also given the privilege of reporting to the government for official appointments. Special high honors were posthumously bestowed upon Su Shih, Ch'eng I, and a select few, the highest going to Ssu-ma Kuang, who was made a companion figure in the temple of the former emperor, Che-tsung.[57]

The interest of Emperor Kao-tsung in recent events opened the door to controversy over the official histories drafted during the seesaw eras when the reform system was first repealed and then restored. The first draft, prepared under the direction of conservative leadership, showed the reformers in a bad light. The second one, drafted after the reform system had been restored, painted a contrary picture to the annoyance of those who cherished the memory of their conservative predecessors. Fan Ch'ung, whose father Fan Tsu-yü (1041–1098) had collaborated with Ssu-ma Kuang in writing the famous chronicle, was appointed the editor to make yet another revision.[58] After Fan Ch'ung did the third draft, several officials who were not conservatives pointed out so many errors arising from his personal and revengeful bias that Kao-tsung was obliged to issue a rescript ordering him to correct its, so to speak, sins of commission and omission by further research. In the end, the court approved this last draft as amended.[59]

The prestige of the conservative gradually rose in the examination hall. In 1132, Chang Chiu-ch'eng (whose lessons in ancient history the emperor preferred to those of Hu An-kuo) placed first among the doctoral candidates and thus took the first step in his fame, which was to spread widely, even into North China under the Jurchens. In 1135, one of Chang's disciples in the doctoral examination again placed first.[60] The emperor saw in this repeated achievement of splendid performance an indication that conservative scholarship was indeed praiseworthy and deserved promotion. He expressed the wish that candidates in the future devote more time to the classics and the writings of the conservative Yuan-yu era, instead of paying so much attention to poetry and poetic-prose. A few years later, he repeated his wish more specifically by saying that the examination essays should test knowledge of statecraft problems, both past and present, and emphasize understanding the Confucian way of self-cultivation, regulation of family life, and their extension to governing the state. This was what the moralistic conservative theory always called for.[61]

Not yet satisfied, many conservatives, and especially the Chu Hsi school later on, asserted that their scholarship was not only the best but the correct one: the true orthodoxy of the Confucian heritage. The issue of orthodoxy was most timely in the realistic context of international rivalry. The Jurchen state by occupying the central plain, the political heartland, had a ready-made claim to political legitimacy. To counter it, the Sung would do well to claim ideological orthodoxy and, by extension, cultural supremacy as the highest civilization. This would serve in their own eyes to compensate for their military weakness as well as to boost their political self-confidence. It would also help to retain the Sung's claim as the central empire vis-à-vis the lesser states around China's other borders. On this score, all Confucians and everyone else in the Southern Sung agreed. What caused debate was the question whether all Confucians had an equal claim to the merit conferred by this orthodoxy. Part of the debate took the form of asking, had the orthodoxy come down from ancient times?

The year 1136 was a fateful one in China's intellectual history. The issue of ideological orthodoxy and its line of transmission sparked a bitter in-fight among the Confucians. It was ignited by Chu Chen (1072–1138), a moralistic conservative from present-day Hupei or the mid-Yangtze region.[62] Following a belief rooted in social conventions, he held that orthodoxy was transmitted through linear succession from a master to a chosen disciple (on rare occasions to a chosen group), much like the line of succession in various religions from a prophet to a disciple or like the imperial succession and, more basically, family primogeniture. Many other Confucians never believed in such linear succession of orthodoxy, nor was there conclusive evidence in ancient literature to support it.

But Chu Chen did not stop there. Instead he made a bold claim. The *tao* or true way, he said, passed from the kings of remote antiquity to Confucius, the greatest sage or the "philosophical king"; from Confucius it passed to Tseng Shen, his leading disciple; from Tseng to Tzu-ssu, Confucius' grandson; and from him to Mencius. Then, after Mencius, the line was interrupted by a long hiatus. Neither legitimate successor nor specific transmission existed for nearly a thousand years, until the line was rediscovered and taken up by the Ch'eng brothers—Ch'eng Hao and Ch'eng I—of the Lo-yang region during the Northern Sung. Henceforth their school was the champion of the true orthodoxy. Then it spread southward, with the implication that the shift paralleled that of the court. Several other followers of this school made similar claims with only slight variations. Some of them drew diagrams to show the transmission like a genealogy. Some of them wrote solemnly as if they spoke by the authority of Confucius and Mencius. But Chu was the first to present the claim formally at court.[63]

No sooner had the claim been made than attacks followed. The line of succession shown by the moralistic conservatives was drawn so narrowly that it could not possibly avoid antagonizing many other Confucians. Leading the attack was Ch'en Kung-fu. How he decided to make the attack is worth repeating in detail, for it epitomizes the style of bureaucratic in-fighting among Confucians. Originally, Ch'en had distinguished himself in leading many young Fellows of the Advanced Institute. He greatly impressed Fan Ch'ung, who recommended him for a higher position. His theoretical criticism of Wang An-shih caused his fame to rise at court. Thus far, he had befriended a number of moralistic conservatives, though he was not one of them. In 1136, he saw the political wind changing and wished to distance himself from them. Fearing he might still be suspect of rallying the support of young Fellows at the Advanced Institute to the conservative cause, he decided to make his own stand clear, to turn against the conservatives, and to please some of his superiors by submitting a stirring memorial attacking Chu Chen's claim of orthodoxy as false and pretentious.[64]

Despite Ch'en Kung-fu's ulterior motives, the first part of his memorial sounded fair. It pointed out that the intellectual-political style of the literati degenerated after Wang An-shih had made them follow his own theories. It would be an equally serious mistake at this time, he argued, to put forward Ch'eng I's theory as the only correct one. Such a mistaken step would only induce many opportunists to join the Ch'eng school for selfish gain or to pretend to follow its teachings in order to win fame. Then Ch'en's memorial turned biting. It said that such distorting scholar-officials would voice strange sayings, attributing them to Ch'eng I. They would wear bulky dresses with big sleeves and raise their eyes while walking in long steps, claiming that it was the Ch'eng manner. This would be absurd. "If Ch'eng I were alive," Ch'en Kung-fu asked rhetorically, "could a man like him really handle state affairs well?"

The alleged transmission of the true way, or orthodoxy, Ch'en Kung-fu continued, was equally absurd. Could the incredible claim that it went exclusively to the Ch'eng brothers be proven? And where was it at present? Such an assertion was a "mad exaggeration, if not a ridiculous boast," he concluded. Others followed Ch'en's lead and heaped attacks on the moralistic conservatives for their presumptuous, impertinent self-aggrandizement in claiming that they alone represented the Confucian orthodoxy.[65]

Having quashed at this juncture the partisan claim to exclusive orthodoxy and its alleged transmission, the critics redoubled their attacks on the teachings of the Ch'eng school. Ch'en Kung-fu was the first to recommend that neither the government nor the civil sevice examinations should officially adopt the private theories of any particular group such as the Ch'eng school, for such theories tended to be biased or distorted. Others went further. They alleged that the Ch'eng teachings were full of exaggerations, lacked utilitarian values, originated in part in Buddhism, speculated on metaphysical voidness, and altogether constituted a deviant heresy.[66] The implication was devastating: Far from teaching the only orthodoxy, the school was itself heterodox.

Indeed the moralistic conservatives had overreached themselves. First of all, they had underestimated the extent of potential opposition to their claim of orthodoxy. They should have realized that their prestige, though considerable, was far from being enough to persuade a sufficient number of officials and literati to support them. For example, shortly before the 1136 controversy, Chu Chen was reportedly going to preside over the next examination. An objection was promptly raised that he would favor those candidates who followed the Ch'eng school. As a result, he never got the assignment. Second, self-importance was a common fault of many moralistic conservatives. Their highminded air offended other scholars. Yet they persisted in their self-righteous claim to orthodoxy, ignoring as irrelevant the numerous criticisms and sarcastic jibes that had been thrown at them.[67]

While the personal integrity and conduct of leading moralistic conservatives were beyond reproach, the behavior of many among their followers was not. Some claimed falsely to have been affiliated with the Ch'eng school; yet the conservative leaders did not bother to check or verify their claims. Others falsified their family background, as northern immigrants who came south often did, and passed themselves off as descendants of the Yuan-yu era worthies so that they could qualify for privileged appointments. Yet others were sheer opportunists. As soon as they heard that Yang Shih and a few other conservative scholars had been promoted to court positions, they came forward unsolicited as disciples of their schools to ask for recommendations. Some conservative leaders, like Chao Ting (see Chapter Six), accepted them all at face value and recommended them for assignments. They had only themselves to blame when these self-seekers failed to live up to expectations, or worse, betrayed them to political opponents.[68]

The controversy of 1136 decidedly put the conservatives in a bad position. Such intellectuals at court as Chu Chen failed to put up a defense. It appeared that Emperor Kao-tsung had inclined to approve or agree with the criticisms against the Ch'eng school. Fortunately for them, this was before Hu An-kuo was dismissed from court; and he rose to defend the conservative position. After all, he said, the Ch'engs had learned from Confucius and Mencius; why then should their philosophy be rejected? In his words, to ban it would be like going into a room without walking through the door; that is, a teaching can be entered only through interpretation. Moreover, Ch'eng I's exemplary conduct had been outstanding in terms of filial piety, brotherly love, loyalty, and sincerity. It was generally known that he would never accept anything unless it accorded with his moral values and particularly his sense of justice; such a philosopher deserved respect. Admittedly, many of his present followers had faults. They were ridiculed for their pretentious mannerism as Ch'en Kung-fu had sarcastically mentioned. But the fault lay with the followers—what did it have to do with Ch'eng I himself?[69]

Kao-tsung was a most subtle ruler. After Hu's defense, he decided to discourage the Ch'eng school without appearing to do so. As a rule in general policy, he did not wish to see his court divided into opposing factions. On the contrary, he preferred a "soft" approach, emulating the example of the restoring emperor Kuang-wu of the Later Han (r. A.D. 25–57), in order to accommodate as many scholar-officials as possible.[70] Early on he had announced that the learning of the Ch'eng school and the scholarship of Wang An-shih each had its respective merits. In the wake of this controversy, he shifted the balance subtly in favor of the majority among the bureaucrats and almost imperceptibly let the moralistic conservatives slip behind. Instead of spelling out this shift in explicit words, he resorted to euphemism. He issued a rescript and later repeated its message a couple of times that "the specialized learning" and "private theories" ought to be "restrained."[71] Nothing was said about rejecting such theories or reprimanding the scholars who held them. After all, scholars should exercise the Confucian virtue of self-restraint themselves. Yet, everyone knew what the code words *specialized learning* and *private theories* stood for. Over the next few decades, the popularity of the Ch'eng school noticeably declined.

In addition to this controversy, a power struggle at the top contributed to the fall of moralistic conservatism. Chao Ting, the leading patron of the Ch'eng school, was no longer the leading councilor.[72] Ch'in Kuei who replaced him soon became the emperor's surrogate. He retained in large measure the style of the Restored Reform era. An astute schemer, he rarely expressed his opinion explicitly, but everyone knew that he did not favor the conservatives or the Ch'eng school theories (see Chapter Five). In 1144, the emperor approved a memorial that reminded the civil service examiners to bar the "specialized" learning and "crooked theories," a more disparaging euphemism than "private theories." Although still a veiled attack, it called for more than "restraint." The same discrimination prevailed at the Advanced Institute.[73] A few years later, Ch'in Kuei's own grandson openly attacked the Ch'eng philosophy in his examination paper. He wrote: "Those who talk about rectifying the mind have not rectified their own minds. Those who talk about making the thoughts sincere have not really done so themselves."[74] He was calling the moralistic conservatives hypocrites. From 1144 till 1155 when Ch'in Kuei died, moralistic conservatism had no active role in state affairs. But no formal ban appeared until long after the reign of Emperor Kao-tsung, a masterful ruler who always avoided extremes and kept a balance among all political elements.

The death of Ch'in Kuei brought neither an end to the veiled discrimination nor a rise in the prestige of the Ch'eng school. With or without Ch'in Kuei, Kao-tsung preserved approximately the same policy during the rest of his reign.[75] The intellectual atmosphere left much to be desired; it was heavily bureaucratically minded and not idealistically inclined at all. As one observation put it, all over the country "the elite are tormented by partisanship; as scholars, they waver according to the rise and fall of a school's current popularity; and as officials, they worry about the civil service merit-rating.[76]

Yet, away from court, moralistic conservatism went on undaunted. The Ch'eng school gave birth to the heir that has become known in Western sources centuries later as Neo-Confucianism. Its proponents succeeded in expanding their influence phenomenally by writing, by printing their kind of books, and especially by teaching. While local official schools in various places declined or degenerated, the Neo-Confucians promoted, started, and enlarged private academies wherever they stayed. They struggled indefatigably for several decades through political storms and stress, even a governmental persecution. Neither trials nor tribulations could prevent them from reaching a crowning victory: The state finally honored their kind of Confucianism as the orthodoxy.

This orthodoxy not only lasted beyond the rest of the Sung period until the end of the nineteenth century in China but also spread to Korea, Japan, and Vietnam. Neo-Confucianism shaped the mind and values throughout East Asia.

FIVE

Autocracy and Councilors

Chinese intellectuals' interest in state affairs was persistent; but their moods and behavior depended on prevailing political conditions, particularly on whether power was exercised exclusively by the emperor; by a surrogate who acted as his proxy; or, as had been normal, by several leading councilors who shared some measure of decision-making power. Increasingly in the late Northern Sung and into the Southern Sung, frustration typified scholar-officials in general as emperors or their surrogates gathered up the lion's share of power, leaving them little room to participate in court deliberations. On occasion, they fought to make their voices heard, but rarely did they succeed in making them prevail. They had two choices, either to continue to serve the government or to get out. When they resigned, the moralistic conservatives were especially inclined to explore long-range avenues for building up their prestige and influence. They publicized their opinions, theories, and scholarship through social channels and, more importantly, through teaching with their eyes on future generations.

The abuse of imperial power dated from about 1100, toward the tragic demise of the Northern Sung. Hui-tsung (r. 1101–1125), the next to last emperor, was one of the most talented and accomplished artists in Chinese history; but politically his reign was a disaster. Among his notable indulgences were his elevation of the Taoist religion and his absurd adoption of the extra title of Taoist supreme ruler; the construction of an extravagant imperial park next to the palace, for which he shipped exotic flowers and rocks from distant places in the Yangtze delta; and his secret but scandalous visits to a house of ill-repute.

As to the country, Hui-tsung left it in the hands of one unworthy surrogate after another. They ostensibly revived the reform system of 1069–1085, but without its original spirit, only with its many defects compounded now by corruption. Political revenge escalated when the court for no compelling reason banished the opposing conservatives to remote places. It was at this time, to add insult to injury, that the government branded them as the Yuan-yu (1085–1093) faction and engraved their names on stone tablets near local government offices. The persecution extended to the future; even their heirs were forever barred from civil service. As a contravention of Confucian principles, the purge was a terrible blow that sent shock waves throughout the ranks of the literati.

What caused greater shock, of course, was the invasion by the Jurchens from Manchuria that caused the shrinking of the Sung Empire. Conventional histories of the Southern Sung have always concentrated on the military hostilities with the Jurchens; issues centering on the peace negotiations; and the struggle to establish internal order in the face of mutinies, uprisings, and too much power in the hands of entrenched generals. More recently, economic histories have concentrated on the growth of cities, transportation, agriculture, and finance, all of which, despite the calamities of war and the conquest of the north continued to expand. (Even trade with the north continued.) But an important area of research has been overlooked. The early to middle twelfth century saw decisive changes in politics that were to have consequences in China for years to come. This study seeks to examine the heart of the changes: the expansion of autocratic power. To do so, it focuses on the sensitive relationship between the emperor and his leading councilors.

In Sung China, the emperor presided over, but normally refrained from dictating to the enormous, centralized, government administration. The bureaucracy was divided into separate branches for general administration, military affairs, and finance, each with separate or supposedly inviolable powers within its own area. The administration exercised executive, legislative, and judicial powers through various scholar-officials, who generally considered themselves to be Confucian gentlemen. It was their responsibility to use their discretionary powers—some appropriated from China's ancient Legalist theories—to govern wisely and flexibly while holding to moral principles. A forerunner of the modern centralized state, the Sung was far from being an all-inclusive or excessively powerful totalitarian state.

A special category of officials were supposed to act as a check on the abuses that could result from the excessive concentration of power in the bureaucracy or the throne. There were the opinion officials (*yen-kuan*), who carried such titles as policy critic-advisors, censors, censorial official, and court academicians. These opinion officials had few or no administrative duties. Their main function was to check up on all other officials responsible for administration, to make recommendations, and in serious cases to prefer charges. In the best of times, the exchanges and debates between the opinion and the administrative side helped achieve consensus. When conflicts led to factionalism, however, resignations and dismissals, abrupt policy reversals, and a general decline in administrative efficiency and bureaucratic morale followed.

The emperor personally held the mandate of heaven (*tien-ming*) that gave legitimacy to the government, so that he is often called an autocrat in Western discussion. Yet he normally exercised authority through councilors or a councilor of state. The term *councilor* is used here in its generic sense. It refers to the ranking ministers who functioned as top executives at court with such titles as *p'u-i* (an archaic formal title for chief councilor), *ch'eng-hsiang* (an informal appellation for the same, often rendered rather inaccurately as prime minister); *t'ung chung-shu men-hsia p'ing-chang shih* (literally, participant in Secretariat deliberations, the standard translation for which is first privy councilor); *ts'an-chih cheng-shih* (literally, associate in political affairs, the standard translation for which is second privy councilor or associate councilor): *shu-mi shi* (military commissioner) *t'ung-chih shu-mi-yuan shih* (coadministrator of military affairs); and the like. At this time, there were usually two chief councilors serving together with some division of labor between them. When the emperor preferred to have only one chief councilor, an associate councilor would play the supporting role. Only on rare occasions did a chief councilor take over completely, reducing the roles of all other nominally top executives to the performance of mere administrative functions. Such a councilor became a sole surrogate.

Because the relationship between the emperor and his councilors determined in reality the way the court functioned, focusing on them is a desirable theoretical short cut for understanding court politics. The historical records, in paying much attention to them, provide us with ample data. This is especially true of the *HNYL,* which is particularly valuable because it has been under-used in the past. The substance of this chapter largely results from searching through its three thousand pages. Also useful is the definitive source, the *HTC.* It reflects the research of the foremost scholars of the eighteenth century, the period when traditional historiography reached its maturity. Neither of these major sources, however, closely ties together the interactions between the emperor, the leading councilors, and the intellectuals. What the present study tries to do is precisely to put this triangle in a theoretical framework.

We begin by posing some perplexing questions. First, on councilors: How did Emperor Kao-tsung choose and dismiss them? From the beginning of his reign to the initial peace negotiations with the Jurchens in 1139, the emperor changed the councilors frequently. Then, Ch'in K'uei became the sole surrogate from 1139 till his death in 1155. The other councilors simply obeyed him. After his death, the pattern of shifts in councilors resumed until the end of Kao-tsung's long reign in 1162. Peace or war did not seem to be the principal factor. What then accounted for these variations?

Second, on military power: Kao-tsung embarked upon the restoration of his empire with only a few thousand troops and never had a large army of his own. Moreover, the leading generals with big armies that they had organized by themselves in several regions tended to follow more often their own inclinations than the wishes of the court. Under these circumstances, how did Kao-tsung succeed in wresting power from the generals and consolidating his autocratic power over all regions of the Southern Sung empire? How did the councilors help to achieve that?

Third, on the controversy over the peace terms of 1139: Besides the territorial loss of North China and the annual payment of tributary money and silk, what the moralistic conservatives found to be most unacceptable was the matter of status. Why did Kao-tsung not seem to mind yielding to the enemy demand of submitting himself as a vassal, subordinate to the superior state of the Jurchens, without his legitimate title of emperor?

Fourth, on the relationship between the autocratic power of the emperor and the surrogate's power: It is commonly assumed that the former became dormant when a surrogate took it over by delegation or usurpation. This is an error based on a false underlying premise that court power is a constant so that when the share held by the surrogate increases, part of the emperor's personal autocratic power decreases by subtraction. The present study proposes a different hypothesis. Both the total court power of the emperor and his councilors and the state power of the government as a whole are variable. State power generally increases with organization, centralization, and assertiveness in controling the society. At court, the personal power of the head of the Sung government, whether the emperor or his surrogate, could increase in either of two ways. It could increase at the expense of power held by the councilors—that is, by the concentration of existing power into the hands of the actual ruler. It could also increase as a part of the expanding state power. Furthermore, the two processes fed each other. By vesting more power in the surrogate than any councilor normally held as well as by delegating his own power to the surrogate, the emperor created a figure powerful enough to exercise highly organized and concentrated power through the state machinery. This meant a great increase in total state power. When the surrogate died or resigned, this increase in total state power remained. Furthermore, if the emperor had all of the surrogate's power revert to himself, his own power or the total court power was also correspondingly enlarged. Did the pattern outlined in this hypothesis hold true for the Southern Sung?

Fifth and last, on the intellectuals, many of whom were moralistic conservatives: In all the storms and stress over the generals, the issue of peace and war, and the way the court wielded its power, what roles did they play? And what happened to them?

To avert the necessity of going through the long and often confusing narratives of political history, Table 2 is offered as a condensation of the key factual information needed for the analytic discussion to follow.

TABLE 2 Chronology of Southern Sung History, 1127–1139

Year	Key Events	Chief Councilors
1127	First bogus regime was established by the Jurchens and lasted thirty-three days.	Li, Huang
	Kao-tsung began his reign and retreated from Kuei-te to Yang-chou on the Yangtze.	
1128	The court was in Yang-chou.	Huang, Wang
1129	The court fled to Hang-chou.	Chu, Lu, Tu
	Mutiny at Hang-chou forced Kao-tsung to abdicate briefly.	Lu, Tu, Fan
1130	Jurchens penetrated deeply south of the Yangtze.	
	Kao-tsung took flight along the seacoast.	
1131	Jurchens set up a second bogus regime, under Liu Yü, in North China	Fan, Lu, Ch'in
	Kao-tsung returned to Shao-hsing near Hang-chou.	
1132		Lu, Ch'in, Chu
1133	Hang-chou became known as Lin-an.	Lu, Chu
1134	Kao-tsung led his first expedition to the Yangtze bank but returned promptly to Lin-an.	Chu, Chao
1135		Chao and Chang
1136	Kao-tsung led second expedition to the Yangtze bank.	
1137	An army disastrously defected.	(Chang dismissed)
	Kao-tsung returned to Lin-an.	Chao and Ch'in
	Jurchens abolished Liu Yü's bogus regime.	
1138	Jurchen envoys were sent to Lin-an for peace negotiations.	(Chao dismissed)
1139	Initial peace and amnesty declared.	Ch'in (surrogate)

Source for councilors: SS 213:5543–5554.
For the full names of chief councilors, see Appendix I.

THE SHIFTING COUNCILORS (1127–1134)

The information in Table 2 makes analysis easy. For one thing, it shows how often Kao-tsung changed chief councilors in the first decade of his reign. Chang Chiu-ch'eng, a young conservative, offered some succinct advice to Kao-tsung. He said it was well known that the rise and fall of empires had depended a great deal on emperors' actions. Not often realized was the fact that it also had much to do with councilors; yet their success or failure in turn depended on what emperor allowed them or caused them to be. This was a major criticism of Kao-tsung's frequent change of councilors, his lack of definite policies for them to carry out, and the degree of uncertainty that resulted. In the early years of the reign, the majority of councilors served about a year. As some critics complained, such instability demoralized the bureaucracy. Few officials, knowing that their superiors would be gone before long, would work as hard as they should.[2] Worse yet, the removal of one councilor and emergence of another unavoidably split the bureaucracy into antagonistic groups, even when no factionalism really existed. Some councilors tried not to choose key officials only from among their own circles, but the mere intention of being impartial was not enough to heal divisiveness.[3]

Kao-tsung did not admit to his early fault of having made the councilors insecure in their positions. On the contrary, he claimed that he always gave their appointments and tenures serious considerations. He said he had never dismissed any councilor till he had found that he must.[4] In his own words, "How can we, secluded in the palace, possibly know among the hundreds of officials who have been doing well and who have not? The only way is for us to look closely at how the councilors are doing."[5] These very words, it seems, betrays a tension between the ruler and his right-hand men. Kao-tsung watched, probably too closely and anxiously. In his inexperience, he tended to be fault-finding, impatient, or quickly dissatisfied with the councilors. The tension mounted when he was on the verge of dismissing a councilor. As Kao-tsung remarked in another context, "The nature of the power a sovereign holds dictates that he has to make single-handed decisions."[6] Either for getting or for getting rid of a top executive at court, the monarchial system had a serious defect: It provided no one for the emperor to consult. But apparently

Kao-tsung learned from mistakes in his early years; later on, he would first decide on a policy orientation and then choose appropriate councilors for its implementation.

According to Kao-tsung, he was quite willing to delegate power. To a large extent, this was true. In the first place, he showed confidence in the councilors by backing them and their actions.[7] Then he sent the former councilors away from court so that they would neither cast any shadow nor exert lingering influence to interfere with their successors. This was a drastic departure from the Northern Sung practice that had usually kept former councilors in some other capacity at court nominally for the benefit of convenient consultation when desired. In the Southern Sung, they were not even allowed to reside near the capital.[8] Thirdly, the new councilors were granted their wishes on changes of personnel so that they would have in key positions the officials they wanted to work with.[9] These personnel changes, though regarded by critics to be a source of bureaucratic divisiveness, were justifiable according to the conventional wisdom in Confucianism that councilors had a major responsibility in "promoting talents and demoting others."[10]

The chief councilors under Kao-tsung did have considerable power, consistent with the trend that had been growing since the Reform, the strong leadership of the anti-reform by Ssu-ma Kuang, and the indulgence of the penultimate Northern Sung emperor. Nevertheless, the normal jurisdiction of the chief councilor had been confined to civilian administration and by extension to the supervision of financial matters.[11] It had not intruded into military affairs, which were under the separate jurisdiction of a military commissioner.[12] The Southern Sung, however, at its beginning had to fight for its life. By necessity, the chief executive official had to attend to both financial and military exigencies.[13] As civilian, financial, and military jurisdiction became concentrated in the hand of the chief councilor, that office became an unprecedented power base. It foreshadowed the coming of an all-powerful surrogate who stood next to the emperor and managed everything. Before 1139, however, this had not happened yet. Usually two chief councilors—one for civilian administration, the other for military matters—took care of state affairs, each with his respective share of pertinent financial jurisdiction.[14]

At the beginning the Southern Sung, with no regular army to speak of, resisted the Jurchen invasions largely by relying on generals who expanded their personal followings and absorbed former bandit groups into sizable armies.[15] These generals had become accustomed to controlling their own regions without much supervision from the central government.[16] It was clearly Kao-tsung's intention from 1131 on to find ways to cut down their regional power. By an explicit order, he gave Lü I-hao, then the chief councilor, discretionary authority to reassert the control of the court over local government in terms of obedience to court orders, appointments, and fiscal matters.[17] While Lü did not succeed decisively, the court did gradually begin to exercise some degree of supervision over various places.[18] This well illustrates how the emperor's delegation of more power to a councilor in the name of centralization built up in due course more power for the court. In other words, autocratic power and its delegated power fed one another; each grew larger.

On the question of why councilors before 1139 fell from office after a short time, there were various reasons, rather than a single answer. The fundamental cause lay with the poor military state of the Southern Sung; not even a clear-headed, strong-willed, and most competent leader could have coped with the situation much better. Faced with the threatening Jurchen forces, which were augmented by non-Jurchen draftees and aided by ethnic Han troops recruited by the bogus ruler Liu Yü, the future of the southern empire looked precarious. As someone commented: "While war would inevitably lead to defeat . . . nor could peace negotiations get anywhere."[19] Caught in this dilemma, the court had no fixed policy and officials could form no consensus of opinion.[20] Often a military setback led to a councilor's being faulted and thrown out of office. His replacement, with inexperienced hands, would most likely try a different policy, steer an unsteady course, and fail to improve the military situation. Under these circumstances, one councilor observed that "he would not dare expect a long tenure of office."[21] In a sense, most councilors in the early Southern Sung were dismissed as scapegoats to enable the emperor to maintain his image as an infallible or blameless autocrat.

Apart from this fundamental cause were personal factors. In 1129, an army mutiny at Hang-chou forced Kao-tsung to abdicate temporarily. Chu Sheng-fei, an extremely skillful chief councilor, used delaying tactics to trick the mutiny ringleaders into refraining from drastic actions till the loyalists came to the rescue and put Kao-tsung back on the throne.[22] Although the chief councilor deserved immense credit in negotiating the crisis, he had seen the emperor in embarrassing circumstances.[23] It would be awkward for him to stay on, for the autocrat could not afford his image to be deflated. In the next case, Fan Tsung-yin (1096–1136), a young and overzealous chief councilor, had to go for he insisted on weeding out those officials who had received unjustifiable appointments because of the emperor's wish to be accommodating.[24] The case of Lü I-hao (1011–1139) was similar. He did well by the emperor and committed no serious mistake. When, however, he had antagonized many other officials and could no longer keep them from voicing their complaints, the emperor saw it best to ease him out politely without reprimand and try to find someone else who could keep the bureaucracy quiet.[25]

To the fundamental military cause and personal factors was added the perennial uncertainty of bureaucratic politics. In 1134 a puzzled Kao-tsung pointedly asked Chang Chün (1097–1164) a question: "Whenever our discussion runs into slight disagreement with the councilors, they seem to be so light-footed that they promptly ask to resign. Why is that?" Chang responded: "As soon as Your Majesty breathes one word about a disagreement with the councilors, some critics who learn which is the favored side line up arguments for it and attack the councilors who happen to have taken the other side. Under mounting attacks, they have no choice but to resign."[26] In other words, councilors were almost invariably the targets of jealousy and rivalry in bureaucratic politics, unless the power delegated to them was sustained by the emperor's steadfast backing. Yet, before the emperor himself acquired enough autocratic power to feel secure, he was inclined to accommodate complaining or criticizing officials, or at least listen to them, for the sake of keeping the support of the dissenters and a balance at court. Furthermore, a councilor who could not deal effectively with criticism in the bureaucracy was a political liability rather than an asset to the emperor.[27]

The Northern Sung stands out in Chinese history as an apogee of the bureaucratic state not only because of the model civil service system it developed but also because of its policy of treating bureaucrats well. It never put to death any high official at all. The government was reluctant to kill even a low-ranking official who was guilty of serious crime. Except on rare occasions, the Southern Sung abided by this tradition.[28] In other ways, however, the autocracy was less considerate than before. Dismissed councilors were not accorded great respect. As mentioned, they were neither kept at court nor near the capital.[29] Some of them appointed as governors or prefects did not last long in office. When criticisms against them persisted, the court would relieve them from such local offices and put them in retirement[30] with the honorary rank and sinecure title of "temple intendancy" by which they would get nothing more than the pension normally due to high officials.[31]

The fate of a dismissed high official could be worse than retirement, depending on political tension. A few outstanding chief councilors who eventually displeased Kao-tsung suffered banishment to distant regions. In extreme cases, they were exiled. More harsh than banishment, exile imposed the additional penalty of surveillance by the local government at the place of exile. The severest punishment for officials was exile of indefinite duration to a place far away, with strict surveillance and the stipulation that the sentence could not be reduced at the next general amnesty.[32]

Exile and banishment, however, were not necessarily for life nor irreversible. A punishment could be reduced later by a court order that permitted the disgraced official to move to a less remote place. Another order could then free him to live anywhere he chose, except the area near the capital, though he was still not readmitted to active government service.[33] True rehabilitation was, of course, the imperial favor of recalling the official by giving him an appointment, usually as a local prefect but rarely at court.[34] Even so, the resumed career was not likely to last.[35] Only in one outstanding exception, the case of Chang Chün, because the emperor remembered a military talent and deemed him to be useful again, did a previously purged high official re-emerge as a new councilor.[36]

THE TEAM OF COUNCILORS (1135–1136 AND AFTER)

The ideal of the Sung court system was to have the chief councilors work as a team, sharing the "same aspirations and values."[37] Under such ideal leadership, it was believed, other ministers would follow suit. Though such a lofty goal seemed too much to expect, Chao Ting and Chang Chün did achieve it for a couple of years. Both were upright and hard-working officials, devoted to the cause of restoring the empire through effective military strength and clean administration. Both served loyally at court with great merit. Their prestige among other scholar-officials remained high through the years. Chang, though a civilian, was best known for his knowledge of military strategies and his command capability. Unfortunately his big campaign using Szechwan as the base to counter-attack Shensi in the northwestern flank ended in a disastrous defeat in 1131. After that, he was in retirement, but not for long.

In 1135, both Chao and Chang were made chief councilors. Their appointments signified the court's determination to organize a stiff defense and to prepare for a counterattack.[38] They cooperated well, upholding high moral standards reminiscent of the Yuan-yu conservative era.[39] A division of labor worked efficiently: Chang in charge of military affairs and Chao for general administration.[40]

Events moved rapidly. The second Jurchen invasion, joined by the armies raised by the puppet Liu Yü, looked ominous at the outset. Stopped by the well organized Sung defense, however, it turned out to be weaker than the first one. Blaming Liu Yü for inadequate logistics, the Jurchens began to think about abolishing his bogus regime, though at the time the Southern Sung had no way of knowing that.[41] In order to boost morale, Emperor Kao-tsung announced an imperial expedition, leading troops from his capital Lin-an to Nanking on the banks of the Yangtze. There he received with great pleasure a report from the front, telling of the victory at Ou-t'ang, about a hundred miles to the north. It was no less than the first major victory the Sung army had ever scored.[42] But he remarked that what pleased him even more was the discipline with which the generals had followed court orders strictly.[43] In his mind, control over the armies counted most: it was a matter of state security.

Ironically, victory brought a fatal split between the two chief councilors. Chao remained cautious, while Chang was bold. Before the victory, Chao had suggested giving up the Huai valley and falling back upon the Yangtze river defense line to insure the strongest possible resistance. Chang's plan to meet the enemy head-on had now been proven right. After the victory, Chao still believed it prudent to reinforce the river defense. But Chang, flushed with confidence, deemed it timely to send the Sung armies northward in counterattack. Given this split and other hidden differences, Chao concluded that he should resign gracefully and neither stand in the way of Chang, his old friend and colleague, nor air the differences between them. Statesmanlike, he regarded himself as less indispensable than Chang and readily replaceable by someone else to take charge of the civilian administration. He advised the emperor accordingly that Chang should follow up this victory and engage in military preparations the way Chang wanted to. It would be a task of great importance. Kao-tsung reluctantly agreed to let Chao go, appointed him as the governor of Shao-hsing near the capital, but told him in a very exceptional way to stand by for recall to court duties.[44]

The esteemed team of councilors thus broke up, and not over strategy alone. There were other unpublicized reasons that had grave implications and consequences. The first was bureaucratic politics. According to Chao, he and Chang had worked together harmoniously like brothers. Unfortunately, some not so worthy officials who found out their difference in strategic outlook deliberately went back and forth between them to sow further discord. Even such old friends as Chao and Chang, who held each other in mutual respect, proved not to be immune to the perennial evil of poisonous tongues.[45] What Chao chose not to reveal was yet another reason: a difference in Confucian theoretical orientation. Chao, a moralistic conservative, chose followers who shared his belief in ethical principles, especially in propriety. Chang, who was not strictly speaking an intellectual, gathered around him men of talent who valued expedience more than morality. Chao promoted the Ch'eng school of learning. Chang, though not attached to any particular school, happened to be socially close to a number of officials whose orientation since the late Northern Sung lay with the restored reform system and the theories of the Wang school. This augmented the frictions between the two statesmen. When Chao supported a new revision of the historical records under a conservative editor he had recommended, Chang disapproved. When it was claimed that the line of transmission of the Confucian orthodoxy had come to the Ch'eng school, Chang again disagreed. In fact, it was just after Chao's resignation that Ch'en Kung-fu unleashed his attack on the conservative claim to the line of transmission. He did so with Chang's acquiescence.[46]

The story did not end there. At the time, Ch'in Kuei (1090–1155) enjoyed high reputation as a neutral figure among the court officials. Accordingly, Chang asked for Ch'in as Chao's replacement.[47] Ostensibly, this formed a new team; but the two men were never close. Chang, eager to get the armies ready for counterattack, replaced a veteran but ineffective general by a civilian official; but this civilian's ineptness provoked a massive defection. Some thirty to forty thousand troops went over to Liu Yü, and a wide gap was exposed in the Yangtze defense.[48] Greatly alarmed, the court returned in haste to the capital Lin-an, a step that Chao had suggested all along.[49] Numerous indictments were made against Chang. Furious, the emperor accused him of having wasted two years of military preparations involving immeasurable funds and manpower. As a result, Chang was again banished, this time for a quarter of a century until another Jurchen attack.[50]

When Chang was dismissed, he declined to recommend Ch'in to succeed him, saying that he found Ch'in devious and furtive. Kao-tsung decided to recall Chao, who pleaded with him to recall Chang also or, failing that, to retain Chang at court in some other capacity.[51] What Chao wanted was at least a partial revival of their team. But Kao-tsung rejected the plea, retorting that Chang had done great harm to the state. Later, when someone mentioned Chang, the emperor was still so resentful that he remarked with intense emotion, or perhaps exaggeration: "We would rather suffer the loss of our state than to employ that fellow again."[52] One suspects that he might have had some other reasons. For example, the emperor may have been afraid that Chang's return to active service could lead to more defections, to antagonizing some generals, or to another adventurous undertaking, any one of which could endanger state security. In any event, Chao's repeated pleas succeeded only in modifying the terms of Chang's banishment to make them less painful.[53]

Unable to get Chang back, Chao asked for Ch'in to stay on as his closest colleague. Ch'in was most grateful but only for the time being.[54] Without really having a team, Chao was unable to do much.[55] He recommended no plan; nor was he prepared for a crucial turning point that was coming up: the peace negotiations.

The Jurchens abolished Liu Yü's bogus regime in the north and offered to make peace by returning the Honan region to Sung rule; sending back the coffin of Kao-tsung's father, Emperor Hui-tsung; and freeing Kao-tsung's mother. (They wanted to keep Emperor Chin-tsung in captivity as a symbol of humiliation and possibly for use as a puppet ruler to dispute the legitimacy of Kao-tsung.) In exchange for their concessions, the Jurchens demanded an annual tribute and recognition from the Sung that it was a vassal state under Jurchen supremacy. Were these terms acceptable to the Sung?

Kao-tsung was in favor of acceptance, considering that the terms, including the recovery of Honan, were actually better than what had been expected. When he asked Chao for his opinion, Chao hesitated to give a categorical answer. As a moralistic conservative, he was in principle against making peace, especially on such degrading terms as vassal status under Jurchen supremacy. But out of loyalty to the sovereign, he would not take a stand diametrically opposed to the imperial wish. Probably as a delaying tactic, he suggested that since it was a matter of war or peace, the leading generals should be consulted.[56] Chao knew some generals objected to the peace negotiations. This was a fatal mistake. The previous incident of large-scale defection had deepened Kao-tsung's dislike and suspicion of generals. Instead of saying so, he resorted to indirection by complaining to Chao that the generals should no longer have anything to do with appointments of local government officials in their regions. This was also an implied criticism of Chao himself, for it was his responsibility to correct such anomalies. Kao-tsung also remarked: "The generals with their troops . . . are like an over-sized tail whose wagging is too much for the dog," a metaphor common to both classical Chinese and English.[57]

While Chao had no plan to curb the generals, Chang Chieh, a veteran official, discussed with the emperor a formula to dissolve the power of the generals by pulling their troops away from them. It was to promote ranking officers under the leading generals to the rank of general also and in command of their own troops. It would leave the leading generals, their former superiors, with no more armies. Kao-tsung responded that it agreed with his own idea but that he would wait for a year or two before carrying it out.[58] Chang Chieh also had a succinct formulation of policy orientation: "Peace in appearance, defense in reality, and war only as the last resort." The emperor liked it and told the councilors to abide by it.[59] Obviously, the emperor was gradually turning to others for advice. The service of Chief Councilor Chao was no longer satisfactory enough.

The peace negotiations threw the court into an uproar. Many a court official thought the Jurchen terms too good to be true and suspected a trick or treachery.[60] But their reservations and objections ran into the emperor's firm rejection, anger, and even rage.[61] Caught in a dilemma between his own inclination and the imperial wish, Chao tried to play it both ways. On the one hand, he instructed the Sung negotiators to insist on the recovery of Honan but never to agree to vassal status. On the other hand, he advised Kao-tsung to reconcile the divided opinion at court by refraining from showing strong reaction to the arguments of the opposing officials. Rather, the emperor might explain that he was inclined toward peace for the sake of his parents in captivity.

The emperor picked up the last point and made a very strong case. He declared that his essential objective in making peace was to fulfill filial piety. It would be, he said, the only means to secure the release of the coffin of his father and the release of his mother from captivity. This was a clever argument, anchored upon the Confucian value system. Who could quarrel with an imperial act motivated by filial piety? The emperor also assured his court that, apart from this essential objective, all the other peace terms would be open to renegotiation at a later date. A number of moralistic conservatives who had supported Chao saw through this argument of filial piety as an excuse, but their continued dissent had no effect. Acting on his own initiative, the emperor invoked his absolutist prerogative in issuing a special rescript that stated once more this compelling reason or excuse for making peace and emphatically forbade the officials from obstructing the imperial wish.[62]

From the wings, Ch'in Kuei edged his way to center stage. Upon the fall of the Northern Sung, he had been taken north by the Jurchens. Then he had somehow eluded their surveillance and joined the court in the south as a high official. Soon he declared openly that peace negotiations would be desirable when conditions ripened. A clever politician as well as a talented administrator, he kept himself well informed on developments among the Jurchens. Despite a lack of concrete evidence, historians have always suspected that Ch'in was a traitor deliberately planted by the Jurchens at the Sung court. There is no evidence on whether he made secret contacts through intermediaries with certain Jurchen generals who grew tired of the war.[63] It seems likely, however, that Ch'in gathered information about the Jurchens from some relatives of his who stayed behind in the north and served in the Liu Yü regime. The present study has made a discovery in the *HNYL*. Ch'in had a cousin named Cheng I-nien (dates unknown), who was a minister and at one time the metropolitan prefect of K'ai-feng in the bogus regime. After the peace, this Cheng came over to the Sung court. Over the protest of censorial officials, the turncoat mysteriously rated the same high rank as he had held in the north, without any explanation why. This exceptional accommodation must have stemmed from some peculiar circumstances. Merely being a cousin of Ch'in is not sufficient ground at all. His having furnished intelligence information as a secret informant to Ch'in is the likeliest explanation.[64]

When Ch'in found the opinions at court to be against peace, he cautiously avoided expressing himself any further on the issue. Instead, he was biding time. When the emperor himself wanted peace, the moment came. First, Ch'in made some preliminary moves to undermine Chao. He told the emperor that Chao was insincere, for what he said to some officials was in a vein quite different from what he said in the imperial presence. Then, Ch'in lined up his cohorts, most of them southerners, to criticize Chao, a northerner. They first attacked not Chao, but those around him. Finally, a confederate of Ch'in's dealt the fatal blow by accusing Chao of secretly keeping in close touch with the generals. Kao-tsung responded quickly that he thought so, too.[65] On this sensitive note, Chao's long and distinguished career ended.

Chao was dismissed. In taking leave, he warned the emperor that someone would take advantage of the Confucian ground of fulfilling filial piety to push him into a hasty acceptance of the Jurchen peace terms without the benefit of careful consideration.[66] Despite his long service, Chao did not grasp the hard reality that the imperial wish stemmed not from Confucian principles, but from power calculations. With Chao gone, like a vanishing sunset, the memory of councilors collaborating in a team to work for defense and dignity faded. A long night of haunted peace had descended upon the Sung.

THE LONG-REIGNING SOLE SURROGATE (1139–1156)

The moment Ch'in Kuei became the sole chief councilor, he proposed to manage the peace negotiations and silence the opposition at court on condition that the emperor would place in him alone full confidence and back him without wavering. Deliberately he asked for no prompt answer but requested the emperor to think it over for three days. After three days, the emperor approved the proposal. Yet Ch'in advised the emperor to take another three days before making it final. Once he had secured the full imperial support, he made it known at court that the august decision was for peace, that he would supervise the negotiations, and that no one else was to interfere.[67] By this unprecedented stroke, he expanded the autocratic power to make an irreversible decision without bureaucratic participation. And he himself derived by delegation the same power held by the emperor. When the peace negotiations were about to be concluded, the court as a gesture did allow officials to voice their opinions once more. But they had to do it within the unheard-of time limit of only one day.[68] Several dozen officials raised strenuous objections, all to no avail.[69]

Why did Kao-tsung accept the humiliating peace terms, especially vassal status for himself? Did he have little regard for the Confucian values of propriety, dignity, and self-respect? Why did he favor peace just when a major Sung victory was followed by some minor ones that made the prospect of counterattack bright?[70] Was he not worried that the peace might sow widespread discontent? To answer these questions will also help explain the long tenure of the powerful surrogate.

The heart of the answer is security, and Ch'in did a great deal to safeguard it. On the eve of peace Ch'in removed the three leading generals from their armies by making them the military commissioners at court, "kicking them upstairs" so to speak. Their former lieutenants were elevated to the rank of new generals, remaining in command of the same troops. Furthermore, these troops were converted to imperial armies under direct command of the court.[71] The reorganization went smoothly; hardly a thing stirred. In fact, some other generals, seeing which way the wind was blowing, volunteered to be relieved of their command. As the early Ch'ing period scholar Wang Fu-chih pointed out, Kao-tsung must have found it gratifying to use this able surrogate in getting things done the way he wanted.[72]

Yueh Fei (1103–1141), the youngest and the most patriotic among the three leading generals, was the only one who let his discontent show and remained openly opposed to the peace. Ch'in, without formally involving the emperor or invoking the imperial power, simply went ahead by his own surrogate power to have Yueh Fei arrested on a trumped-up charge of treason and put him to death in prison.[73] This injustice was so infamous and flagrant that from the next century to the present day, it has been the subject of popular plays and novels.[74]

To return to the main point, peace with the Jurchens insured external security, and the removal of the generals' military power signified internal security. Safety meant much to Kao-tsung. As emperor, he had struggled for over ten years, in successive flights, hardships, and narrow escapes; and he was often in fear of military men on account of the mutiny early on that had forced him to abdicate, the recent massive defection, and the opposition to peace voiced by several generals. Now, after what Ch'in had done, he had little to fear. And if something should go wrong later on, he could make Ch'in a scapegoat—as he eventually did after Ch'in's death. Meanwhile, so long as nothing serious happened, he would reign by letting Ch'in the surrogate rule for him. The few dissenting officials and any discontented intellectuals outside the government could be suppressed by political measures and silenced. Thus from his standpoint, the empire stood in fine shape.[75]

The frequency with which councilors were appointed depended in the final analysis on how secure the emperor was feeling. When the empire was insecure and its policy unsettled, Kao-tsung responded to various exigencies—internal, external, personal, or in combination—by trying out new councilors in rather rapid succession. When the situation was stable, exactly the opposite happened. As the sole chief councilor, Ch'in held an unusually long tenure of nearly eighteen years till his death in 1155. Moreover, the associate councilors under him did not change often either. During all these years, there were only four of them.

What the surrogate did after having made peace with the Jurchens was to remove the known political dissidents and others suspected of being such. Kao-tsung was behind him. A perceptive official had predicted that "once the emperor succeeds in making peace by invoking his imperial power, he will have much less regard than before for scholar-officials in general."[76] Kao-tsung himself described the trouble with scholar-officials in this way: "They have little faith. Nor do their diverse opinions and discussions help state affairs."[77] Worse, he said, they distract the attention of the country: "Since the peace, nothing serious happens in the country. The only thing we watch are those scholar-officials who mistakenly set forth their diverse opinions and disturb the court."[78] For those already banished to distant places, the emperor ordered a close watch by local governments.[79]

Important among these banished were the former councilors whose prestige made them natural leaders among scholar-officials. Soon after the peace in 1139, the court in a reconciliating move appointed every one of them a prefect.[80] On one excuse or another, however, they all lost their positions the following year and went back to retirement or banishment or even exile.[81] Their plight is illustrated by the case of Chao Ting, discussed in the next chapter. Suffice it to say here that a condition somewhat similar to excommunication was imposed upon these elder statesmen. Their own relatives, let alone old friends, did not dare keep in touch with them.[82]

Ch'in also instituted a pre-modern kind of thought control. Though not much publicized, it has been referred to in a few histories as a "ban on learning" (*chin-hsueh*) during the Shao-hsing reign. To begin with, he ordered official records edited in order to remove undesirable information.[83] A ban was repeatedly ordered on the printing and circulation of private historical accounts that contained political slanders.[84] A descendant of Ssu-ma Kuang, the famous conservative statesman, was so afraid that he disowned a book of anecdotes long in circulation, declaring it had not been written by his illustrious forefather.[85] Not only books about politics were suppressed, but also those containing what were called heretical theories, strange ideas, and even slanderous poetry.[86] For a book to remain in print, a copy had to be sent to the Imperial Library for inspection. If it did not pass inspection, the printing blocks were supposed to be destroyed. The regions of Szechwan and Fukien, where printing flourished, were singled out for close attention. Fortunately, the rules were enforced unevenly and intermittently so that not all dissident thought disappeared. For instance, the Ch'eng school of learning, seemingly in eclipse, managed to go on among private circles, especially in Fukien.[87]

Under this suppression, however, most scholar-officials ceased to engage in political discussion. Their silence led Kao-tsung to observe that "in recent years there has been a paucity of writings on serious matters of state affairs."[88] In peace time, he told Ch'in, the chief councilor should relax.[89] What he did not quite realize was that Ch'in felt a compulsive need to keep himself incessantly occupied not only in hunting out dissenting scholar-officials but in eliminating their potential influence. It was rumored that a few days before his death, Ch'in was making out a list of fifty-three officials to be censured and removed.[90]

A FORMER COUNCILOR SERVING ELSEWHERE (1161–1162)

While getting rid of those he disliked, Ch'in openly practised nepotism, putting his family members and maternal relatives in various key government posts. When he was dying, his son, a high official by his side for years, asked to take his place. Emperor Kao-tsung, after rejecting the audacious request, promptly turned against the Ch'in family. He dismissed the sons from court and ordered them to leave the capital by going back to their native place.[91] Since the empire had been well consolidated, it no longer needed a surrogate. On the contrary, Kao-tsung wished to improve his imperial image by remedying some of the harm Ch'in had done.

The emperor decided to take over the general administration himself.[92] Local governors and intendants were told to report directly to the court, instead of by the short-circuiting procedure Ch'in had used that channeled their reports straight to concerned ministries without going through the court.[93] More significant was a new order that redressed past injustices by rehabilitating the banished former councilors as well as other officials who had been dismissed with them. Those rehabilitated received new appointments, or had their former titles restored, or were at least granted permission to live wherever they pleased. Chao Ting, who had died already, received posthumous honor.[94] The only glaring exception was Chang Chün. Allowed to make a trip home in Szechwan for his mother's funeral, he nevertheless had to report back to his place of banishment.[95]

Did Kao-tsung remove the councilors who had served under Ch'in? On the contrary, he kept them for a while as the policy orientation largely remained the same. But these councilors were no longer immune from attack by those who surfaced after rehabilitation.[96] One of them, for instance, was soon denounced as just another Ch'in.[97] Consequently, they did not stay on at court for long. The pattern of frequently shifted councilors reappeared, and apathy among the bureaucrats revived.[98] Flattery at court was in ample supply. One high official obsequiously presented a "theory of power holding," postulating that the emperor "who takes Heaven as the model" holds all-inclusive power and should exercise it in the same way.[99] Praising absolutism sky high was no cure for a sick government; it was a symptom.

The cost of Ch'in's suppressive measures was demoralization. Once fearful of political risks, few scholar-officials would step forward or speak up, even though the atmosphere changed.[100] Some ministers advised that since scholar-officials had a strong desire for fame, the emperor should encourage them to voice their opinions with a promise of no penalty. The emperor demurred, seemingly afraid of opening a floodgate.[101] Instead, he tried a different tack. All bureaucrats were told to submit their opinions on how to save government expenses, a technical topic of little political sensitivity. Half a year went by and no one spoke up at all.[102]

The bureaucratic apathy was not an acute ill. Far more alarming was the renewed Jurchen invasion in 1161, after a long interval of twenty years. It was their third attempt to end the Sung as an empire. The Sung had been observing the treaty carefully and assumed that peace would hold.[103] What could not have been foreseen by anyone was the rise of a Jurchen usurper, who, as he put it in a poem, wished to ride his horse on top of the hills overlooking Lin-an.[104] When the news broke that the former Emperor Chin-tsung had died in captivity and the Jurchens would retake Honan and advance toward the Yangtze, panic spread. But Kao-tsung, rejecting a eunuch's advice to relocate the court farther south in Fukien, took steps to mobilize for defense.[105] Setting himself as an example, he led an imperial expedition to Nanking, though he stayed there for only two weeks.[106] At the same time, in order to appease the

the pro-peace group and get ready for negotiations with the Jurchens, he summoned back to court a former councilor who had succeeded Ch'in and was still popular in some quarters.[107] To appear completely impartial, he pardoned the descendants of condemned councilors who, at the end of the Northern Sung, had been for peace, as well as the descendants of the martyr-general Yueh Fei, who had stood for war. The belated recognition of the general pleased many patriots and conservatives.[108]

One card seemed missing from the hand: Former councilor Chang Chün, a leading hawk with military expertise, was still banished. But Kao-tsung finally reversed himself. First, he recalled Chang to active service by making him a prefect near his place of banishment.[109] Before Chang could catch his breath, he was appointed governor of Nanking, in charge of its defense.[110] Before he could get there, however, the Sung forces had already scored a major victory—though not because the generals had fought well. Surprisingly, a scholar-official named Yü Yun-wen (1110–1174), had happened to be at the front, got the troops regrouped, rushed into a battle, and won.[111] Shortly after the battle, the Jurchen troops who were tired of the war, assassinated their usurper-leader, abandoned the invasion, and withdrew. The resumption of peace was in sight.[112]

Chang, arriving in Nanking, promptly crossed the Yangtze to plan for counterattack in the Huai River valley.[113] His prestige from the past stood so high and his efforts now were so energetic that many people expected him to become the next chief councilor. But this hope never materialized.[114] When Chang asked to join the councilors and associate councilors at an audience to discuss with the emperor the military situation, the request was denied.[115] For the emperor did not want a hawk like Chang to be near him or to upset his own plan. The hawks idealistically wished to reconquer the north, but Kao-tsung was realistic with respect to the immediate and actual. In his calculation, security came first and further improvement of security next. The continuation of war involved great risk. In his mind, the recent victory did not change the desirability of peace.[116] Instead, the victory should be seized as a great opportunity to renegotiate for better terms, such as restoration to the Sung of the proper title of emperor and an end to addressing the Jurchen as the superior state.[117]

Someone advised Chang to resign and go home, since his opinion was apparently at odds with the court policy for resumption of peace. But Chang stayed on in Nanking, taking care of routine administration. In part, he may have been biding his time; but his argument was that people regarded him as a symbol of defense, and his leaving active service would cause a general uneasiness injurious to the state.[118] Biding his time was probably the right thing for him to do; under the next emperor he did get another chance to attempt a large-scale counterattack, though this one, too, was unsuccessful.[119]

In 1162, having ruled the country for thirty-six years, Kao-tsung chose to abdicate in favor of his adopted heir,[120] eventually known as the Emperor Hsiao-tsung (r. 1163–1189). Perhaps Kao-tsung felt tired after the recent military emergency; perhaps he felt much gratified after the conclusion of the second peace to be able to turn over to his young successor an empire as secure as it could be. In any event, as the Sovereign Emeritus, he enjoyed perfect health in his old age and continued to exercise from behind the throne an indirect supervision over vital state affairs. Had it not suited his purpose well in the past to have a surrogate do what he himself wanted? If so, the new emperor was now it.

More importantly, Kao-tsung left the legacy of an autocratic power extending toward absolutism. It became crystal clear to a number of intellectuals at the time that everything now depended on the emperor. He alone, without the bureaucrats, made state policy. Hence, the intellectuals realized that statecraft must begin with the enlightenment of the emperor himself, all the rest being secondary. This was precisely why the philosopher Chu Hsi in later days memorialized the new ruler at great length on the fundamental importance for the emperor "to rectify his mind" so as "to make his thoughts sincere" through an honest "investigation of things," thereby "reaching for the utmost knowledge."[121] Many others regarded these philosophical concepts to be politically naive; but in the context of absolutism, what Chu Hsi spelled out was from his standpoint most realistic, pointing right at the heart of the problem. If an emperor alone made decisions at court, then his personal values and ideology would directly affect the welfare of the state. A good Confucian, therefore, must ask, What besides the emperor's conversion to Confucian philosophy can make a good state and society come true?

SIX

A Case Study: From Excellence to Exile

The preceding account of the political conflict between the moralistic conservatives and the more pragmatic realists at the court of Emperor Kao-tsung seems to be at an end—but not quite. For the conservatives, though down, were not out. Somehow in adversity they maintained their beliefs and hopes. The example of someone who had made a determined struggle to render his best service according to what they considered correct principles could have helped sustain their morale and hold out hope to the young intellectuals who would come after them. Even a loser in war or politics can be an inspirational model; indeed a reversal can demand an added measure of heroic spirit. The sadder the reversal, the stronger the message that the search for other avenues toward the same goals must go on.

To understand the mood and the actions of the idealistic intellectuals who were out of favor and out of power, especially during the surrogacy of Ch'in Kuei and in the years immediately after his death, it is helpful to understand what sort of man they admired. Who among the participants in the events of the early Southern Sung could have served as a model for the young men who came along later, the men who became what we call transcendental moralists? Whose career offers a case study in the application of conservative principles to actual events and offers insights into the implications of this school of Confucian thought?

WHO QUALIFIED AS A MODEL?

Would the intellectuals choose General Yueh Fei as the model? Though a stirring symbol of pure loyalty who also aroused deep sympathy for his martyrdom, he was, after all, only a military man who had begun as a common soldier and was not a scholar-official. In fact, he never had an opportunity for formal schooling. Some writings of his, particularly a patriotic poetic-song that remained popular as recently as World War II, were probably ghost-written by members of his staff or otherwise attributed to him. In any event, this most famous poetic-song was not known at all in the mid-twelfth century.[1] Even though they could admire General Yueh, the intellectuals would not identify with him.

Would Chang Chün qualify as a model for many idealistic intellectuals? As is generally acknowledged, he stood well above his contemporaries as a patriotic, talented, bold, far-sighted, and determined statesman, who had the ability to organize large-scale military operations. Unfortunately, Chang never won a victory; and on three occasions, he failed miserably. In 1130, he fought an ill-advised battle in Shensi. In 1137, he caused a massive defection by General Li Chung and his troops at the front when he planned to remove the general, just at the time of a pending enemy offensive. Under the next emperor, in 1163, he broke the peace by taking the initiative in counterattacking the Jurchens with a sizeable army; but defeat soon followed, and the Sung had to sue for peace again.[2] His scholarship was also open to doubt. He was at times critical of the moralistic conservatives and their concept of history,[3] though his son Chang Shih (1133–1180) became one of their leading exponents and a close friend of Chu Hsi.[4]

Generally speaking, to be a model with whom intellectuals, particularly the moralistic conservatives, would have a sense of identity required the combination of at least two qualifications: first, an active scholarship that was influential among scholars; and second, a distinguished career with significant contributions to the state. An eminent scholar-official usually scored high on only one test, seldom on both.[5]

Chao Ting was the rare statesman highly qualified in both ways. Although his statesmanship and scholarship were well recognized at the time, and although some of his writings were collected in a Ming period anthology of memorials by famous statesmen through the ages,[6] histories have underestimated his significance as a model for intellectuals. At court he was a leading exponent of moralistic conservatism, setting forth opinions that were anchored in classical Confucian principles and pointing out defects in the conduct of state affairs, from the reform system to his own day. As a chief councilor, he helped advance the careers of many whom he regarded to be good Confucian scholars. Yet distressingly, despite his loyal and distinguished service, he was sacrificed on the altar of the humiliating peace that Emperor Kao-tsung chose to accept. In his old age, Chao was banished for no proven offense to exile in a remote corner of the empire, where, after writing his memoirs, he chose death by fasting.[7]

Both his illustrious life and its sad end aroused intense feeling as well as moral indignation among many intellectuals. Open admiration and profound sympathy, however, did not get expressed till he was posthumously rehabilitated in 1163 when Hsiao-tsung became the new emperor and bestowed upon him the highest honor, with the title Duke of Chung-chien. Together, *chung* meaning "loyalty" and *chien* meaning "unfulfilled, high aspirations" not only encapsulated the character of Chao's career but captured the essence of why a great number of intellectuals identified with him. These literati deeply felt that they, too, were loyal but frustrated. The title of his collected works (*Chung cheng te wen chi*) carries these descriptive words: "loyal, upright, virtuous, and cultured (in the Confucian way)." From the reign of Emperor Hsiao-tsung on, many scholar-officials, and certainly the conservative intellectuals, agreed that he had been the best minister of the early Southern Sung. The case study that follows in the rest of this chapter will show why.

RISE TO DEPUTY MILITARY COMMISSIONER

Chao Ting, a native of Shansi in the north where the Yellow River bend turns from its southward flow to the east, had close contacts in Lo-yang, less than two hundred miles away. There, in the cultural center of the Northern Sung empire, he studied as a young man under Shao Po-wen (1057–1134), whose father had been a friend of both Ssu-ma Kuang and the Ch'eng brothers. At an early point in his official career, Chao returned there as a magistrate.[8] Then, serving as a minor official in the capital, Kai-feng, he personally witnessed the tragic fall of the Northern Sung. The puppet regime installed by the Jurchens tried to get scholar-officials to join it; and years later, when Chao was in exile, retroactive accusations alleged that he had debased himself by collaborating with the puppet regime, climbing into a high office in it, and even trying to stop loyal volunteers from moving toward the capital. Chao's memoir refuted every bit of the slander as deliberate smears instigated by his enemies. Historians since have agreed that these charges were false. What Chao did was to evade the overtures of the puppet regime and then escape to the south.[9]

In the early days of the Southern Sung, Chao was not yet well enough known to merit an appointment at court till he was recommended by his friend Chang Chün. What soon brought him fame was his stern discussions of the fundamental cause of the national debacle. It was his opinion that the Reform had been the source of mistakes which Ts'ai Ching had merely aggravated. He said that the most damaging effect of Wang An-shih's policy had been the waste of talents, who were guided to the wrong path and even corruptive practices. (It should be pointed out that because it was improper in Confucian principles to criticize former emperors, blame nearly always fell on ministers, in this case Wang An-shih.) Although similar views were expressed by a few others such as Yang Shih, it was Chao's opinion that caused a great stir.[10] Eager for a new image, the court found Chao's thesis attractive and promoted him three times in rapid succession: first to be a policy critic-adviser, then a censorial official, and finally a general censor.[11] Chao's initial attack, reinforced by what some other conservatives said, resulted in removing the tablet of the reformer previous honored in the temple of Emperor Shen-tsung.[12]

Chao discharged his censorial duties feverishly. He submitted forty recommendations in three months and the court approved nine-tenths of them. Among those rejected was an idea of moving the court to a point below the Yangtze gorges for safety.[13] In 1129, the Jurchens mounted their largest offensive and crossed the Yangtze. After retreating to Hang-chou, Kao-tsung was forced to abdicate briefly by the army mutiny that contributed to his lifelong distrust of the military. Pursued relentlessly by the Jurchens, he had to retreat even further along the Chekiang coast. Chao, noted for his loyalty and steady service to the emperor during the mutiny and abdication crisis, was sent ahead to that area to make advance preparations and then rejoined the court in successive flights.[14] Surveying the situation, he outlined three options: to keep on fighting, to choose a defensible position, or to avoid the enemy by evacuation. Because the Sung forces were outnumbered, he agreed with the chief councilor in recommending evacuation or escape by sailing into the sea in the last lunar month of 1129 (equivalent to January 1130). For his steadfast service in time of danger he was promoted once more to be executive censor.[15]

No Chinese court had ever been on the high seas. The very idea turned many officials pale. They faced a terrible dilemma: between the Jurchen devils and the blue sea, a danger dreaded and a risk unknown. Once the emperor had decided to sail, he took with him from the court only the councilors and six other courageous officials, Chao included. The rest were told to disperse to nearby places wherever they could find haven. Before sailing, the soldiers, uncertain of the future, were in an uproar. Recalling the experience of the recent mutiny, the emperor decided to prevent a similar occurrence by dispensing with most of them. On his voyage, he took only a minimum number of regular soldiers and about three thousand troops under the command of the chief councilor. There was neither a fleet nor naval forces, only a hurried assembling of ordinary ships. While we do not know how many ships there were, we do know each ship carried sixty soldiers. So the total should be at least fifty ships. Nor do we know the size of these ships; but it must have been fairly large, for we are told that each soldier was allowed to have with him two family members. Counting the sailors themselves, the average capacity of the ships should be over two hundred or probably around three hundred persons.[16]

The imperial voyage ran into a heavy storm for three days, followed by a most depressing lunar New Year of 1130, and a narrow escape. With native help at the coast, the Jurchens sailed after the emperor, and almost caught up with him. Fortunately, the vessels of the pursuers were small and the Sung captain was able to drive them away with his larger ships.[17] Nevertheless, the emperor and his group felt safer the farther south they went. They got as far as Wen-chou, near Fukien, but reports continued to be bad. The Jurchens also crossed the Yangtze upriver in central China in pursuit of the empress dowager and her entourage in Kiangsi. The troops escorting her mutinied and robbed the imperial party; bandits took what was left. A prefect in the area (none other than the father-in-law of Ch'in Kuei) not only surrendered to the Jurchens but had his son requisition valuables for the enemy.[18] Back in Nanking, Tu Ch'ung, a chief councilor who had been expected to defend the city, shocked most people by giving it up without a fight; and even more surprisingly, he surrendered himself to the Jurchens, something no Sung councilor before or after him ever did. When this terrible news came, the emperor had no appetite for several days.[19]

Most fortunately, insufficient manpower and over-extended supply lines led the Jurchens gradually to the north from spring 1130 on. The return voyage of the Sung emperor, however, was not entirely without accident. Surrounded by a dense fog, the imperial ship was thought to be missing for nearly half a day.[20] Finally, the emperor landed and put his headquarters in Shao-hsing, named after his new reign title.

During all this time Chao rendered excellent service. In the course of the evacuation, he was temporarily assigned from time to time to look after military affairs, thus acquiring some expertise in them. A rumor even claimed that he played a part in repulsing some Jurchens.[21] Such a rumor, however, did not help Chao's career, for it made other officials jealous.

After the Jurchens withdrew, Chao was eager to straighten administrative affairs and did not hesitate to engage in political struggles. Having discovered shortcomings in the chief councilor, Lü I-hao, especially with regard to financial and personnel policies, he repeatedly declined promotions and used the refusals as opportunities to voice his complaints against Lü in a dozen memorials. The emperor finally consented to send Lü away by making him a regional governor. Although the governor took care to declare that Lü had committed no serious mistake,[22] Chao had won the fight. In view of Chao's recent military experience, he was eventually promoted to deputy military commissioner, an office ranked right below that of the councilors. With no military commissioner on active duty at the time, furthermore, Chao became virtually equal in importance to the highest officials.

Although Chao held rank and power, he was not able to achieve everything he wanted. He tried first to restore the Military Commission to its normal independence from the chief councilor and his associates, an effort which, though justifiable, was neither wise nor practical.[23] Wartime exigencies demanded councilors to extend their jurisdiction to military affairs. Secondly, Chao saw, as several other officials did, the need to impose supervisory control over the generals with personal armies, who frequently acted on their own. The emperor heartily agreed. Nevertheless, when Chao wanted to reprimand a leading general severely for having disobeyed a court order to send rescue forces to a neighboring army, the emperor told him to use gentle words instead.[24] The emperor, who became more astute in politics than his idealistic minister was, also insisted that on any strategic deployment of various armies Chao must consult the generals and get them to agree.[25] Thirdly, the political wind changed. Chang Chün, who was Chao's close friend, tried to turn around the hard-pressed military situation of the Sung in the coastal areas by a great northward counterattack from the southwestern hinterland in fall, 1030. Unfortunately, this was a premature and ill-prepared flank movement that resulted in bad defeat. The dismissal of Chang had adverse effects on the political standing of Chao, who had supported him.[26]

In winter, 1030, Chao was transferred away from court, ostensibly because he had contravened the imperial wish over a few cases of promotion and other minor matters.[27] These cases, however, involved neither sensitive issue nor serious error on Chao's part. What really damaged him was cumulative criticism and the charge that a scholar like Chao who did not know enough about military affairs often offended colleagues, officers and civilians alike. In short, Chao caused friction. When a number of colleagues wished to see him go, the emperor, who always wished to retain majority support at court, agreed.[28]

THE TEAM OF COUNCILORS AND STATE POLICY

Chao's departure from court was a mere setback, not a fall from grace. Undaunted, he continued to do his energetic best wherever he served. First appointed governor at Soochow, within a few months he was transferred to the strategic city of Nanking, with the concurrent title of pacification commissioner of the eastern Yangtze region. Nanking was a hard place to administer; for serving there were a number of high officials and generals with their troops, many of whom had been bandits and were accustomed to getting their own way. Even those who were not former bandits might be engaged in what is known as "regimental economy": Officers used their soldiers to engage in shipping, trading, brewing, even smuggling. They sometimes kept their units deliberately under-sized so that they could pocket the difference in provisions between the normal, reported figures and the actual number. Some did not give their men what was due them. Unfair treatment often led to small, local mutinies. Chao's prestige helped impose order on Nanking: With him around, everybody behaved. But Chao had difficulties getting enough provisions shipped in; and from this failure to fulfill one of his major responsibilities fully, some dissatisfaction arose.[29]

In 1133, another transfer made him governor at Hung-chou (present-day Nan-chang), which overlooks Lake Po-yang in mid-Yangtze, and concurrently pacification commissioner of the Kiangsi region. He succeeded in gradually eliminating various notorious bandit groups. In connection with these operations, he gave full support to Yueh Fei, the general who was later to become a martyr, but who was at this time a rising figure.[30]

To Chao, putting the regional administration back in order and engaging in post-invasion reconstruction were no more than preliminary steps; restoring the Sung empire was the great ultimate task. He advised the court on the strategic significance of Hsiang-yang as the best forward base from which to recapture the old capitals of K'ai-feng and Lo-yang. The court did not regard the advice as feasible; soon Hsiang-yang was lost to the enemy. As the retreating troops scattered southward, the court ordered Chao to regroup them along the Yangtze and place them under his command. Having done so, Chao recommended the strengthening of the garrisons at E-chou (present-day Wu-chang) and Chiang-chou (present-day Chiu-chiang) in mid-Yangtze. As soon as the bandits were under control, Yueh Fei began to build up the regrouped forces in preparation for a northward campaign.[31]

Suppressing banditry was vital to internal security, and preparing a counterattack helped external security. Much pleased with Chao's progress on both scores, the emperor decided that his service could be even more valuable at court.[32] In 1134, Chao was summoned to become associate councilor. Presumably he had learned a lesson from his previous frictions with other officials. His political style became less stern and his cooperation with the chief councilor, Chu Sheng-fei, though not without stress, produced no serious dispute.

It was a time of shifting the appointments of the councilors. Chu was replaced by Lü I-hao, whom Chao had attacked several years before. The emperor, who knew about the hard feelings between the two, chose to send Chao out again—this time not as a mere governor, but as the governor-general (*tu-tu*) with discretionary power over the extensive area of both Szechwan and Shensi. He was to prepare a counterattack on the northwestern flank, the same mission Chang Chün had undertaken in 1030 but failed.[33] To get ready for his misison, Chao asked for somewhat more funds and supplies than Chang had been given. Lü, the chief councilor, allotted him much less. After Chao complained, he got a little more but not nearly enough. He protested. If while still at court he could not get adequate support, he argued, how could he be expected to carry out a mission of tremendous scale when he would be thousands of miles away from the seat of power?[34]

The dispute, instead of being resolved, was unexpectedly shelved; for an emergency arose and canceled Chao's mission. Up to this time, the Sung had been in touch with the Jurchens through peace overtures made by informal emissaries. The Jurchens' insistence on retaining the central plain for the bogus regime of Liu Yü made agreement impossible.[35] Then, without warning, the Jurchens sprang a general offensive in the Huai valley, with the help of Liu Yü's armies.[36] Caught by this unexpected storm, the court needed Chao to help steady the ship.

Some timid souls reminded the Sung court of the old formula that had worked once before: The emperor should go further south along the coast, as far as Fukien, and the officials should disperse to various other places of safety. Even some generals agreed that the court might do so and leave the Yangtze defense to them. While the emperor wavered, Chao recommended exactly the opposite. He pointed out that the last time the Jurchens had crossed the Yangtze, they had lacked enough manpower to stay, but that this time they were coming with the additional troops of the bogus regime. If they were able to cross the river again, they would not stop, but continue their advance to wherever the emperor went. This invasion in the long-term perspective pointed to the ultimate challenge from which the court had no room to retreat. The only realistic course of action was to meet it head on immediately. Fortunately, in Chao's cool estimation, the Sung had a good chance to blunt the enemy's impact right away. For the Jurchen forces were not at their strongest; they came this time at the request of Liu Yü, not at their own initiative, nor by their own choice. The additional troops of the bogus regime would not change the picture as a whole.[37] Chao assured Kao-tsung that the Sung forces, having had several years of preparation, should be equal to the task. The time was at hand to prove their worth. This stirring line of reasoning convinced the emperor. He, too, felt that it was more than a question of security: At stake was the survival of the state itself.

Picking Chao to be both chief councilor and military commissioner, Kao-tsung declared that he was embarking from Lin-an toward Nanking in order to assume personal command, though he sent palace personnel to Wen-chou where he had last sought safety and to Ch'üan-chou farther south in Fukien.[38] Taking Chao's advice, he informed the generals that under his personal command they were assured of equal provisions and ample rewards in victory, but they were expected to cooperate with one another in effective defense. The armies in a heightened morale did score several initial victories.[39]

Kao-tsung also undertook a political offensive. Up to this time, the Sung had patiently refrained from denouncing or belittling the bogus regime, so as not to offend unnecessarily the Jurchen master behind it. In the renewed hostilities that threatened to be a life-or-death struggle, Kao-tsung issued one edict after another, bitterly denouncing the puppet Liu Yü and calling upon everyone under him to surrender and return to the Sung fold.[40] Encouraged by initial victories, the emperor himself considered going northward from Nanking across the Yangtze. Chao demurred. The best strategy, he suggested, was to stay on the Yangtze line long enough to deprive the enemy of its initiative and momentum. At the same time, he cautioned, to stay on at Nanking implied that the emperor was determined to fight on without retreat even if the Jurchens should penetrate the defenses along the river. If later the emperor should fall back, it would trigger the retreat of the generals, a dispersal of their forces in various directions and the collapse of the entire defense. Even with its dangers, the emperor accepted this strategy.[41]

As military operations intensified, Chao felt he could not handle the situation alone and requested the recall to court of Chang Chün, his old friend. Chang, he pleaded was the leading military expert among the civilians; his dedication to state service was beyond reproach; his vitality always inspired military men; and his dismissal had been a general disappointment to them. The severe criticisms that had led to his dismissal, Chao explained, had been motivated by the personal enmity of those whose requests had been rejected by Chang. Many allegations against him had been either groundless or exaggerated. Chang's disastrous defeat had been a failure, not an offense, for which he should have been reprimanded, not dismissed from active service. The request was so persuasive that Kao-tsung felt obliged to issue a special edict repudiating the previous charges against Chang and forestalling any censorial objections to his appointment as the new commissioner.[42] The emperor instructed Chang in turn to cooperate with Chao in a team; for, he said, Chao was a strong-minded and upright statesman.[43] It was a perceptive appraisal.

Prospects for the Southern Sung began to brighten. Standing beside his emperor at the head of the government, and assisted by his respected old friend, Chao felt more convinced than ever that uplifting moral principles in application were the best guidelines for state affairs.

THE POLITICAL STYLE OF MORALISTIC CONSERVATIVES

The Chao-Chang team—their good progress and regrettable break-up—has been discussed (Chapter Five). What is to be analyzed here is Chao's political style as illustrative of the moralistic conservatives in general. Chao furnished us with a revealing insight when he said, "Believing in my own conviction, I go straight forward."[44] Conviction is a matter of principle; this was particularly true of the moralistic conservatives. However, when to express a conviction and how to do it are matters of tactics in the art of politics. Is it politically wise, for example, to go "straight forward" often? In a crisis that calls for difficult but decisive action, this style helps; but in normal bureaucratic proceedings, it is frequently inadvisable. As it happened, the moralistic conservatives were apt to get the two levels mixed up and treat normal encounters as confrontations over high principles.

Chao and other conservatives immersed in Confucian teachings tended to be theoretical in their opinions. Chao, for example, admitted that he was often criticized for being "unrealistic and irrelevant" (*yü k'uo*).[45] With some truth, his administrative style was said to stress "conventional formalities" (*hsu wen*) over substance.[46] For instance, after the emperor had just returned from the sea, when even routines were hardly settled yet, Chao submitted a memorial asking the emperor to discard his military clothing in favor of imperial attire so as to uphold his exalted dignity.[47]

Like many moralistic officials, Chao resented bureaucratic evils. Whenever he had the power to do so, he hastened to clean up negligence and abuses among clerks, subordinate officials, and army officers.[48] In his belief, councilors should carefully select regional intendants and governors who would clean up the local administration.[49] The need was acute for the government to revitalize itself in order to carry out existing laws rather than to reform the laws, to change them, or to devise novel administrative measures. Through simple enforcement, Chao was, in fact, able to produce good results in improving the state finance in hard times and supplying the armies with adequate resources. And when he was demoted to be mere governor in Shao-hsing at the end of his career, he practiced exactly what he preached: nothing but "restraining the officials and the clerks and relieving the burden of the people."[50]

The moralistic conservatives are usually described as being too rigid in applying their principles. It is true that some of them were rigid on all points, yet two objections can be raised. First, they can be criticized for having been too rigid on minor matters when their intellectual pride simply made them obnoxious; but it is unfair to criticize them for having been absolutely steadfast on major issues. In major policy decisions, they stood by their principles because integrity demanded it and so did their understanding of the consequences of the actions being decided. Second, not all moralistic conservatives were, in fact, totally rigid and unyielding. Even in matters of some importance, Chao Ting, who was basically a moralistic conservative in outlook, was able to make judgments partly on the basis of circumstances as well as on principle. For example, Kao-tsung moved back and forth several times between his capital and the Yangtze, either to recoil before the threatening enemy or to face up to it. How did Chao advise? His advice was often based on caution. If the enemy was too strong, if the emperor was in very insecure territory, or if the Sung troops would be dangerously overextended if he did not retreat, then Chao advised avoiding direct confrontation in order to protect what was still held. The general principles of moralistic conservatism taught that the emperor should fight to defend the kingdom, not run away. Some moralistic conservatives, therefore, criticized Chao for his advice; but they are examples of those who were absolutely rigid, not proof that everyone of their persuasion was unyielding. Nevertheless, on occasions Chao urged the emperor to move forward. Basically, he agreed with the principle that the emperor must defend the empire and thought that the enemy challenge must be met.[51] When he offered this advice, the more pragmatic, non-conservative scholar-officials accused him of failing to appreciate the value of flexible expediency.[52] This was unfair. He did act flexibly; but he also had backbone. He saw the need to take circumstances into account, but he also saw limits to the value of bending with every wind. Indeed, the question always remains, Is there a principle that can decide how much flexibility is desirable?

The most troublesome practical issue in the Sung bureaucratic government was personnel selection. To put it in over-simplified terms, as the Sung scholar-officials habitually did themselves, the burning question was: Who were the worthy Confucian gentlemen (*chün-tzu*) and who were the unworthy petty men (*hsiao-jen*)? It was a problem as old as Confucianism. While all the bureaucrats claimed to be worthy, obviously some were not. To distinguish between them required clear-cut criteria, if possible. At an imperial lecture in his early days at court, Chao suggested a way.

By comparing the conservatives, who opposed Wang's Reform, and those who followed it in the late Northern Sung, Chao pointed out that the conservative-minded officials were likely to be honest, kind, dignified, and mature. In local government they preferred to rely on the service customarily furnished by reputable upper-grade households or leading elements in the community. On the other hand, the reform-minded ones were likely to be talented, capable, vigorous, and smart. Under the reform system of hiring service, they chose to employ subordinates and clerks who were also like that.[53] Later, Chao added another, and what was to him incisive, distinction: The Confucian gentlemen were relatively forgiving, while the petty men would attack their adversaries mercilessly in order to get ahead. This was because the true Confucians hoped to transform people through moral influence, while those who deviated from the Confucian principle had no such consideration at all.[54]

To clarify this age-old controversy, one may say in modern language that the differences lay essentially between a regard for efficacy and a regard for propriety. For anyone who was realistic about running an effective government (or playing bureaucratic politics), *politics is power.* Exercising power was what counted. Decisions should be made on the basis of what would best achieve desired goals; success could be measured by results; and civil servants should be chosen for their ability to be effective. To a moralistic conservative, or indeed to anyone else who believed that a theory of government was inseparable from a theory of morals, this was not so. To them *politics is proper government.* Ensuring that actions conformed to moral theory was what counted. Decisions should be based on doctrinal precepts; success was defined as conformity to correct teachings; and officials should be chosen for their adherence to moral standards.

This opposition in orientation was not a peculiarity of Sung China. It can be found in many places and many ages. Each position has its strengths and weaknesses. The regard for efficacy, represented in Sung China by the reformers, can lead to the implementation of innovative, beneficial policies; it can also lead to the worst abuses of opportunism. A regard for propriety, represented by the moralistic conservatives, can offer inspiring leadership and prevent abuses of power; but it can also lead to narrow-minded self-righteousness in judging others and a tendency to miscalculate or disregard the real impact of policies on actual situations. In the early Southern Sung, moreover, as probably in most times and places, men of one persuasion were likely to view the least admirable examples of the opposition as the most representative.

To cut through a lot of argument, the matrix given in Table 3 shows

TABLE 3 Contrasting Political Types

	Valued propriety	*Valued efficacy*
High-minded idealists	Leading moralistic conservatives, who believed that moral exmaple would bring about a transformation of society	Original Reformers who sought to devise governmental policies to bring about their vision of a better society
Second-rate followers	Stubborn, narrow-minded dogmatists, who were more interested in the rigid application of precepts than in consequences	Opportunistic, cynical hacks with low moral standards, who were willing to use any means to achieve selfish or expedient goals

schematically the basic comparisons and contrasts among the men who stressed morality and those who stressed power when they are viewed at their best and their worst. It makes clear that theoretical differences in orientation form the major division between the two camps; but it also makes clear that the contrast between high and low quality within each camp is just as major a division. In idealism, vision, dedication, and imagination the leaders of each side were more like each other than like some of their own followers. But, sad to say, even wise leaders often judge their opponents by looking at the worst examples rather than the best. More important, events influence opinions.

Wang An-shih and his early followers had been idealistic and certainly had believed themselves to be good Confucians. Their emphasis, nevertheless, had been on what could be achieved by government within Confucian bounds rather than on what bounds would be imposed on government by Confucianism. Their achievements had not, moreover, been universally accepted, nor were they unqualified successes. Furthermore, after the first generation of reformers had passed on, their successors were less idealistic than they. When the dynastic crisis was brought on by the Jurchen invasion after the Restored Reform, opponents perceived the disaster as the result of the reforms. This interpretation was made easier by the fact that the younger scholar-officials who had grown up with the reform system as the status quo were less idealistic than its original formulators. To the moralistic conservatives, the low moral standards and self-serving reactions of these second- and third-generation reform bureaucrats to the dynastic upheaval were proof that something was terribly wrong. They believed that by opening the floodgate, the original reformers had been responsible for the fault and were therefore as guilty as their followers. Not only was the efficacy of the Reform questionable, but worse, an emphasis on getting things done led to an acceptance of any expediency and degenerated into abusive trickery and the manipulation of the system for selfish aims.

The moralistic conservatives believed that only propriety in government action could inspire and nurture the popular support needed to hold the empire together. Moral values would have to be cultivated by public-minded discussions among the bureaucrats, by an inspiring mode of conduct among the literati, and by a response from the common people. In the twelfth century, a widely believed myth held that applying half of Confucius' *Analects* had been enough to establish good order at the beginning of the Sung dynasty.[55]

Nevertheless, in practice as opposed to theory, they found themselves to be at a disadvantage. To put it as Chao Ting did, in the struggle between the two sides, the petty men were likely to win; for they would use any means to reach their end against the Confucian gentlemen. To put it more objectively, power seekers know best how to win in power politics, while moralists face a dilemma. If they play by the rules of the power game, they must on occasion abandon their principles and thereby lose their identity. If they do not, they lose power. This is analogous to the "Prisoner's dilemma" in game theory in which a cooperator fares poorly and a competitor does very well.

When Chao was in power, the two sides were joined in a struggle over appointments. Chao claimed that he recommended everyone who appeared to be worthy, regardless of political, social, or personal connections. In fact, he insisted on this strict policy in order to eliminate factionalism and to raise morale among the scholar-officials.[56] Yet Chao had his own bias. As illustration, two examples may suffice. Choosing tutors for the prince was a pivotal matter, for the determination of what intellectual influences the young man would be subject to in the present had political implications for the future. The first tutor whom Chao recommended was Chu Chen of the Ch'eng school, the same person who subsequently initiated the claim of Confucian orthodoxy and stood against Ch'in Kuei in opposition to peace.[57] Next Chao recommended Fan Ch'ung, a man of similar intellectual persuasion, to be another tutor for the prince. He was the same scholar-official appointed to revise the controversial records of the Reform and the Anti-Reform.[58] He was also related to Chao through the marriage of their children. Obviously, Chao chose to put forward both men at least partly because they were on the same political side as he was. And while no one denounced him as habitually nepotistic, it can hardly be denied that he sometimes practiced favoritism. At least, it would have been hard to convince Chao's opponents that he was free from partiality. The most that can be said was that in Chao's mind political and social connections did not carry decisive weight. Yet, intellectual affinity did weigh to a significant extent. To his realistic-minded adversaries, this constituted partisanship. The claim of Confucian orthodoxy meant power if it was recognized; so did the control of historical records to serve as a background guide to current politics. Those who were opposed to this intellectual-political bias insisted that they did not want the Ch'eng school "to confuse and disturb the country."[59]

When it came to such vital issues in state affairs as the relative status of the Jurchens and the Sung, and the related issue of war or peace, Chao stood firmly on his conviction and would not oblige even his sovereign. At the root of his conviction was belief in the ideal of a single emperorship, one supreme ruler on earth. On this principle that the true emperor was sovereign and supreme, Chao could conceive of no compromise. Propriety in abiding by it was what made the state a state; otherwise the state would cease to deserve the name. Even security was not so important as this principle. But he could not change the mind of the realistic emperor. To Kao-tsung, security always came first, even at the cost of compromising propriety for the time being by nominally admitting the Jurchen to be the superior state and the Sung to be its vassal.

This is a convenient point to sum up the major traits of Chao's political style. As these traits are applicable to a large extent to the conservatives in general, they stand in contrast to the characteristic political style of Ch'in Kuei's followers and many other bureaucrats who excelled in power politics. Chao, a moralistic conservative, was straightforward in criticism but rather backward in tactics. Likewise, he was eloquent in theories but would have been hard put to prove their relevancy to existing problems. He was good at improving administration but not necessarily resourceful in handling delicate matters or in exploring new alternatives. He tried to make honest personnel selections but did not take enough care in seeking allies and cultivating support in order to protect his own political position. His great merits were on the paramount issues of the state. Always resolute, he would not bend just to please his imperial master. His loyalty belonged *to the state*, not what was to him a mistaken decision made by the emperor.

FROM PEAK TO PIT

Chao Ting's determination to govern on the basis of moral conservative principles met its ultimate test when the war reached the crisis of peace negotiations. These came in the period after Chang Chün had been dismissed and Chao had been returned to power with Ch'in Kuei as the other chief councilor next to him. If Chao thought his calm, "go-slow" policy of improving the administration would bring about stability, he was sadly mistaken; for decisions by the enemy and antagonism from those at his own court precluded its success.

In 1138, the Jurchen posture changed radically. For domestic reasons of their own, they wanted peace, at least on certain conditions.[60] Ch'in Kuei had always hoped that the Jurchens would abandon the bogus regime and make peace with the Sung; Emperor Kao-tsung himself had on occasion sent similar signals to the Jurchens,[61] and the Jurchens finally came to this position themselves. Ch'in, who had feigned gratitude to Chao for retaining him as chief councilor, was eager for action. To get the peace negotiations going, he must get rid of Chao.[62]

Whether to negotiate and how to deal with the Jurchen demands were great questions. When Chao made the mistake of suggesting consultation with the generals,[63] he irritated Kao-tsung, who was usually suspicious of their loyalty. It was at this time that Ch'in (who was ready to implement a plan to dissolve the military power held by the generals)[64] began surreptitiously undermining Chao by instigating indirect criticism of him.[65] On the surface, however, no break yet occurred; and since the emperor insisted on the peace negotiations, Chao as a loyal minister withheld his own reservations.

When the Jurchen envoys arrived at court, protocol required Chao to receive them. He did so with courtesy and dignity at the chancelery, dutifully sparing the emperor from seeing them in person.[66] The negotiations, while narrowing the gap, were not yet conclusive. A Sung envoy was to be sent north to bargain on further specifications. He asked for instructions and Chao gave them to him point by point in a tense session. Briefly, the points were as follows: The Sung was willing to send the annual tribute of 250,000 taels of silver and an equal amount of silk. The return of expatriates from the Sung to the north and several other demands of similar magnitude were negotiable. The Sung envoy at his discretion could agree to some compromise.

The next two issues were of such importance that the envoy was instructed to break off negotiations rather than yield to enemy pressure or compromise in any manner. The first issue was the boundary. It must be drawn along the Yellow River, specifically its old course and not, as the Jurchens demanded, to the south along its new course that had been formed by flood during war time. To refuse compromise on this issue, Chao explained, was to secure the heartland in the central plain and the highland to its west. The second issue was status. The Sung "absolutely refused to submit to a Jurchen investiture" or any other formality that "would remove or damage the supreme title" of the emperor. Chao told the Sung envoy that he was not to give a single inch.[67]

Given the military stalemate between the two countries, Chao did not stand categorically against the peace negotiations. But the principles he believed in required him to weigh the terms most carefully. He did not quite realize that the emperor was too eager for peace to insist on these two issues about which Chao was adamant. Indeed, he may have failed to see that he was losing the emperor's confidence. He was suddenly dismissed. Ch'in Kuei, who then became the sole chief councilor, quickly concluded the negotiations by simply accepting the terms the Jurchens had proposed.[68] Ch'in also pleased the emperor by relieving the generals of their armies.[69]

At his dismissal, Chao was assigned again to Shao-hsing as governor. As one censorial official friendly to him protested: Why had Chao been recently recalled to court so urgently? Why was he so hurriedly dismissed? And why, after the dismissal, could he not in some way be near the emperor to give advice?[70] Neither this protestor nor many other officials could see at the time that Chao's adversary Ch'in would promptly deliver to the emperor peaceful borders, peace in the country, and peace from Chao's stern moralizing.[71]

If Chao felt that leaving the court would mean the end of his political conflicts, he could not have been more mistaken, for his personal trouble was just beginning. At Shao-hsing, he heard the announcement of peace and general amnesty. Out of sustained loyalty, he sent a memorial reporting grave anxiety among local scholar-officials and common people, lest the emperor should relax and trust the unreliable Jurchens.[72] He got no response from the court but heard that several censors were attacking him retroactively for duplicity: Having done little for peace, they alleged, he slipped away to protect his own reputation as a supposedly blameless councilor. This was, according to the critics, a disloyal evasion of duty and a stealthy maneuver for fame.[73]

Chao resigned immediately, but his resignation was refused. At the time, the court wished to compensate for the humiliating treaty abroad by building a good image at home. One way for the emperor to be popular among scholar-officials was to honor those who had been their leaders. Thus, every former councilor was appointed as governor in one region or another. Since Ch'in did not want his adversary to be near the capital, Chao was transferred to Ch'üan-chou in southern Fukien, despite his complaint of old age and hardship in travel.[74] None of these governors stayed long in office. As to Chao, he was soon stripped of his titular high honors when he was impeached for having used several hundred local guards on his way to his post.[75] The next year, 1140, he was put into retirement. In private life at Shao-hsing, he was charged with "having former subordinates and factional cohorts running" between his home and the capital. Accordingly, he was banished to Hsing-hua (present-day P'u-t'ien), again in Fukien.[76]

Later in the same year, the Jurchens, led by a usurper, broke the initial peace and resumed attack. The correctness of Chao's earlier prediction that the Jurchens could not be trusted only made Ch'in, and perhaps the emperor, angry at him. Ironically, Chao was exiled further south, first to Ch'ao-chou and then to Chang-chou, both on the Kwangtung-Fukien border. His alleged offense was that he had greeted the news of the resumed invasion with pride and pleasure.[77] Around the same time, Yueh Fei, the fighting general who was Chao's friend, was imprisoned and put to death.[78]

Additional accusations were made against Chao in a number of memorials. Though no formal charge was brought, the court did not accept Chao's defense by refutation in answering memorials. First, he was accused of having received from General Yueh Fei a gift of 50,000 taels of silver. Though Yueh was now dead and no longer available to disprove it, Chao said, there must be some witnesses available to testify, if it were true, about moving the extremely heavy load of cash. But no such witness existed. Second, Chao allegedly had taken for himself a modest amount of money from his previous office. Again, there was no supporting evidence, whereas Chao could account for all his actions in office. Third, he was indicted for having received gifts from an imperial clansman who befriended both him and Yueh Fei. Chao said that there had been gifts, but that they consisted of only ten bottles of wine plus some fish and game, and that he had reciprocated in kind. Fourth, Chao allegedly conspired to get back to high offices. The truth, according to Chao, was that some petty person had deliberately tried to put words in his mouth to that effect but that he had not risen to the bait.[79]

Other attacks were more serious. It was alleged that at the collapse of the Northern Sung court Chao rendered active service to the first puppet installed by the Jurchens. After he rejoined the Sung court, he planted confederates to be the tutors of the prince. Then, it was insinuated, at his instigation, General Yueh Fei asked the emperor to designate the prince as the heir apparent. For a military man to do so was quite out of place. Last but not least, Chao and his friend Chang Chün seemed to engage, so the enemies alleged, in some kind of dark or even possibly treasonable plot. These accusations pieced together a composite picture of a disloyal conspirator from beginning to end. They were meant to shatter Chao's moralistic Confucian image. In defense Chao gathered all the concrete facts in order to shatter every accusation that was raised against him.[80] But signs from the court indicated that it remained suspicious of him.

A firm peace was finally made in 1141. The persecution intensified against the surviving hawks on the pretext that their objection to the peace meant disloyalty to the state. Consequently, Chao in banishment was excluded from the general amnesty in celebration of the peace.[81] In 1144, the persecution was extended to those reported to be in touch with the banished former officials like Chao.[82] Chao himself was exiled to Chi-yang in Ya-chou, an isolated southern tip of Hainan Island in the South China Sea on the vague ground that he had used followers to go around engaging in "unfathomable conspiracies." This was a cleverly constructed accusation that by its own circular definition would need no demonstratable evidence to corroborate.[83]

Ultimately, Chao told his son: "Ch'in Kuei is determined to have me killed. If I should die now, you and others in the family need not worry anymore. Otherwise, the whole family might perish."[84] In 1147, at that remotest place of exile, he fasted for days and passed away. After his tragic death, continuing troubles bothered his son. Some minor officials were accused of communicating and conspiring with him. The government authorized an investigation. A raid was made on the Chao house in Shao-hsing in the hope of seizing incriminating documents, but none were found.[85]

By this time, the Ch'eng school was known to be in official disfavor.[86] For the most part, during Kao-tsung's reign, it was referred to in government quarters as the Ch'eng and Chao learning.[87] Having vanquished Chao the official, Ch'in turned to smearing Chao the scholar. The emperor, however, interceded. What the court disliked, he explained, was specialized learning of particular persuasion, whether of Ch'eng or Chao or someone else.[88]

It was in 1156, a year after the death of Ch'in, the surrogate, that the court ordered the series of rehabilitations and remedial measures mentioned in Chapter Five.[89] Titular honors were posthumously restored to Chao and the patronal privileges normally given to the offspring of a minister were granted to his descendants.[90] The court also called upon Chao's disicples to come forward for appointments; but only three appeared, an indication that Chao never had a school or large personal following.[91]

The case of Chao left an indelible mark on the minds of many idealistic intellectuals, especially the moralistic conservatives. Given such a distressing precedent, how could they afford to become active in politics or to have high aspirations beyond routine government service?

They knew Chao's outstanding record: He shared the perils of the imperial sea voyage, rendered excellent service in consolidating the Yangtze delta region, put down the banditry in Kiangsi, regrouped the forces in mid-Yangtze, advised the emperor to take personal command against the resumed invasion, implemented the strategy of a firm defense along the river, repaired the damages caused by Chang Chün, and despite personal reservations took care to explain to the Sung envoys quite specific instructions on what to give in to if necessary and what never to give up during peace negotiations. His record consisted of truly a long string of royally shining pearls. This was not all. Chao also promoted both learning and learned scholars. In the end, a great deal was forgotten by the court. A number of merits were turned and twisted into demerits. Was there any justice in his banishment, exile, and tragic end, a virtual suicide, rather a virtual murder by incessant mental torture?

By the highest Confucian moral standard, a loyal minister owed his sovereign the obligation of absolute devotion and service, including his life, with neither expectation of reward nor complaint. In actuality, however, not many Confucians believed that the virtue of loyalty should be so one-sided. Moreover, it was a great regret to them that Chao's long service produced or left nothing lasting. His high ideal of educating and transforming scholar-officials remained unfulfilled. The bureaucratic mode and the intellectual mood both continued to deteriorate. To many who came after him, the question was inescapable: Was this kind of struggle meaningful?

A question must have arisen in the minds of some inquisitive intellectuals: What sort of government was this that permitted itself so arbitrarily to abuse such a fine official that much? But the tradition, the convention, the law, and current practice absolutely forbade any such question from being raised. To paraphrase a Western fable, no one would be permitted to hint, let alone to cry out, that the emperor had no Confucian clothing on.

In distress and frustration, many an intellectual could not help turning to introspection and retrospection. Introspection led them to place more emphasis upon self-cultivation and less upon government, as their writings clearly indicate. Retrospection led them to believe that certain deficiencies in the Confucian heritage should be made up by reinforcing them with better parts. These parts were metaphysics as the foundation, knowledge through specialized studies, and non-elitist education for the general public. Only after they had succeeded in rebuilding a moral society, could they have a chance to remold the state. This became the leading intellectual trend from the middle part of the Southern Sung on. It continued for centuries.

In the meantime, some intellectuals would become officials. What should they say? They knew that the state was an autocracy that relapsed from time to time into absolutism, though one must not say so. But the supreme autocrat was the sole key. If he could be remolded, he would redirect the government. This was why the great Neo-Confucian Chu Hsi advised the emperor that to govern the state rightly depended on regulating the family and to regulate the family depended on cultivating the person which, in turn, depended on rectifying the mind. Therefore, the superior man must make his thoughts sincere.[92] People other than dedicated Confucians might well regard such advice irrelevant to state affairs. But the Neo-Confucians, the heirs of the earlier moralistic conservatives, were convinced that this was truly the authentic Confucian medicine for the disease of autocracy that no conceivable institutional reform nor any other means could possibly cure.

Part Three
The Pyrrhic Victory
of Neo-Confucian Orthodoxy

SEVEN

Neo-Confucians as Transcendental Moralists: Dissension, Heresy, and Orthodoxy

The gate to the reform path was closed. The restoring emperor shut it with the help of many scholar-officials, the moralistic conservatives included. But the conservatives did not succeed in opening their gate to moral uplifting either. What would be the prospect of these politically frustrated intellectuals? Several decades later toward the turn of the century, an innovative branch grew up stoutly from the old roots of Confucianism. It reached a great height in metaphysical and transcendental directions. At the same time it spread its shade over the ground of daily life.

Inasmuch as it reoriented and reinvigorated the Confucian heritage, it deserves to be called Neo-Confucianism, the name bestowed upon it later by the Jesuits. However, at the time of its formulation, it was given several other names drawn from its different aspects. From its most distinguished Northern Sung pioneer, Ch'eng I, and its great synthesizing leader, Chu Hsi, it was called the Ch'eng-Chu school. As it claimed to be the only true orthodoxy, it was called Tao-hsueh, the school of the way or the true way, a name coined sarcastically by critics but later taken over by faithful adherents. Finally, from the word *li*, which means both "principle" and "reason," it was also known as Li-hsueh, the school of principle or reason, because its metaphysics rested on belief in a principle held to be ever present in everything everywhere and accessible to reason. To distinguish them from their predecessors, the moralistic conservatives, the present study calls its followers transcendental moralists.

In general, differences among the varying appellations do not matter much; the terms are largely interchangeable.

The philosophy of this great school needs no repetition here. It is well covered in all standard works on Chinese history and thought. Strange as it might seem, however, the story of its phenomenal ascent from the teachings of a few small groups of struggling intellectuals to the highest possible status as the state orthodoxy has rarely been told.[1] By no means merely the result of a development in philosophical formulation, this ascendancy was partly brought about by politics, further complicated by miscalculated maneuvers with unforeseen results. Starting off as a dissenting doctrine and then branded as heresy, Neo-Confucianism had difficulties in surviving, but its followers held on to their profound convictions. By the force of changed political circusmtances, a reversal of fortune bestowed upon it the honor of state orthodoxy, with great social influence, though the transcendental moralists did not share political power.

A SCHEME OF ANALYSIS

For a long time during the Northern Sung, most scholars became officials. From the late eleventh century on, however, the supply of accomplished scholars exceeded available government posts, with paradoxical results. Because of rising standards, a limited number of positions, and sharp competition, many supposedly Confucian candidates resorted to various tricks to cheat at the examinations.[2] Successful degree-holders vied with one another for civil service appointments in an overcrowded bureaucracy. Differences of political opinion as well as other factors—such as regional partisanship, kinship affiliations, personal friendship, patronage, ingratiation, favoritism, nepotism, and even bribery—intensified bureaucratic and personal frictions. A number of high-minded scholars became either frustrated or disgusted. Particularly from the twelfth century on, not a few learned intellectuals preferred to remain in private life, often after a brief government career that proved ungratifying. Their concerns became predominantly intellectual, philosophical, and educational. Standing at the edge of the establishment, they were critical of it.

The continued presence of the Jurchens in the north remained a gall to many intellectuals. Courageous scholars like Ch'en Liang advocated reform in the military to prepare for an irredentist effort in the north, but to no avail. After the abdication of Emperor Kao-tsung, his successor, Emperor Hsiao-tsung, did initiate war against the Jurchens in 1163–1164. Though the Sung was not victorious, this war led to improvements in the peace terms. The southern ruler regained the right to call himself an emperor; the annual tribute to the Jurchens was reduced by 100,000 units; but the south gave up some border territory. After this peace, the stalemate between the Southern Sung and Jurchen empires was the stable political reality for some seventy years. To many an intellectual who still regarded the peace relations a great humiliation, a soul-searching question remained inescapable: What had gone wrong? What should be done to make the Sung supreme? On these questions, the transcendental moralists emerged as particularly vigorous in their advocacy of strict adherence to classical Confucian principles according to their new elucidations and interpretations. Although this group was neither a faction nor politically active, when it extended its influence and criticized the establishment, those in power regarded it as a potential threat. Official repression pointedly labeled the teachings of this School of the True Way as the False Learning (Wei-hsueh) and proscribed it in state examinations. The word *false* included varying shades of connotation, such as misguided, misleading, masquerading, sham, bogus, and falsifying. The ban was, however, short-lived, lasting only from 1195 to 1202. Once it was rescinded, this school gradually gained much wider acceptance, recognition, and prestige. By 1240 it was honored as the state orthodoxy. Irresistible is the question, how did these zigzag turns take place?

An analytical framework helps to clarify the picture. The Confucian state was a composite that came under the direction of two interlocking elements: Confucian ideological authority and state power. In some respects, the two elements overlapped and functioned together; but in others, they were often at odds.[3] The intellectuals who were most committed or most concerned with ideology often tended in some way to stand apart from the exercise of state power. They were likely to be oriented to universal concerns different from or even opposed to the organizational priorities of the bureaucrats who were most concerned with state power.[4] In acting out their ideals, such intellectuals developed a mode of life distinct from the prevailing norms of the ruling class.

The polarizing tension between the two dispositions tended to rise in direct proportion to advances in learning, increases in the number of intellectuals in private teaching, and the intensity of their ideological concern.[5] It reached a critical stage when factions had a dispute over ideological authority or when a dissenting school, supported by some friendly scholar-officials, posed a claim to orthodoxy. The government could ill afford to ignore an open dispute; it had to make a decision. There were three options. The first was acceptance. In this case, the state recognized a claim to be outstanding and officially adopted it as the orthodoxy. A political reform or some moderate restructuring of the state power often followed. The second option was repression. Superficially effective in the short run, repression eventually became counterproductive. On the one hand, the state power was not widespread enough to uproot the intellectual and the social prestige of respectful, though dissenting, scholars. On the other hand, the reliance upon sheer power to suppress admittedly Confucian ideals damaged the image of the state itself. Between acceptance and repression existed a third alternative: accommodation or co-optation by sophisticated manipulation. The government drew into its service a few renowned dissenters and granted honor to their theories but went no further. It did not undertake reform or restructuring. Forced to act under normal organizational constraints, those who joined the government were able to realize only some of their ideals in such limited areas as rites, state examinations, official pronouncements, and the like. They had little to do with military affairs, diplomacy, financial policies, appointments to decision-making positions, or other vital concerns.

In the Northern Sung, the court had exercised the first option when it accepted Wang An-shih's New Learning and restructured the state by means of his New Policies. The Southern Sung at first banned the School of the True Way but then switched from the second to the third option, that is, from repression to accommodation. The question is, why did it make the change? The answers lie in the content of the True Way doctrines, the means by which the transcendental moralists propagated them, and the reaction among scholar-officials to the effects of measures used to suppress claims that at first seemed so inept and even odious.

Saddened by the tragic fall of the Northern Sung and faced with the deplorable situation of the Southern Sung, many idealistic intellectuals came to the realization that conventional Confucian education was ineffectual.[6] Something basic must be lacking. If so, what was it?[7]

Chu Hsi and his friends found the answer in the writings of the five philosophers in the Northern Sung: Chou Tun-i, Shao Yung, Chang Tsai, Ch'eng Hao, and his brother Ch'eng I. These masters had not been very influential during their lifetimes, nor shortly thereafter.[8] The main intellectual thrust at that time had not stressed metaphysics, the area of their major contributions. To Chu Hsi and his friends, however, the neglect of metaphysical theory was precisely the fatal flaw. Confucian moral philosophy needed a universal and cosmological basis to interpret the classics, to incorporate compatible non-Confucian thoughts, to meet effectively the Taoist and particularly the Buddhist challenges, to integrate the entire heritage as a whole into a systematic philosophy, and to redefine a detailed value system accordingly. Only thus could Confucianism give man and his society an integrated way of life with meaning in everyday activities. To approach this ideal, a true Confucian must examine himself inwardly and then understand all things—the material world, social relations, and the cosmos—through investigation. This approach did not exclude statecraft but made it secondary.

The Chu Hsi school developed the paired concepts of *li* the immutable, immaterial principle in all things that gives them their form, and of *ch'i*, the material force that brings them into individual and actual existence. A third concept is also central to Neo-Confucianism, as it is to most Chinese philosophy. This is *tao*, the way. The school reinforced an old Confucian belief in a deep, underlying principle throughout the universe by stressing that this principle, far from being intangible, is vital in man himself, his very nature, all social relations, the entire cosmos. Hence it is imperative to know *tao* and to keep on striving to make oneself superior by following it so that it might prevail in the world. To these Neo-Confucians or transcendental moralists,[9] education thus acquired a much deeper meaning than before; for it became the means of a heightened consciousness of the universal order, awareness of the natural world, and sensitivity to one's fellow man. Only through disciplined self-cultivation could a man commit himself to his own moral well-being and the welfare of other people, and thus also contribute to a general moral transformation—to a "greening of China," so to speak. Perhaps in half a century, by Chu Hsi's optimistic estimation, the dawn of a truly Confucian society might arrive.[10]

This vision inspired the transcendental moralists to teach tirelessly with a sense of urgency, immediacy, and piety approaching religious faith. Rising above the debris of futile reforms, decadent government schools, and the dynastic disaster, they surged ahead toward a better life. The transcendental moralists taught what was in fact a new approach in character-building, more fundamental than policy-making. But they said it was only a new wave that had flowed from the genuine ancient teachings. It came from Lo-yang, the longtime capital of China during several dynasties in the past, the favorite place for Buddhists and Taoists to meet for intellectual debates, then the center for the leading culture of the Northern Sung, and so it happened, the home base of the school's pioneers. Although Lo-yang had unfortunately fallen into enemy hands, invoking its name probably involved a psychological compensation to deny the Jurchens the right to inherit the tradition.

The prestige of Lo-yang, however, was not enough proof that theirs was the original Confucianism. From the term *tao*, or the way, they went one step further in stressing the concept of *tao-t'ung*, meaning the lineage of legitimate transmission of the orthodoxy.[11] It was a double borrowing: on the one hand, borrowing the historiographical concept of legitimate dynastic successions known as *cheng-t'ung*; on the other hand, borrowing the Buddhist practice of transmitting teaching from one patriarch to the next, especially in ch'an or zen Buddhism. The Chu Hsi school thereby asserted that the transmission of the teachings contained in the classics had come down from antiquity to Confucius, then to his grandson Tzu-ssu, and to the latter's disciple, Mencius. A long period of interruption followed with no worthy successor at all. This point first made by Han Yü of the T'ang period had not been generally accepted.

As seen by the transcendental moralists, it was the five pioneers in the Northern Sung who rediscovered the orthodoxy and reactivated the line of transmission.

Attitudes differed on the question of orthodoxy. For example, another important school at the time, led by Lu Chiu-yuan, called the School of the Mind, did not bother with transmission lineage at all. To many others of varying Confucian persuasion, the exclusive claim of the Chu Hsi school to legitimacy and orthodoxy looked pretentious and either probably or definitely unwarranted. Some scholars, annoyed by their incessant use of the word *tao,* sarcastically gave them the nickname Tao-hsueh, implying an indulgence in empty talk about the "way." But the self-righteous transcendental moralists did not mind. To the surprise of those who had coined the nickname, it became a respectful designation.[12]

A CONCERN FOR THE PROPAGATION OF IDEAS AND MORAL FELLOWSHIP

Intellectually, the Tao-hsueh or True Way school was in more ways than one superior to its contemporary competitors. Its dedication to propagation also accounted for a great deal of its eminence.[13] One may reconstruct a composite picture of its masters and activities from the *SYHA.* This source is partial to the school and omits the petty, personal criticisms found in less formal sources; but it is reliable in recording the positive aspects of the school and allows us to see clearly what was new and forceful about it.[14]

Teaching in this school was not confined to formal sessions. In residence, travel, or exile, many of its masters expounded on questions raised by students, friends, visitors, or themselves.[15] They advised people, mostly literati and others fairly well-to-do, on how to behave, how to cultivate themselves, how to correct mistakes, how to govern the family, how to conduct rituals properly. In short, they promoted personal and group well-being in kinship and in community.[16] Chu Hsi and his close colleague Lü Tsu-ch'ien (1137–1181) subsumed all these topics under the rubric "reflections on things at hand" (*chin ssu lu*), which was used as a title for their compilation of passages from various writers.[17] What does it mean? It means "relevant to concrete life," and the approach it represents offers instructions on a way of integrating life by applying these ideals to everyday activities while relating all things to universal principles. This integration makes the True Way a system of great appeal.

The transcendental moralists sought to infuse the entire society with a revitalized spirit, class barriers notwithstanding. Most of their followers who did advanced studies presumably came from fairly well-to-do families, though not necessarily from the elite. There were also a few disciples of relatively humble social origin.[10] Also, many a master held public sessions from time to time for community people, both high and low. In contrast, in many official academies, the low-ranking officials who served as instructors had little to offer. The students were like parasites who received boarding, stipends, and such privileges as quasi-official status, tax and labor service exemptions. They paid little attention to studies. These schools were deplorable. The educational leadership thus went by default to private intellectuals, particularly transcendental moralists.

Through active and intense propagation in the late twelfth and early thirteenth centuries, the teaching of the True Way School spread. It had its largest following in the economic and political core of the empire, roughly present-day Chekiang, Kiangsi, and Fukien. Then it expanded to present-day Hupei, Szechwan, and Hunan, the last being culturally a frontier area.[19]

The promotional efforts of its proponents multiplied. They devoted attention to local welfare institutions and helped to build memorial halls in honor of early Confucians who had a local tie. These halls were more than decorations; they helped to raise local pride into a constant reminder of moral standards. Promoting education was another worthy area of their activity. Many a master reorganized existing schools; others obtained enough support to revive defunct ones, private as well as government-supported. All such promotion depended on getting private donations and, more often than not, local government appropriations. These, in turn, depended on winning the respect of local elite and officials who were themselves Confucian scholars.[20] The True Way approach, however, did not consider it essential for a school to have an extensive library. What was crucial was for a good master to set out a proper curriculum to ensure an orderly progression of studies. For a basic philosophical orientation, they started with the "Four Books"—*The Great Learning* (*Ta-hsueh*), *Centrality and Commonality* (*Chung-yung*), the *Analects* of Confucius (*Lun-yü*), and the *Mencius*. They continued with the *Book of Rites* (*Li Chi*), *Book of songs* (*Shih-ching*) and other classics to further the guidance of daily conduct, and went on to other areas of lesser immediacy.[21]

While teaching and promoting, a master had to sustain himself. If his prestige rose, so did the number of his visitors. Occasionally disciples stayed on at his residence or a nearby place through his arrangement.[22] How did a master meet these expenses? Rarely was there formal tuition, but most disciples followed the social custom of presenting gifts to show respect. When these were not enough to cover the expenditures,[23] a master relied in part upon goodwill donations from well-to-do families, local officials, personal friends, and admirers elsewhere. Moreover, the True Way masters were not unworldly philosophers unmindful of practical finance. They earned income from literary works: calligraphy; the composition of poems, essays, prose, encomiums, funeral odes, and tomb epitaphs; and sometimes a combination of calligraphy and composition, such as a colophon to authenticate and comment on a painting.[24] They also invested in land, had their schools print books for sale, and took an interest in other trades.

Hardly any of these private scholars and former scholar-officials who took up private teaching in retirement could be called wealthy. Some of them, by a combination of personal and family income, lived modestly; others slightly better. Some masters built a detached house next to their residence or at a short distance from it, usually named a *ching-she*.[25] The term had a long historical evolution. Briefly, in ancient aristocratic times it meant a study of refined style. When the Taoist religion was influential, the term denoted a secluded apartment for meditation, deep reflection, religious devotion, or such occult arts as alchemy. After the coming of Buddhism from India, the term was picked from existing Chinese vocabulary to translate the Sanskrit term *vihara*, meaning a house of religious devotion. In the twelfth century it came back into Confucianism with an aura of religion or mysticism, to mean a "house of devoted learning." Such a house was used for meditation, concentrated studies, intensive reading, and serious discussions. Its essential characteristic was its solemn atmosphere, imparting a feeling of introspection, communion with the ancient sages, and the spirit at one with the way or *tao* of the universe.

The dedication of these masters was matched by the enthusiasm of their disciples. Some came from nearby communities and others from a great distance, even several hundred miles.[26] Some stayed with the master for years; some accompanied him on long journeys.[27] Others made short visits but remained in touch. In some cases they went away to visit a kindred master who had something else to offer. Besides disciples, others came as friends to discuss learning. These friends were classified by the SYHA into three categories in ascending order: companion-in-learning (*t'ung-tiao*), fellow-in-learning (*hsueh-lü*), and fellow-in-explication (*chiang-yu*).[28] One may refer to the last category in the English of academia as discussants. Indeed, dialogues and discussions were their favored teaching formats.[29]

In short, the True Way School went beyond the conventional, bookish type of Confucian teaching. It was an innovative branch of Confucianism that put its emphasis upon systematic philosophy, most significantly metaphysics; upon incessant teaching through lectures, encouragement of questions, and discussion; and upon self-cultivation in thought and conduct. Furthermore, although it did not have a formal organization, its deeply committed followers were joined in an intellectual-moral fellowship.

AN ALIENATING MODE OF LIFE

Intense concern with learning made many True Way intellectuals serious-minded to a fault. It kept them from giving priority to other pursuits. For instance, they considered literature a time-consuming art without corresponding importance, often a distraction from moral responsibilities and self-cultivation, by which they meant disciplined daily introspection, reflection, study, and attention to actual conduct.[30] Few of them ranked among the best essayists or poets, quite unlike the eleventh-century notables. Some of them printed their rhymed quotations for effective communication to the less educated, as rhymes were easy for them to learn and then recite by themselves; but the literary quality of such compositions was not very high.[31]

Noble as their beliefs were, their approach to education was rather narrow and sometimes self-defeating. Their historical studies emphasized moral lessons to be learned far more than factual information. In their view, neither the Han nor the T'ang empire commanded much respect because they seemed to lack a proper Confucian orientation. Other periods were seen as even worse because of disunity or decadence.[32] The True Way intellectuals were devoted to the classics and pertinent commentaries and interpretations. With the exception of the five revered philosophers, all other well-known intellectuals and scholar-officials in the Northern Sung, despite their various contributions were held to deserve only qualified respect because they all had faults in private life or in official conduct, and particularly because their interpretations of the classics were held to have gone astray or failed to go deep enough. While quick to criticize their predecessors, however, they were slow to agree among themselves. Nearly every Neo-Confucian or True Way master tended to set forth his own interpretations. Since there were so many interpretations, were all of them correct? Even Chu Hsi once sighed that some of his fellow thinkers had voiced rather strange ideas.[33] Of course, this statement applied not to his own theories.

The True Way school criticized the examination system for putting a premium on literary qualities. They often belittled those who excelled in examinations and little else as mere literati, rather than genuine Confucian intellectuals.[34] The criticism was valid insofar as literary ability could hardly reflect the potentialities or forecast the qualities of civil servants in the future; but it was not new, having been raised many times before. Moreover, the alternative of emphasizing knowledge of the classics instead, as the Reform had done, had led to disputes. This put the True Way intellectuals in a dilemma. Having found many faults with the Reform, they could not possibly advocate a similar change.[35] Nor did they have other practical or feasible suggestions to make. Their only hope was to have as much influence as possible on both examiners and candidates, mainly through their promotion of the commentaries on the classics they approved and what they composed themselves. In other words, they had to accept the existing institutional framework and hope to change its contents by boring from within.

The same was true with regard to a bureaucratic career. While in it, they felt alienated. For example, although Hu An-kuo lectured at court, in a span of four decades, from the time of his degree to his death, he spent only six years in active service, the rest in private life.[36] Chu Hsi repeatedly declined appointments. Apart from a dozen years at local posts, he served at court for only forty-odd days.[37] Many intellectuals of this school openly stated their aversion to fiscal duties in the belief that such duties tended to compromise their moral integrity. On this ground, they requested transfers.[38] When their antipathy to bureaucratic careers was seized upon by their adversaries as evidence of their empty talk and administrative incompetency, the two sides became further polarized.

With profound conviction and feelings of alienation, the True Way minority sought to create for themselves a strong identity of their own. This was manifest chiefly in two areas: rites and manner. Rites meant to them more than ceremonies or formalities: Rites were means to condition human feelings and rectify moral attitudes. Many scholars of this persuasion insisted upon rites in a solemn atmosphere, almost like a religious service. Discarding the conventional rites as below standard, they advocated the revival of archaic forms.[39]

The True Way manner had interesting manifestations. Though times had changed, they searched among Northern Sung portraits and records to recover bygone styles and dressed accordingly. They mostly chose to wear, for example, a tall hat with a pointed top for formal attire, a beret-like gear for informal wear, a roomy gown with broad sleeves, and a fine, white, gauze shirt underneath. Their deportment was strict: They sat squarely with straight back; walked in measured steps, looking straight ahead; bowed slowly and deeply; and spoke in a dignified fashion with few gestures.[40] Their critics looked upon their lofty air as strange, stupid, snobbish, arrogant, or as more Taoist than Confucian. According to the School of the Mind's Lu Chiu-yuan, a disciple of Chu Hsi had a peculiar way of greeting as well as an odd vocabulary.[41]

The Buddhist and Taoist influence on the True Way school manner was evident. In retirement, members of this school called themselves *ch'ü-shih* or lay devotee and *yin-chün* or eremitic master, titles that were conventionally used by Budhists and Taoists respectively.[42] For another example, Chu Hsi in his discussion of an ancient, eclectic, religious work commented that studying books was analogous to alchemy.[43] By that he meant that real study leads to the internalization of the values derived from reading, which, in turn, produces a transformation of personality, like a chemical process. Yet such borrowings from non-Confucian religions, including a mystic flavor, were used by the opponents of the True Way School to deflate their Confucian claims, to attack their allegedly false pretensions, and to condemn their way as false learning.[44]

The Miscalculated Ban of the "False Learning"

How did the True Way school come to be officially proscribed in the years 1195–1202 as the False Learning?[45] To put this puzzling question in another way, How did these intellectuals, who were mostly not active in politics, get into such serious trouble? Many historical accounts regard it as another factional dispute, often recurrent in Chinese history. This is misleading. A faction is a cohesive political group consciously engaged in a power struggle. In the present case, however, the attackers lacked cohesion beyond a common dislike of the True Way followers, while the victims engaged in no coordinated political actions. Only certain key officials, feeling insecure, regarded this school as a potential threat to their own power. But since this school had ideological and social prestige, those who did actively oppose it saw that an effective way to knock it out would be to humiliate it intellectually as false and to dismiss it politically as a subversive influence.

Frictions had begun in the early Southern Sung. Chao Ting, as discussed, favored the teachings of Ch'eng I, whereas many others, Ch'in Kuei among them, were accustomed to the established ways. The emperor, who wanted no divisive controversy, decreed in 1136, it will be recalled, that in neither examinations nor government service should intellectual differences be made the grounds for discrimination. His successor repeated the order in 1178.

Devoted as they were to teaching and propagation of their doctrines, few True Way intellectuals were actively involved in court politics during these decades. Nevertheless their claim to legitimacy and orthodoxy to the exclusion of others, their alienation and critical attitude toward the establishment in general, and their distinct, supercilious manner put off many conventional scholar-officials. In time, personal and political antagonism accumulated. An initial skirmish occurred between Chu Hsi and T'ang Chung-yu (c. 1131–ca. 1185), while both served in the same region in Chekiang. In 1183, Chu in reporting to the court censored T'ang for various misconduct. T'ang was a distinguished poet and a scholar versed in both classical and historical studies, but Chu severely denounced his alleged lack of moral integrity in such terms that he did not seem to be a Confucian at all. The attack was politically unwise or miscalculated. A harsh moral judgment against a well-known official who had high standing intellectually alarmed many others in the establishment. Several friends of T'ang at court counterattacked by finding fault not so much with Chu personally as with his leadership of this particular school, whose pretentious claim seemed to be building up his influence in order to voice his critical opinions. The court, upon sophisticated counsel, diffused the dispute as if it were shadowboxing between two rather emotional scholar-officials.

Paradoxically, this counterattack had unforeseen effects. It made the Chu Hsi school better known in the country; at the same time it accelerated the polarization. In 1188, when Chu Hsi came to the capital awaiting a promotion, his enemies criticized his disruptive influence in having a misguided following. As a result, Chu Hsi did not get his expected appointment and quietly returned to his local post. Several outstanding scholar-officials, including Yeh Shih, who were neutral in the controversy sadly warned that such retaliatory discrimination against Chu would eventually lead to serious troubles for all intellectuals, if not most literati. They pleaded that alienation toward the established order should not be misconstrued as a threat, nor intellectual disagreement as a demerit in government service, nor an academic following as political subversion. Unfortunately, the court pigeonholed their good advice.

The year 1195 saw a crisis in the imperial succession. Emperor Kuang-tsung (r. 1190–1194), mentally ill, was forced to retire in favor of his son, Ning-tsung (r. 1195–1224). The reign was hardly stabilized when Han T'o-chou (1152–1207) wanted to get rid of the prestigious chief councilor Chao Ju-yü (1140–1196). Han, a relative of the empress dowager and an uncle of the new empress, had much power. In order to undermine Chao, who had a distinguished career, some excuse had to be found. The accusations against the True Way school provided it. Since Chao had recommended Chu Hsi and other True Way scholars, he was accused of plotting to spread their influence. Chao was banished and the school denounced as False Learning, as if it were a faction.

Han recruited support from a few opportunistic or unprincipled scholar-officials. At his instigation, in one memorial after another, they alleged that the True Way followers gathered frequently in the middle of the night, listened to strange doctrines delivered in a mysterious atmosphere, dressed themselves strangely, revered their leaders while slighting other scholar-officials, attempted to gain advantages in state examinations through the influence of their friends, and tried to influence court policies. In this light, the school was made to appear much like a subversive religious sect. On the basis of these charges, Han had this alarming strawman crucified. The court ordered that each candidate at state examinations must declare in a sworn statement that he had no connection with False Learning. But how could one know for sure that none of his teachers from former days could be regarded as having belonged to that school? It was not till a year later, in 1197, that the court publicized a list of fifty-nine individuals as the leaders of the proscribed False Learning.

Several points are significant. First, it took as long as two years to take various steps in imposing the ban. Second, even then, there was no evidence that this school ever took political action beyond individuals' occasional criticisms of those in power. The influence of what fifty-nine critics had said in scattered words, could hardly be a threat. Third, the persecution of the individuals was cynically varied. Chu Hsi, the best known, did not draw the heaviest penalty; he was simply stripped of his official rank. Yet Ts'ai Yuan-ting, a private scholar who was not even in government service, suffered exile. These points betray that the government had difficulty in making the image of a faction stick to the True Way school. Because Chu Hsi had a high standing among so many scholar-officials, a harsh punishment might arouse either sympathy or protest. But Ts'ai, who had no influential friend to help him, conveniently served as the leading scapegoat.

The ban of False Learning, based as it was on feeble, fabricated grounds, did not last. Many bureaucrats, while refraining from opposing it outright, withheld strict enforcement. Others privately considered it outrageous. In the end, the image of the Confucian state itself suffered more than its persecuted critics. Chu Hsi died in 1200. By 1202, only seven years after its imposition, the court had rescinded the ban. Even Han himself regretted it as having inadvertently gone too far. What caused the repression of the True Way school was not any policy issue but politics compounded by the proponents' claim to ideological orthodoxy. In fact, they were largely the pawn in a power play over which they had no control.

FROM CRISIS TO STATE IDEOLOGY

Most historical sources have followed the Tao-hsueh or the True Way orientation. They leave the impression that once the ban was lifted, this school by its superior teaching naturally acquired such wide acceptance that it soon became the state orthodoxy. They imply that although the Southern Sung failed to apply its teaching soon enough to save the dynasty from invasion, the Mongol conquerors were persuaded before long to accept the same orthodoxy. This is not so. The ascendancy to state orthodoxy was determined not by intellectual considerations, but by political expediency.[46]

The lifting of the ban merely restored the condition prior to it. The spreading influence of the True Way school during the next few decades was at best gradual. After the assassination of Han T'o-chou, both the political and the intellectual winds were reversed. Those who had suffered from his repressive measures stood to gain admiration. The court, upon the recommendation of some officials, granted appropriate honors to its masters: Chu Hsi in 1208 and three of the five Northern Sung forerunners in 1220. The decree that posthumously honored Chu Hsi referred to his scholarship as correct learning without saying anything about the transmission of Confucian truth. In 1212 the Directorate of Education took a step further in honoring his learning by adopting his commentaries on the *Analects* and *Mencius,* but not yet those on the first two of the Four Books that according to Chu Hsi were the basic introduction to Confucian education. As yet, no mention was made of state orthodoxy.

It was another crisis in imperial succession that helped to make the rise of the Chu Hsi school politically desirable. When Emperor Ning-tsing died in 1224 without an heir apparent, Shih Mi-yuan (1164–1233), chief councilor since 1207, arbitrarily set aside the elder adopted prince and made the younger one emperor. Almost a usurpation, this action had no legally justifiable basis. To make the matter worse, after the elder prince had been sent away to Hu-chou, an uprising took place there in his name, denouncing the succession as illegitimate. The prince himself had no prior knowledge, nor did he approve it. When the rash uprising collapsed, however, the innocent prince was implicated and forced by court agents to commit suicide. The first injustice was thereby compounded by what amounted to a political murder. These events greatly damaged the image of the court among the literati, as well as Shih Mi-yuan's personal standing in scholar-official circles. To remedy the situation, the chief councilor resorted to the manipulative politics of borrowing prestige for window decoration. In an act of political accommodation, several veteran leaders of the True Way school were appointed to high court positions. They were not given much power, however, nor did they have long tenure of office.[47] Nonetheless, the fact that the court turned to them enhanced the prestige of this school politically as well as intellectually.

The further rise of the school involved both court politics and mounting international trouble. In 1227, when the emerging Mongols took the Hsi Hsia Kingdom in Inner Mongolia, the court began to concern itself with this new challenge in diplomacy and defense. Political consolidation and intellectual reinforcement also became desirable. Chu Hsi's commentaries on the Four Books were made official in the belief that learning correct interpretations of basic Confucian teachings would make the country orderly, resolute, and strong. In 1233, the Mongols, having penetrated the Great Wall line, took the advice of Yeh-lü Ch'u-ts'ai and built a new temple in honor of Confucius at what is today Peking.[48] Besides establishing their military superiority, the nomads claimed to be a Confucian empire as well. In the same year, Shih Mi-yuan died and Cheng Ch'ing-chih (1176–1257) who succeeded him as chief councilor promoted to court two True Way leaders, Wei Liao-weng (1178–1237) and Chen Te-hsiu (1178–1235). Already old and unable to make policy changes, they merely relied upon moral appeals to raise morale. The situation went from bad to worse next year. The Mongols, having destroyed the Jurchen empire, directly faced the Southern Sung, its next target.

The southern empire in efforts to boost political prestige and self-confidence resorted to cultural propaganda. The five Northern Sung philosophers of the True Way school were worshipped in the Confucian temple.[49] This implied that, no matter how Confucian the Mongol empire might try or pretend to become, the legitimate line of true Confucianism had been exclusively transmitted to the south through Yang Shih, a leading disciple of Ch'eng I, and on to the True Way school. Knowing this would heighten the awareness among the Sung people that theirs was the true Confucian empire, making them, so it was believed, more determined than ever to defend it. A councilor behind this move had studied under one of Chu Hsi's closest associates, but he was not sure that most scholar-officials would support this step that so honored the True Way school. Cautiously he finessed the proposal by having a friendly but inconspicuous medium-rank official recommend it to court. The recommendation went through without a hitch.[50]

Political competition carried out at the cultural level continued between the Mongols and the Southern Sung. In 1237 the Mongols instituted civil service examinations.[51] In the same year, the Southern Sung emperor, it was later said, composed an imperial eulogy, endorsing the True Way claim of having inherited the orthodoxy. In 1240, in addition to the external threat, the Southern Sung faced internal dangers—a great famine in the capital and several uprisings in mountainous regions in the deep south.[52] The next year, with impressive rites, the court formally proclaimed the learning of the True Way school to be the state orthodoxy, in order to improve the Confucian image of the country and to enhance the people's confidence that the truth was with them. Since it had been known as the Tao-hsueh when it was banned, use of that early name would be awkward, hence the alternate designation of Li-hsueh or the School of Principle. The imperial eulogy, allegedly composed earlier in 1237—an indication of imperial foresight—was released to the whole country.[53] This was the official Neo-Confucianism. From then on, state examinations and those who studied in preparation for them abided by it.

It was hoped that the state orthodoxy would help rally scholar-officials to act loyally, properly, and wisely in defense of the realm. Its theories, however, were not applied to state affairs; nor were its current leaders in power; nor did morale in general rise significantly. Only a small number of transcendental moralists received appointments, none in vital posts and some merely in local academies.[54] Although in his rare appearances in court the emperor listened to lectures on Neo-Confucian teachings, he paid scant attention to them; for he was interested mostly in such un-Confucian indulgences as wine, women, and song.[55] The state orthodoxy notwithstanding, state affairs made no progress.

The Sung Dynastic History, compiled later under the Mongols, departed from the standard format for dynastic histories by including a special chapter on leading Neo-Confucians under the alternate name of Tao-hsueh. The same history excuses the failure of the emperor to put Tao-hsueh into practice; for, it said, in establishing the state orthodoxy he had paved the way for future rulers.[56] After all, the emperor was honored with the posthumous title of Li-tsung, or the Emperor of Principles, for elevating Li-hsueh.

As is well known, the True Way philosophy, especially the synthesis of Chu Hsi, was much more comprehensive and systematic than earlier Confucianism. The relative darkness of the Mongol occupation did not obscure it: It was already culturally a part of the establishment, and it continued to inspire and encourage scholars in private teaching.[57] In spite of, or perhaps because of, the country's being completely under alien occupation for the first time, the Chinese belief in their own cultural superiority and identity became stronger than ever. Through the spreading effects of urbanization, particularly vernacular literature and the performing arts, the orthodox Confucian ideals upheld in teaching also pervaded the general society gradually. These ideals translated into simplified concepts influenced even the illiterate. Thus the state orthodoxy of Neo-Confucianism became the common ideology that helped to integrate and cement the whole culture.[58]

Yet Neo-Confucianism moved toward an inward growth, enriching itself within its established bounds. Adjustments and innovations were incremental, not transformational. Education in this tradition took on increasingly doctrinaire tones. What may be called the neo-traditional period had a tremendous inertia that perpetuated its own bounds century after century. Another factor contributing to the country's political and cultural stability, and later stagnation, was the relationship between Neo-Confucianism and the state. While orthodoxy supported the hierarchical order of the establishment, the state had the power to channel it, to manipulate it, and even to distort it for the sake of political control.

The pyrrhic victory gained by establishing their doctrines as state orthodoxy left the Neo-Confucians in subsequent centuries with considerable ambivalence. First, gratified with their ideological supremacy and social respect, they tended to mute their political criticism, even though they were not happy with the autocracy or its worse form, absolutism. Second, when their political opinion did not prevail despite recommendations, protests, and their own actions for improvement within their jurisdiction as officials, they rationalized and postponed their hope into the future, albeit an elusive future of uncertain prospects. Third, even when a number of Neo-Confucians became disillusioned about both the present and the future, what options did they have? They had little information on an alternate or reform approach. Was it possible for them to depart from tradition? It was hard to leave what they had been brought up with. To criticize the orthodoxy as a political failure? That would be both treason and heresy. To denounce the autocracy? That was unthinkable. To demand thoroughgoing reform? The whole bureaucracy or establishment was adamantly against it. All such departures were impossible. Furthermore, the disillusioned at any given time were a small number of isolated particles scattered within the frozen immensity of the tradition. Though it had been something new a long time ago, Neo-Confucianism aged. Neo-traditionalism permeated the culture so completely that it lost the power to transform.

Epilogue

Prosperous, agrarian, neo-traditional China—the leading empire in history before the industrial age—lasted from the Sung dynasty to the dawn of the twentieth century. It went through a period of native-led splendor, the Ming (1368–1644), that came after the Mongol conquest (Yuan, 1279–1368) but was replaced by the Manchu conquest (Ch'ing, 1644–1911). Autocracy persisted, sometimes expanding, sometimes degenerating into a tyranny of absolutist violence. The Neo-Confucian ideology was locked in with the state, functioning in a symbiosis. It generally supported the autocracy but stubbornly reflected idealistic dimensions as well as developing its own refinements within constraints.

This then is the story, probably told here with many inaccuracies by either commission or omission. In any event, one major complaint is anticipated. Legion are the admirers of Neo-Confucianism. They are bound to ask why has the present study left out its philosophy? Was the philosophy not extensive, expansive, and outreaching in scholarship as well as in daily life? Are its metaphysical and cosmological theories not the best China has ever produced? The present study by design stays away from philosophy, whether of the reformer Wang An-shih or that of the conservatives, Neo-Confucians included. There are already a number of excellent books on these subjects. Some are the history of ideas as formulated by great masters, without the general historical, or at least without the political, context. The version prsented here is something that has rarely been told elsewhere. It tries to weave together the political and the intellectual developments, or, more specifically, to provide the political context needed for understanding the ebb and flow of intellectual tides and the ups and downs of a few key individuals.

Neo-Confucian philosophy was preoccupied with the question of how the superior man, the "Confucian gentleman," cultivates himself. Its "reflections on things at hand,"[1] to use the title of its famous primer, mainly referred to the concerns of scholar-officials, fairly well-to-do literati, and other superior elements in the society. What it taught was not much connected with such practical problems as peasants, village life, townspeople, religious practices, social conditions, and the art of governing even though its leaders occasionally mentioned these topics in their writings. On the whole, Neo-Confucian philosophy tended to emphasize the inward-looking side of Confucian ethical thought, the introspective discipline, and internalized moral values within the individual person rather than in the patterns and structures of society and the political order.[2]

To be bold, a generalization may be suggested. The longer the Sung conservatives and Neo-Confucians devoted themselves to essentially introspective formulations and the deeper they pondered metaphysical and cosmological topics, the less they tended to be oriented toward mundane and objective social realities and the less they tended to seek verification of their philosophical theories by relating them to the actualities that should also be "at hand."

However, what about the case of Chu Hsi? Would it not demolish this generalization right away? It is true that the range of Chu Hsi's knowledge was extremely broad, his investigations in many branches of learning penetrated deeply, his original findings appeared as numerous as they were striking, and above all his systematization of extensive knowledge was the most impressive in Chinese history.[3] It seems equally true that, while the Northern Sung produced at least half a dozen intellectual giants at par with one another, the Southern Sung had hardly any one else comparable to the giant stature of Chu Hsi. From the standpoint of the present study, he was not exactly an exception to the generalization. He stood as the great decisive figure between the two centuries and the herald of a major change. In more ways than one, the broad dimensions, the intellectuality, and the magnitude of his scholarship made him a kindred spirit of the eleventh-century pioneers as well as a crowning successor who surpassed them all. This was why he was able to lead his twelfth-century contemporaries. None of his friends, companions, or disciples ever achieved nearly as much as he did. His followers in the thirteenth century fell further behind like pale reflections.

Despite the greatness of Chu Hsi, who often reached out beyond philosophy, the generalizaton stands. It suggests also a long-range trend in Neo-Confucianism: It would not run into other avenues of knowledge, such as what came to be known as the natural sciences. Uppermost in the mind of the Neo-Confucians were self-cultivation and inner thoughts. They tended to turn inward. This by no means downgrades the great contributions Neo-Confucians made in Chinese history.[4]

Another major problem is whether Neo-Confucians tried to look *out* or outside the system for possible ways to change it? The answer tends to be, "no," for they worked hard on improvements *within* the system. They were not strictly speaking conservatives in the sense of standing pat. They were *inward*-looking.

Yet another complaint is bound to arise. Is not the present study generally unsympathetic to the Neo-Confucians? The contrary is true. They deserve much sympathy and respect for having endured so much struggle and hardship and yet managed to become so influential. They did try to revitalize the political system by cultivating good men who would improve it from *within*. The failure to modify, or perhaps even to transform the autocracy was not the fault of the Neo-Confucians alone. Much later, when Li Chih, the Ming period dissenter, blamed the orthodoxy since Confucius for the absence of critical intellectual spirit in China, he foreshadowed the thunder of the May Fourth movement of 1919; but he neglected to take account of the realities and severe constraints. Politics was in command much of the time.[5]

It must be emphasized that although the Sung was known to treat scholar-officials well, their share of power generally diminished vis-à-vis the autocracy between the eleventh and twelfth centuries. In mid eleventh century, a conservative minister named Wen Yen-po (1006–1097) had the audacity to tell his emperor candidly: "Your Majesty does not share the country with the common people [*pai-hsing*, or "the hundred surnames"]; Your Majesty shares it with scholar-officials [*shih ta-fu*]."[6] Few since his time would dare to say so. In the twelfth century, to paraphrase this striking statement, the emperor shared power with few officials except his surrogate.

Could scholar-officials get together to make themselves heard effectively? It was hardly possible, for the autocracy did not permit them to organize. Factionalism was punished. Nor did they have a forum to discuss common concerns and to develop a consensus among themselves. The state also monopolized political communication. Even social organizations other than kinship groups were not quite acceptable. For instance, a Neo-Confucian philanthropist of only modest means set up private soup kitchens to feed literally thousands of famine-stricken people in his native area year after year. What he did was probably the world's largest charitable operation at the time. But he never thought of setting up a permanent organization like the United Way to do it. Instead, he made *ad hoc* arrangements every time.[7] Politically speaking, by the late Sung, scholar-officials were in essence dispersed, individual members of the elite, almost like the peasants under them, who were dispersed on fragmentary farms.

State power was not alone to blame. The scholar-officials tended to divide among themselves. Leaving all other divisive factors aside, there was one central issue of conflict in the Confucian bureaucracy: the conflict between those in favor of institutional reform and those in favor of moral reconstruction. Reformers preferred administrative ability, while moral reconstructionists stressed trustworthy personality. In the old adage of Confucian language, it was *ts'ai* (talent) versus *te* (virtue). Could the two sides compromise, reconcile, and collaborate? It would be difficult. When the issue inevitably involved numerous other factors, it was hopeless. This was not a particular fault of the Sung scholar-officials. Talent versus virtue, long conceptualized in Chinese sources both before and since the Sung period, actually appears under different labels and in different forms in other cultures. It reflects a permanent problem that vexes various bureaucracies, modern studies in public administration notwithstanding.

Nevertheless, state power was at the center of the stage in traditional China. The crux of the culture lay with government and ideology (*cheng-chiao*).[8] This combination dominated everything else, the economic area included. As the state orthodoxy within the ideology, Neo-Confucianism despite its growth could not reshape or alter the political-intellectual complex or specifically change the subculture of power politics into a subculture of ethical values. Nor could increasing productivity, expanding trade, rising commercialism, or growing urbanism.[9]

In conclusion, the sympathy for Neo-Confucians should be extended to their modern heirs, the present-day educated Chinese—scientists, technocrats, bureaucrats, intellectuals, writers, artists, and the like. They remain dispersed or unorganized outside the highly organized modern state system that has taken over the political-intellectual complex. They have no choice but to serve. In agony, they equally deserve empathy.

Appendix
Notes
Bibliography
Glossary-Index

Appendix
Alphabetic List of Chief Councilors, 1127–1139

Chao Ting (1085–1147)
Chang Chün (1097–1164)
Ch'in Kuei (1090–1155)
Chu Sheng-fei (1082–1144)
Fan Tsung-yin (1099–1137)[a]
Huang Ch'ien-shan (?–1129)
Li Kang (1083–1140)
Lü I-hao (1071–1139)
Tu Ch'ung (?–1140)[b]
Wang Po-yen (dates unknown)
Yeh Meng-te (1077–1148)[c]

[a]Fan was made a chief councilor at the age of 33, one of the youngest in Chinese history (*HNYL*, 658).

[b]Tu was the only chief councilor who surrendered and served under the Jurchen (*HTC*, 2822; *LCSC*, 690).

[c]Yeh was an associate councilor but once, for fourteen days, filled in the role of chief councilor (*HNYL*, 413).

Abbreviations Used in the Notes

Complete bibliographical information for the works listed below can be found in Section B of the Bibliography.

CCTWC: Chao Ting. *Chung-cheng Te-wen chi*
CS: T'o-t'o et al., eds. *Chin shih*
CTYL: Chu Hsi. *Chu-tzu yü-lei.*
HNYL: Li Hsin-ch'uan. *Chien-yen i-lai hsi-nien yao-lu.*
HTC: Pi Yuan. *Hsu tzu-chih t'ung-chien.*
PMHP: Hsu Meng-hsin. *San-ch'ao pei-meng hui-pien.*
SS: T'o-t'o et al., eds. *Sung shih.*
SSCSPM: *Sung-shih chih-shih pen-mo.*
SYHA: Huang Tsung-hsi and Ch'üan Tsu-wang. *Sung-Yuan hsueh-an*
SYHAPI: Wang Tzu-ts'ai and Feng Yuan-hao. *Sung-Yuan hsueh-an pu-i*
TMTY: Ch'i Yun. *Ssu-k'u-chüan-shu tsung-mu t'i-yao*
WHTK Ma Tuan-lin, *Wen-hsien t'ung-k'ao*
YS: Sung Lien, *Yuan shih*

Notes

1. A FOCUS ON CONTRASTS

1. Chang Chia-chü, *Liang-Sung ching-chi*; Chi, *Key Economic Areas*; Liu Tzu-chien, "Pai-hai li-kuo."
2. Chan, *Source Book*, 450–653; Ch'ien Mu, *Kuo-shih ta-kang*, 396–430; James T. C. Liu, "Neo-traditional Period"; Tonami Mamoru, "Sōdai shitaifu"; Reischauer and Fairbank, *East Asia*, 183–242.
3. Aoyama Sadao, "Godai Sō ni okeru Kōsei no shinkō kenryō"; Ch'ien Mu, "Lun Sung-tai hsiang-ch'üan"; Chin Chung-shu, "Sung-tai san-sheng"; Gong, "Participation of Censorial Officials," "Usurpation of Power," and "Role of Censorial Officials"; Liang T'ien-hsi, "Pei-Sung t'ai-chien"; Lin t'ien-wei, *Sung-shih shih-hsi*; Miyazaki Ichisada, "Sōdai kansei"; Yanagida Setsuko, "Sōdai Chūō."
4. Mumford, *City*, 259–260.
5. Meng Yuan-lao, *Tung-ching meng-hua lu*, the only account of K'ai-feng; the 1956 punctuated edition used also has four accounts of Hang-chou appended. See Chang Chia-chü, "Chung-kuo she-hui"; Ch'üan Han-sheng, "Sung-tai Tung-ching" and "Sung-tai Kwang-chou"; Finegan, "Urbanism"; Gernet, *Daily Life*; Liang Keng-yao, "Nan-Sung ch'eng-shih"; Ma, *Commercial Development*; Shiba Yoshinobu, "10–13 seiki ni okeru Chūgoku toshi no tenkan" and "Sōdai no Kōshu"; Sogabe Shizuo, *Kaihō to Kōshu*; Umehara Kaoru, "Sōdai chihō shōtoshi" and "Sōdai no chihō toshi."
6. Ch'üan Han-sheng, "T'ang Sung cheng-fu shui-ju yü ho-pi"; Ferenczy, "On State Regulations of Money"; Hartwell, "Evolution of the Early Northern Sung Monetary System" and "Classical Chinese Monetary Analysis"; Kato Shigeru, *Kingin no kenkyū* and *Shina keizaishi kōshō*; Kusano Yasushi, "Nanso Kozai kaishi"; Miyazaki Sadao, *Godai Sōsho no tsūka mondai*; Sogabe Shizuo *Nichi Sō Kin kahei kōryōshi*.
7. Amano Motonosuke, "Chin Fu no *Nōsho* to suitōsaku"; Hino Kaisaburo, "Tōsaku taikyūshu"; Ping-ti Ho, "Early-ripening Rice"; Kato Shigeru, *Shina keizaishi kōshō*; Liang Keng-yao, *Nan-sung ti nung-ts'un ching-chi*.

8. Chi Tzu-yai, "Sung-tai shou-kung-yeh"; Hung Huan-chun, "Sung-tai ti sheng-chan chi-shu"; K'o Ch'ang-chi, "Sung-tai ku-yung kuan-hsi," a partial translation in James T. C. Liu and Peter Golas, eds., *Change in Sung China;* Su Chin-yuan, "Lun Sung-tai k'e-hu ti jen-shen"; Wang Fang-chung, "Sung-tai min-ying shou-kung-yeh"; Wu T'ien-ying, "Lun Sung-tai ssu-ch'uan chih-yen-yeh."

9. Amano Motonosuke, "Chūgoku ni okeru nōgu no hattatsu"; Fang Hao, "Sung-tai ti k'e-hsueh"; Hung Huan-chun, "Shih chih shih-san shih-chih Chung-kuo k'e-hsueh ti chu-yao ch'eng-chiu"; Nakayama and Sivin, *Chinese Science;* Yabuuchi Kiyoshi, *Kagaku gijutsushi* and his other works listed in the Bibliography.

   For the unique scientist Shen Kua, see Chang Chia-chü, *Shen Kua;* Chang Yin-lin, "Shen Kua pien-nien"; Hu Tao-ching, *Meng-ch'i pi-tan;* Sivin, "Shen Kua," in *Dictionary of Scientific Biography.* The notes here do not include specific references to Shen Kua's medical knowledge.

   For references to Sung mathematics, see Ch'ien Pao-tsung, ed., *Sung Yuan shu-hsueh-shih;* Lam, *Critical Study of "Yang Hui San Fa";* Libbrecht, *Chinese Mathematics in the Thirteenth Century;* Yabuuchi Kiyoshi, *Chūgoku no sūgaku.*

10. Chang Chia-chü, "Chang-kuo she-hui chung-hsin"; Makino Tatsumi, *Kinsei Chūgoku shūzoku kenkyū;* and Twitchett, *Land Tenure.*

11. Hui-chen Wang Liu, *Traditional Clan Rules* or "Analysis of Chinese Clan Rules."

12. Dawson, *Chinese Chameleon.*

13. De Bary, Chan, and Watson, eds., *Sources;* de Bary and Bloom, eds., *Principles and Practicality;* Fairbank, ed., *Chinese Thought and Institutions;* Nivison and Wright, eds., *Confucianism in Action;* Wright, ed., *Confucian Persuasion;* Wright and Twitchett, eds., *Confucian Personalities.*

14. Chang Meng-lun, *Sung-tai hsing-wang shih;* Fang Hao, *Sung shih;* T'ao Chin-sheng, *Pien-chiang-shih;* and Yao Ts'ung-wu, *Tung-pei-shih.*

15. Meng Yuan-lao, *Tung-ching meng-hua lu.*

16. Ch'i Hsia, *Wang An-shih pien-fa;* James T. C. Liu, *Reform;* Teng Kuang-ming, *Wang An-shih;* Williamson, *Wang An-shih: Chinese Statesman and Educationist.*

17. *SYHA*, 24:42 and 40:98.

18. Chu Hsi, *I-Lo yuan-yuan lu*, 1:3 and 2:11.

19. *SYHA*, 32:89.

20. For present-day or late-twentieth-century relevancy, see an article by Nathan Glazer, *The New York Times*, Feb. 26, 1984, the book review section.

21. Aoyama Sadao, "*Sō Kaiyō.*"

22. *TMTY,* 1070–1071; *HTC*, 2600, 2618; Ch'en Lo-su, "*San-ch'ao Pei-meng hui-pien k'ao;* Wang Te-i, "Hsu Meng-hsin."

23. *HTC*, 2600 and 2618; *TMTY,* 1041–1042; Wang Te-i, "Li Hsin-ch'uan."

24. Wang Chi, "*Hsu Tzu-chih t'ung-chien.*"

25. *HNYL*, 2287, 2431, 2660, 2769.

2. SUNG LEARNING

1. Aoki Masaru, *Shina bungaku shisōshi;* Ch'ien Chung-shu, *Sung-shih hsuan-chu;* Hu Yun-i, *Sung-shih yen-chiu.*
2. James T. C. Liu, *Ou-yang Hsiu,* 135–136.
3. Liang Kun, *Sung-shih p'ai-pieh lun;* and Shuen-fu Lin, *Transformation of the Chinese Lyrical Tradition.*
4. Hsia Ch'eng-t'ao, *T'ang Sung tz'u;* Hu Yun-i, *Chung-kuo Tz'u-shih;* James Y. C. Liu, *Major Lyricists;* Irving Yu-cheng Lo, *Hsin Ch'i-chi;* Malmqvist, "On the Lyrical Poetry of Hsin Ch'i-chi"; Chang K'ang-i Sun, *Evolution of Chinese Tz'u Poetry;* T'ang Kuei-chang, *Sung tz'u.*
5. Chang Chien, *Sung Chin ssu-chia wen-hsueh;* Ch'ien Tung-fu, *T'ang ku-wen yun-tung;* K'e Tun-po, *Wen-hsueh shih.*
6. Lü Tsu-ch'ien ed. *Sung-wen chien;* Chin Chung-shu, "Ku-wen yuan-tung."
7. *TMTY,* 2, 11–25, 30–48, 51, 55, 115.
8. *TMTY,* 218–235, 303–307, 314, 319.
9. *TMTY,* 363–367, 371–372, 389, 391, 399, 431–432, 438–441.
10. *TMTY,* 529–531, 536–549.
11. *TMTY,* 719–725, 728, 731, 735–736.
12. *TMTY,* 1900, 1904, 1907, 1912–1914, 1919–1920, 1937–1938, 1942.
13. *TMTY,* 982–987, 1004–1010; James T. C. Liu, *Ou-yang Hsiu,* 100–113.
14. *TMTY,* 1005, 1007.
15. James T. C. Liu, *Ou-yang Hsiu,* 3, 175.
16. *TMTY,* 1028–1029, 1041–1047, 1840–1841.
17. *TMTY,* 1069–1072.
18. *TMTY,* 1095–1099.
19. *TMTY,* 1134–1136, 1142–1153.
20. Chu Shih-chia, *Sung Yuan fang-chih chuan-chi,* preface; *TMTY,* 1461–1465, 1492–1493, 1513–1516, 1525–1526.
21. *TMTY,* 1527–1528; Meng Yuan-lao, *Tung-ching meng-hua lu.*
22. *TMTY,* 1093–1095, 1702–1704.
23. *TMTY,* 1729–1732.
24. Ch'ien Mu, *Chu-tzu;* Mou Jun-sun, "Ts'ung Chung-kuo ti ching-hsueh k'an shih-hsueh"; Yoshikawa Kōjirō, *An Introduction to Sung Poetry.*

3. SUNG CONFUCIANISM

1. Liu Po-chi, *Sung-tai cheng-chiao shih.*
2. Kenneth K. S. Ch'en, *Chinese Transformation of Buddhism;* Chikusa Masaaki, *Chūgoku Bukyo shakaishi;* Huang Min-chih, "Sung-tai ssu-kuan yü chuang-yuan;" Tsukamoto Zenryn, "Sō no zaiseinan."

3. Ch'ien Mu, *Chu-tzu;* James T. C. Liu, "How Did a Neo-Confucian School Become the State Orthodoxy?"

4. See Chapter One, note 13.

5. *SYHA,* 22:106, 23:117; *SYHAPI,* 23:7.

4. THE MORALISTIC CONSERVATIVES

1. *HNYL,* 560, 2093, 2616; *PMHP,* 123:9 10.

2. *SYHAPI,* 38:2.

3. *Ching-kang pai-shih,* No. 5, p. 1, and No. 6, p. 2.

4. *Nan chin chi-wen lu,* 34–35.

5. *Ch'ieh fen hsu-lu,* 11–12.

6. *Ching-kang pai-shih,* No. 6, p. 1, and colophon at the end, dated 1909; Chou Mi, *Ch'i-tung yeh-yü,* 18:1–2.

7. Ch'ien Shih-sheng, *Nan-Sung shu,* preface; *HTC,* 2585, note.

8. *HNYL,* 125–127, 138–139, 160–161, 240, 323; *HTC,* 2580, 2623–2624, 2637, 1702; *Huang-Sung chung-hsing,* 395, 420, 465, 508; *PMHP,* 110:1, 120:1–13; *SYHA,* 22:108; *SYHAPI,* 22:43.

9. *HNYL,* 524–525; *PMHP,* 108:2.

10. *HNYL,* 873, 1348; *HTC,* 3037–3038; *Huang-Sung chung-hsing,* 1228; *PMHP,* 164:9 and 172:10–12; Yang Yao-pi, *Wei Ch'u lu.* See also Chu Hsi-tsu, *Wei-Ch'u-lu chi-pu;* and Shen Ch'en-nung, "Sung-tai Wei-chu-chih chih shih-mo."

11. *HNYL,* 1004–1005.

12. *HNYL,* 2009, 2016, 2022–2024, 2027–2028, 2172; *HTC,* 3298, 3307, 3310–3311; *PMHP,* 155:17, 161:4–11, 162:1–11, 163:1–12.

13. *HNYL,* 2276.

14. *HNYL,* 2292–2293.

15. *HNYL,* 2355.

16. *HNYL,* 2645.

17. *HNYL,* 2430; *Huang-Sung chung-hsing,* 773.

18. Chu Hsi, *I-Lo yuan-yuan lu,* appendix, 4:6; *HNYL,* 149; Hung Mai, *Yung-tsai sui-pi,* 2:58–59; *PMHP,* 108:1–2; *SYHA,* 32:91.

19. *HTC,* 2562–2564, 2579, 2608–2609, 2615–2616; *Huang-Sung chung-hsing,* 398, 410, 433–434; *PMHP,* 78:9–11, 79:4–9, 79:13, 80:3–4, 84:5–8, 105:11–12, 106:1–2, 134:14–15, 135:1–3, 138:3; Wang Ming-ching, *Hui chu lu,* item 435.

20. *HNYL,* 1700–1701; *HTC,* 2667, 2802–2805, 3246; *Huang-Sung chung-hsing,* 411–412.

21. *HNYL,* 912.

22. *HNYL,* 148–149, 2078–2086; *HTC,* 2878; *Huang-Sung chung-hsing,* 773; *PMHP,* 141:11 and 145:8–9; Liu Tzu-chien, "Lueh-lun sung-tai wu-kuan ch'ün."

23. Chuang Cho, *Chi-li pien,* 67; *HNYL,* 148–149, 2078, 2086; *HTC,* 2638–2639, 2655, 2685, 2781, 2843, 2921, 2936–2937, 2946, 2966, 2977; *Huang-Sung chung-hsing,* 429, 482, 859, 923, 967–968, 1174; Wang Ming-ching, *Hui chu lu,* item 339.

24. Ning K'o, "Sung-tai chung-wen ch'ing wu"; Liu Tzu-chien, "Lueh-lun Sung-tai wu-kuan ch'ün."

25. *HNYL,* 836, 1334; *Huang-Sung chung-hsing,* 806, 1674.

26. Aoyama Sadao, "Hokusō o chūshin to suru shitaifu no kika"; Kinugawa Tsuyoshi, "Sōdai hōkyū ni tsuite"; *HNYL,* 1059, 2150; *PMHP,* 134:8.

27. *HNYL,* 1492.

28. Ch'i Chueh-sheng, "Nan-Sung hsien-ling chih-tu;" *HNYL,* 1745, 2133–2134.

29. *HNYL,* 297, 494.

30. *HNYL,* 1449; *Huang-Sung chung-hsing,* 803–804.

31. Ch'en Yuan, *Mo-t'ang chi,* 16:13; Ho Hsiang-fei, "Wang An-shih p'ing-cha."

32. Ch'en Yuan, *Mo-t'ang chi,* 17:9, *HNYL,* 494, 542, 831, 1290, 1296–1297, 1449; *HTC,* 2771, 3019.

33. *HNYL,* 512–513, 782, 1375, 2446.

34. James T. C. Liu, *Reform,* 98–113.

35. Chu Chia-yuan, "Tan-tan Sung-tai ti hsiang-ts'un chung-hu"; McKnight, *Village,* 20–97; Sudō Yoshiyuki, *Tō Sō shakei keizaishi;* Wang Tseng-yü, "Sung-ch'ao, chieh-chi chieh-kou."

36. *HNYL,* 2544, 2970–2971, 3610; Wang Huai-ling, "Yu-kuan Sung-tai chai-i", Wang Te-i, *Sung-shih Yen-chiu lun-chi,* 1:233–262.

37. James T. C. Liu, *Reform,* 83–84.

38. *HNYL,* 530, 1395, 1419, 1769.

39. *HNYL,* 1971, 2447, 2449.

40. *HNYL,* 1158, 1971, 2447.

41. *HNYL,* 2941–2942; Hung Mai, *Yung-tsai sui-pi,* 4:5–6; *SS,* ch. 281.

42. *HNYL,* 2967.

43. *HNYL,* 645, 1869, 1886, 1974.

44. Bol, "Culture and the Way"; Bush, *Chinese Literati on Painting; HNYL,* 322, 832; *HTC,* 2672; Yutang Lin, *Gay Genius.*

45. de Bary, Chan, and Watson, *Sources,* 448–452; Freeman, "Lo-yang and the Opposition to Wang An-shih"; Hsiao Kung-ch'üan, *Chung-kuo cheng-chih Ssu-hsiang-shih,* ch. 16; *HTC,* 2662–2663; *Huang-Sung chung-hsing,* 493–494, 630, 1280–1282, 1294, 1308; Sariti, "Monarchy, Bureaucracy, and Absolutism in the Thought of Ssu-ma Kuang."

46. *HNYL,* 297, 1047, 1199; *HTC,* 2999.

47. *HNYL,* 861, 1733, 1832; see the Classic *The Great Learning,* tr. James Legge, Ch. 5–7. See also Gardner, *Chu Hsi and the "Ta Hsueh."*

48. Chin Chung-shu, "Pei-Sung Ke-chü chih-tu;" *HNYL,* 1184–1275, 1428–1429, 1560, 2835; *HTC,* 2995, 3472; *Huang-Sung chung-hsing,* 1104–1105, 1132–1133.

49. *HNYL,* 200; *SS,* ch.459.

50. Chu Hsi, *I-Lo yuan-yuan lu,* 10:5 and 10:8; *HNYL,* 289, 313; *HTC,* 2645; *Huang-Sung chung-hsing,* 433, 493, 502; *SS,* ch. 428; *SYHAPI,* 25:22–23.

51. *HNYL,* 978–979, 1399, 1774, 1960–1961; *Huang-Sung chung-hsing,* 935, 953, 1133; *SYHA,* 9:14, 34:17.

52. *HTC,* 2675, 2919–2920, 2938, 3128; *Huang-Sung chung-hsing,* 511–512, 815, 875–881, 893–894, 1152, 1341, 1390; Li Hsin-ch'uan, *Tao ming lu,* 3:8; *SYHA,* 34:116–121; *SYHAPI,* 34:32.

53. Chu Hsi, *I-Lo yuan-yuan lu,* 11:11; Fu, "Huang Ting-chien's Calligraphy"; *HNYL,* 1501, 1625.

54. *HNYL,* 2048, 2703; *Huang-Sung chung-hsing,* 1181, 1213, 1245, 1291, 1352–1353, 1375, 1382, 1425–1426, 1432, 1499–1500, 1516, 1519–1521, 1555; *PMHP,* 178:1, 185:6, 189:6–9, 191:4.

55. *HNYL,* 259, 297–298, 313; *HTC,* 2645, 2662–2666.

56. *HNYL,* 472, 633, 677–678, 732, 753, 1509; *HTC,* 2759, 2900, 2909; and *Huang-Sung chung-hsing,* 697, 804–805, 815.

57. *HNYL,* 832, 1712.

58. *HNYL,* 1253–1254, 1419, 1547, 1708–1709; Wang Te-i, *Sung-shih Yen-chiu lun-chi,* 1:32–38, 2:87–106.

59. *HNYL,* 1801, 1804, 1817, 1862; Ho Hsiang-fei, "Nan-Sung Kao-tsung Hsiao-tsung liang-ch'ao Wang An-shih p'ing-cha," 161–180; *HTC,* 3017–3018; *Huang-Sung chung-hsing,* 1032, 1038–1039, 1045–1047, 1121, 1195–1196, 1395.

60. *HNYL,* 423–424, 1510, 1531, 1551; *SYHA,* 32:11–12; *SYHAPI,* 32:94; Wang Ming-ch'ing, *Hui chu lu,* item 329.

61. *HNYL,* 1510, 1832.

62. *SYHA,* ch. 37.

63. *HNYL,* 1660; Li Hsin-ch'uan, *Tao ming lu,* 3:3–4; *SYHA,* 32:10.

64. *HNYL,* 1747–1751; *Huang-Sung chung-hsing,* 1319–1320, 1326–1328, 1331–1332; Li Hsin-ch'uan, *Tao ming lu,* 3:8; *SSCSPM,* 80:212; comment by Chang P'u; *SYHA,* 34:117.

65. *HNYL,* 1747–1748, 1754, 1759; Li Hsin-ch'uan, *Tao ming lu,* 3:5–6.

66. *HNYL,* 1759, 1785, 1802, 2712, 2723, 2766.

67. Li Hsing-ch'uan, *Tao ming lu,* 3:1–2, 3:12.

68. *HNYL,* 200, 1137, 1477, 1598; Li Hsin-ch'uan, *Tao ming lu,* 3:9–10, 3:14–15; Shao Po, *Shao-shih Wen-chien hou-lu,* 75; *SYHA,* 34:34, 48:3–6.

69. *HNYL,* 1754–1756; and *Huang-Sung chung-hsing,* 1328–1329.

70. Liu Tzu-chien, "Pao-yung cheng-chi." For a discussion of this "gentle" approach, see also under rubric "Kao Tsung's handling of bureaucrats," *Encyclopaedia Britannica,* 15th ed., *Macropaedia* 4:337.

71. *HNYL,* 2431–2432, 2469, 2704, 2750, 2847.

72. Li Hsin-ch'uan, *Tao ming lu,* Preface.

73. *HNYL,* 2427, 2431–2436, 2447, 2453, 2456; Li Hsin-ch'uan, *Tao ming lu,* 4:3–5.

74. *HNYL,* 2712.

75. *HNYL*, 3162; Li Hsin-ch'uan, *Tao ming lu*, 4:3–5; Liu Tzu-chien, "Lueh-lun Sung-tai ti-fang kuan-hsueh yü ssu-hsueh."

76. *HNYL*, 2056 and 2252; *PMHP*, 193:8.

5. AUTOCRACY AND COUNCILORS

1. Li T'ang, *Sung Hui-tsung; SSCSPM*, ch. 48–51; Ts'ai T'iao, *Tieh-wei-shan;* Wang Ming-ch'ing, *Hui chu lu*, items 101, 117, 143, 380, 388.

2. *HNYL*, 43, 1399, 1485, 1979; *PMHP*, 216:6; *SS*, ch. 360, Comments; *SYHA*, 40: 97–98.

3. *HNYL*, 635, 1554, 2172.

4. *HNYL*, 492, 1531, 1947.

5. *HNYL*, 1685.

6. *HNYL*, 2279.

7. *HNYL*, 375, 1591.

8. *HNYL*, 1374, 1928–1983.

9. Precedent in 1131–1132, see *HNYL*, 989–993, 996–999.

10. *HNYL*, 1315, 1413.

11. Chou Tao-chi, "Sung-tai tsai-hsiang ming-cheng"; *Huang-Sung chung-hsing*, 602; *HNYL*, 1728; *HTC*, 2760.

12. Chin Chung-shu, "Sung-tai san-sheng chang-kuan"; Kinugawa Tsuyoshi, "Sōdai saishō kō"; Kracke, *Civil Service*, 38–39.

13. Ch'ih Ching-te, "Sung-tai tsai-shu fen-li"; *HNYL*, 658, 1418; *HTC*, 3470; Wang Ming-ch'ing, *Hui chu lu*, item 125.

14. *HNYL*, 951, 1397.

15. Hsu Ping-yü, "Sung Kao-tsung chih tui Ch'in cheng-ts'e."

16. *HNYL*, 989–999.

17. *HNYL*, 907.

18. *HNYL*, 1109.

19. *HNYL*, 1980.

20. *HNYL*, 1399, 1413, 2173.

21. *HNYL*, 1411; Teraji Jun, "Shin Kai go."

22. Chia Ta-ch'üan, "Lun Pei-sung ti ping-pien"; *HTC*, 2728–2752; *Huang-Sung chung-hsing*, 559–588; Wang Ming-ch'ing, *Hui chu lu*, item 268.

23. *HNYL*, 507; *HTC*, 2757–2758; *Huang-Sung chung-hsing*, 598, 622–623.

24. *HNYL*, 827–828.

25. *HNYL*, 634, 1146–1147; *PMHP*, 137:11–12.

26. *HNYL*, 1353.

27. *HNYL*, 1591 and 1718.

28. *HNYL*, 664, 890, 2821, 3288; Wang Ming-ch'ing, *Hui chu lu*, items 128, 356.

29. *HNYL*, 1374, 1982.

30. *HNYL*, 365, 375, 404, 407, 439, 481.

31. *HNYL*, 1153; Liang t'ien-hsi, "Sung-tai chih ssu-lu chih-tu"; Wang Ming-ch'ing, *Hui chu lu*, item 25.
32. *HNYL*, 363, 401.
33. *HNYL*, 570.
34. *HNYL*, 836–837, 895, 903, 1397.
35. *HNYL*, 1047, 1052.
36. *HNYL*, 951, 1325, 1397.
37. *HNYL*, 1709; *HTC*, 2929, *PMHP*, 166:14–15.
38. *HNYL*, 1397; *HTC*, 3053; *Huang-Sung chung-hsing*, 1111–1113.
39. *HNYL*, 1717, 1721–1727.
40. *HNYL*, 931, 936, 1397.
41. *HNYL*, 1730.
42. *HNYL*, 1721–1722; Yamauchi Masahiro, "Chō Shun" and "Nansō no Shisen ni okeru Chō Shun to Go Kai."
43. *HNYL*, 1731.
44. *HNYL*, 1727, 1737, 1739–1740; *HTC*, 3080–3086, 3091, 3097–3099, 3110–3112; *Huang-Sung chung-hsing*, 1173, 1269, 1304–1305; *PMHP*, 170:6–7.
45. *HNYL*, 1727; *PMHP*, 193:7; *SYHAPI*, 96:60.
46. *HNYL*, 2056; Li Hsin-ch'uan, *Tao ming lu*, 3:14–17.
47. *HNYL*, 1759–1761, 1911.
48. Chia Ta-ch'üan, "Lun Pei-Sung ti ping pien"; *HNYL*, 1822–1825; *HTC*, 3130, 3135–3136, 3142–3144; *Huang-Sung chung-hsing*, 1354–1356, 1372–1374; *PMHP*, 178:2–4.
49. *HNYL*, 1873; *Huang-Sung chung-hsing*, 1296–1297, 1305; *PMHP*, 183:1–2.
50. *HNYL*, 1834, 1840, 1858; *SSCSPM*, 809–818; *SYHAPI*, 44:15.
51. *HNYL*, 1860, 1867; *HTC*, 3144, 3152, 3170; *PMHP*, 178:9.
52. *HNYL*, 1857–1859; *HTC*, 3478; *PMHP*, 200:11; Wang Ming-ch'ing, *Hui chu lu*, item 284.
53. *HNYL*, 1867; *HTC*, 3147.
54. *HNYL*, 2762.
55. *HNYL*, 1868–1869, 1886.
56. Chu Ch'i, "Sung Chin i-ho"; *CS*, ch. 79; *HNYL*, 1900; *Huang-Sung chung-hsing*, 1420–1421; *PMHP*, 161:4.
57. *HNYL*, 1904; Koiwai Hiromitsu, "Nansō shoki gunsei"; Liang T'ien-hsi, "Nan-sung Chien-yen Yü-ying-ssu" and "Nan-Sung chih tu-fu chih-tu."
58. *HNYL*, 1915, 1924; *PMHP*, 145:7–8, 175:11–12.
59. *HNYL*, 1970.
60. *HNYL*, 1944–1950; *PMHP*, 173:1–5, 176:16; Wang Ming-ch'ing, *Hui chu lu*, items 275, 320; Wang Ming-sun, "Chin-ch'u ti kung-ch'en," 217.
61. *HNYL*, 1983–1986; *PMHP*, 167:4–9, 168:1–9, 170:2–4.
62. *HNYL*, 1955; *HTC*, 3179; *PMHP*, 188:7–8; *SYHA*, 39:82.
63. *HTC*, 2859–2860, 2864–2865, 2899, 2943; *Huang-Sung chung-hsing*, 750, 758–

759, 805, 897; *SS*, ch. 473; *SSCSPM*, 733–764; Ting Ch'üan-ching ed., *Sung-jen i-shih hui-pien*, 751–770.

64. *HNYL*, 975, 1635, 2116–2117, 2149, 2174–2175, 2330–2331, 2336, 2339, 2351, 2360–2361, 2364; Ch'ien Shih-sheng, *Nan-Sung shu*, 31:10.

65. Wei Ai Gong, "Participation of Censorial Officials"; *HNYL*, 1954, 1956, 1967–1968, 1972–1974; *HTC*, 3188; *Huang-Sung chung-hsing*, 1455–1459; *PMHP*, 183:3; *SYHA*, 35:12.

66. *HNYL*, 1974.

67. *CS*, ch. 77; *HNYL*, 645, 1869, 1886; *Huang-Sung chung-hsing*, 1606; *PMHP*, 172:10–12.

68. *HNYL*, 1974–1975; *PMHP*, 185:4.

69. *HNYL*, 1990–2004, 2019–2020; Lin Jui-han, "Shao-hsing shih-erh-nien"; *PMHP*, 188:7–8.

70. *HNYL*, 2193–2197, 2203–2205, 2211–2212, 2236; Wang Ming-sun, "Chin-ch'u ti kung-ch'en," 215.

71. *HNYL*, 2244–2249, 2253–2254, 2258; *HTC*, 2918, 3281–3282; *Huang-Sung chung-hsing*, 1429, 1432–1433, 1438, 1622–1623.

72. *HNYL*, 2188, 2261, 2265; Wang Fu-chih, *Sung lun*, ch. 10.

73. *HNYL*, 2264–2272, 2282, 2298–2304; *HTC*, 3287–3289, 3294, 3300–3301; *Huang-Sung chung-hsing*, 1630–1637, 1643, 1653–1655; *SSCSPM*, 723–726; Teng Kuang-ming, *Yüeh Fei chuan*; Wang Tseng-yü, *Yüeh Fei hsin-chuan*.

74. Li An, "Sung Kao-tsung t'zu Yüeh Fei ssu" and "Yüeh Fei chai Nan-Sung"; James T. C. Liu, "Yüeh Fei (1103–1141) and China's Heritage of Loyalty."

75. *HNYL*, 2775.

76. *HNYL*, 2045, *HTC*, 3193, 3344–3346, 3416, 3429–3430, 3448, 3456; *SYHAPI*, 35:29, 96:60; Wang Ming-ch'ing, *Hui chu lu*, items 279, 300.

77. *HNYL*, 2072, 2425; *Huang-Sung chung-hsing*, 1665.

78. *HNYL*, 2359.

79. *HNYL*, 2387; Hung Mai, *Yung-tsai sui-pi*, 4:78.

80. *HNYL*, 2050–2054, 2066–2069; *HTC*, 3208–3209.

81. *HNYL*, 2126, 2152, 2164, 2293.

82. *HNYL*, 2699.

83. *HNYL*, 2382; Shao Po, *Shao-shih Wen-chien hou-lu*, 78; Wang Ming-ch'ing, *Hui chu lu*, item 127.

84. *HNYL*, 2433, 2599, 2641; *HTC*, 3343, 3404, 3461.

85. *HNYL*, 2477, 2599, 2604.

86. *HNYL*, 2382, 2399, 2496, 2736; *SYHA*, preface: 18, 44:69–70; *SYHAPI*, preface: 64, 34:63.

87. *HNYL*, 2432, 2745, 2811; *SYHA*, 32:95.

88. *HNYL*, 2660.

89. *HNYL*, 2287.

90. *HNYL*, 2431, 2769; Hung Mai, *Yung-tsai sui-pi*, 2:142; Teraji Jun, "Shin Kai go";

Yang Shu-fan, "Sung-tai tsai-hsiang chih-tu"; Yueh K'o, *T'ing-shih*, 79, 134.

91. *HNYL*, 2769–2774.
92. *HNYL*, 2794.
93. *HNYL*, 2724, 2824.
94. *HNYL*, 2781–2789, 2793, 2801–2806, 2930, 2887.
95. *HNYL*, 2885–2888.
96. *HNYL*, 2928.
97. *HNYL*, 2942–2948, 3123–3131.
98. *HNYL*, 2818–2819, 3028–3032.
99. *HNYL*, 2909–2911.
100. *HNYL*, 2824.
101. *HNYL*, 2939.
102. *HNYL*, 3014.
103. *HNYL*, 3100–3108.
104. *HNYL*, 3172–3175.
105. *HNYL*, 3211, 3233, 3243.
106. *HNYL*, 3295, 3306–3310.
107. *HNYL*, 3247, 3250.
108. *HNYL*, 3252.
109. *HNYL*, 3144, 3181, 3191.
110. *HNYL*, 3250, 3257; *HTC*, 3616.
111. *HNYL*, 3260–3272; Shen Ch'i-wei, *Sung Chin chan-cheng;* T'ao Chin-sheng, *Pien-chiang-shih yen-chiu-chi: Sung Chin shih-chi.*
112. *HNYL*, 3281–3287.
113. *HNYL*, 3294, 3301, 3357, 3376.
114. *HNYL*, 3315.
115. *HNYL*, 3319; *HTC*, 3617.
116. *HNYL*, 3313–3314.
117. *SSCSPM*, 823. The humiliating fact that the Sung lost imperial status vis-à-vis the Jurchen was not made clear to the Sung people until 1164 when Kao-tsung as Emperor Emeritus directed his successor to fight another war and through renewed peace negotiations got the imperial status restored to the Sung.
118. *HNYL*, 3335.
119. *SSCSPM*, 809–818.
120. *HNYL*, 3377, 3382–3385.
121. *HNYL*, 3389; *SSCSPM*, 827–845; see also the Classic *The Great Learning*, tr. James Legge, ch. 5–7.

6. A CASE STUDY: FROM EXCELLENCE TO EXILE

1. Teng Kuang-ming, *Yueh Fei chuan,* insists on the traditional view that the famous poetic-song was a genuine composition of Yueh Fei himself. Hsia Ch'eng-chu, however, in *T'ang Sung tz'u,* has speculated that it was likely to have been written by someone else around 1500 in celebration of a Ming dynasty victory in Inner Mongolia, but retroactively attributed to Yueh Fei. The present author plans to argue in a short note in the near future that the poetic-song was probably written with some collaboration of a ghost-writer on Yueh Fei's staff.

2. *SSCSPM,* 809–818.

3. Li Hsin-ch'uan, *Tao ming lu,* 3:13–17.

4. *SYHA,* 44:61.

5. James T. C. Liu, *Ou-yang Hsiu,* 2.

6. Huang Huai and Yang Shih-ch'i, *Li-tai ming-ch'en tsou-i.*

7. *CCTWC,* works of Chao Ting; *SS,* ch. 360, biography of Chao Ting.

8. *CCTWC,* 3:9–10; cf. biography of Shao Po-wen in *SS,* ch. 433.

9. *CCTWC,* 3:4–17; *HNYL,* 52, 68.

10. *CCTWC,* 1:4–7, Chu Hsi, *I-Lo yuan-yuan lu,* 10:5, 10:8; *HNYL,* 472, 494; *Huang-Sung chung-hsing,* 616; *SS,* ch. 360, 362, 428.

11. *HNYL,* 498, 507, 526; *Huang-Sung chung-hsing,* 626–627, 632–633, 662.

12. *HNYL,* 1375, 1487–1497, 1508–1509.

13. *HNYL,* 526, 559; *Huang-Sung chung-hsing,* 699.

14. *HNYL,* 558–562.

15. *HNYL,* 578–579. Chao merely suggested retreat; the idea of sailing into the sea came from Lü I-hao, then the chief councilor.

16. *CCTWC,* 7:9–12; *HNYL,* 584–589; *PMHP,* 134:3–4; Wang Ming-ch'ing, *Hui chu lu,* items 269, 307, 358.

17. *CCTWC,* 7:14; *HNYL,* 603.

18. *CCTWC,* 7:10, 7:13; *PMHP,* 135:1–3.

19. *CCTWC,* 7:15.

20. *CCTWC,* 7:17.

21. *HNYL,* 611–612.

22. *CCTWC,* 7:18; *HNYL,* 631–636, 645, 674, 679, 855; *HTC,* 2830; *PMHP,* 137:11–12; *SS,* ch. 362; Wang Ming-sun, "Chin-ch'u ti kung-ch'en."

23. *HNYL,* 645–649.

24. *HNYL,* 695, 713–714, 724–725; *PMHP,* 145:8.

25. *HNYL,* 728.

26. *HNYL,* 711–713, 1218–1225.

27. *HNYL,* 733; *HTC,* 2863–2864.

28. *HNYL,* 1085, 1233, 1286.

29. *HNYL,* 1025, 1049, 1065; *Huang-Sung chung-hsing,* 926–927.

30. *CCTWC,* 2:12–13; *HNYL,* 1079, 1206; *Huang-Sung chung-hsing,* 943, 1014; *PMHP,* 155:15.

31. *HNYL,* 1110, 1109, 1121, 1137, 1152, 1161, 1172–1173, 1191, 1194, 1241, 1250; *PMHP,* 161:6, 162:6–7.

32. *HNYL,* 1222, 1263, 1281.

33. *HNYL,* 1290–1291; *Huang-Sung chung-hsing,* 1201, 1047–1049; *PMHP,* 161:1.

34. *CCTWC,* 2:15–29, *HNYL,* 1305–1306; Li Hsin-ch'uan, *Chiu-wen cheng-wu,* 51–52.

35. *HNYL,* 1196, 1199, 1202, 1283, 1306–1307, 1311.

36. *HNYL,* 1313, 1318, 1321.

37. *HNYL,* 1323; *HTC,* 3023–3028, 3041; *Huang-Sung chung-hsing,* 1056–1059, 1063, 1087.

38. *HNYL,* 1337–1338, 1344; *PMHP,* 157:1, 164:1.

39. *HNYL,* 1370, 1668–1669, 1695–1697.

40. *HNYL,* 1346–1348, 1354, 1362–1363.

41. *HNYL,* 1356–1357; *PMHP,* 164:5, 164:10–11, 165:1.

42. *HNYL,* 1305–1306, 1325–1326, 1349–1352; *HTC,* 3026, 3046; *Huang-Sung chung-hsing,* 1054–1055; *SS,* ch. 361, biography of Chang Chün.

43. *HNYL,* 1354. There was a precedent: see *SS,* ch. 362, biography of Lü I-ho.

44. *CCTWC,* 4:10.

45. *CCTWC,* 1:8.

46. *HNYL,* 1591.

47. *CCTWC,* 1:24.

48. *CCTWC,* 1:14–15, 1:30–32.

49. *HNYL,* 1649, 1652.

50. *HNYL,* 1741; *HTC,* 3114–3115; T'ang Keng, *Mei-shan chi,* 1:3.

51. *CCTWC,* 3:5–6, 3:19, 8:21–22; *HNYL,* 1226–1228; *HTC,* 2829.

52. *CCTWC,* 4:9.

53. *CCTWC,* 3:17; *SYHA,* 40:89; *SYHAPI,* 39:2, 98:60.

54. *CCTWC,* 8:20; Ch'en Yuan, *Mo-t'ang chi,* 16:18; *Huang-Sung chung-hsing,* 1085, 1115–1116, 1395–1396, recording the views of Kao-tsung, Chang, and Chao respectively.

55. *CCTWC,* 1:9; Hung Yeh, "Chao Pu i Pan-pu *Lun-yü.*"

56. *CCTWC,* 4:8.

57. *CCTWC,* 3:7, 8:19, 9:21–22; *SS,* ch. 33; *SYHA,* 37:45, 43:51.

58. *CCTWC,* 4:24, 8:18; *HNYL,* 1248, 1289–1290; *Huang-Sung chung-hsing,* 1173.

59. *CCTWC,* 8:17–19; *Huang-Sung chung-hsing,* 1123.

60. *HNYL,* 1894, 1898.

61. *HNYL,* 1782, 1924.

62. *CCTWC,* 8:24.

63. *HNYL,* 1900, 1932, 2029.

64. *HNYL,* 1943–1944; *SSCSPM,* 723–724, 754–755.

65. *HNYL*, 1954, 1967–1968, 1970–1974.
66. *HNYL*, 1945–1947; *HTC*, 3197–3202.
67. *CCTWC*, 9:1–4; Franke, "Treaties"; *HNYL*, 1955; *HTC*, 3183; *Huang-Sung chung-hsing*, 1449–1450; Shen Ch'i-wi, *Sung Chin chan-cheng*.
68. Chu Hsi, *Chu-tzu yü-lei*, 5047, where he admitted that the Sung could not win the war. See also *SS*, ch. 360, "Comments"; *SYHAPI*, 44:4; Wang Ming-ch'ing, *Hui chu lu*, item 282.
69. *HNYL*, 1974–1975.
70. *HNYL*, 1982, 2007.
71. *HNYL*, 2098, 2123, 2197.
72. *CCTWC*, 3:27–28.
73. *HNYL*, 2011, 2348; *PMHP*, 204:1, 204:4.
74. *CCTWC*, 4:10–11.
75. *HNYL*, 2067, 2097, 2102.
76. *HNYL*, 2162, 1194.
77. *HNYL*, 2196, 2223.
78. *HNYL*, 2298–2303; *SSCSPM*, 723–726.
79. *CCTWC*, 9:17–22.
80. *CCTWC*, 9:14–17, 9:22–23; *SS*, ch. 361.
81. *HNYL*, 2368, 2431; *PMHP*, 212:4.
82. *HNYL*, 2372, 2445.
83. *HNYL*, 2491, 2514, 2531; *PMHP*, 213:2.
84. *HNYL*, 2537; *HTC*, 3375–3376, 3468; *PMHP*, 216:1–3.
85. *HNYL*, 2616, 2760; *HTC*, 3411, 3460; Yueh K'o, *Ting shih*, 134.
86. *HNYL*, 2453, 2512.
87. *HNYL*, 2703–2704, 2723.
88. *HNYL*, 2847.
89. *HNYL*, 2770–2775.
90. *HNYL*, 2806, 2838, 3122; *HTC*, 3473.
91. *HNYL*, 2881.
92. See the ancient Classic, *The Great Learning*, tr. James Legge, ch. 6–9.

7. NEO-CONFUCIANS AS TRANSCENDENTAL MORALISTS: DISSENSION, HERESY, AND ORTHODOXY

1. In addition to the earlier version of this chapter (Liu, "How Did a Neo-Confucian School Become the State Orthodoxy?") see Julia Ching, "Truth and Ideology: The Confucian Way"; Schirokauer, "Neo-Confucianism under Attack."
2. Liu Tzu-chien, "Sung-tai kao-ch'ang pi-tuan."
3. Nivison and Wright, eds., *Confucianism in Action*, 22.
4. Liu Tzu-chien, "Jukyō kokka."

5. For a parallel in the experience of present-day American intellectuals, see the interview with Kenneth Keniston in the *New York Times,* 7 February 1971, section VI, p. 12; and his letter of response, *New York Times,* 28 February 1971, section VI, p. 4.

6. Sung hui-yao chi-kao, "Tsung-ju" segment, 2:14. See also Araki Toshikazu, "Sōdai Kakyo seido"; Ch'ien Mu, "Sung Ming li-hsueh kai-shu"; Fumoto Yasutaka, "Hokusō ni okeru Jugaku"; Hsia Chün-yü, *Sung hsueh;* Lee, "Life in the Schools and his *Government and Examination;* Liu Tzu-chien, "Lueh-lun Sung-tai ti-fang kuan-hsueh"; Terada Gō, *Kyoikushi.*

7. Chu Hsi, *Chu-tzu yü-lei,* 107:4306, 128:4975–4976. For a comprehensive analysis of Chu Hsi's ideas, see Ch'ien Mu, *Chu-tzu hsin hsueh-an.*

8. Wang Ch'eng, *Tung-tu shih lueh,* a standard Sung work, put the biographies of all the leading philosophers in ch. 114, with the sole exception of Shao Yung, who was relegated to the next chapter. See also Winston Lo, *The Life and Thought of Yeh Shih,* 163, n. 40.

9. Professor William Theodore de Bary, Professor Wing-tsit Chan, and other colleagues of the Neo-Confucian Seminar at Columbia University have often used the term "transcendental moralists."

10. Chu Hsi, *Chu-tzu yü-lei,* 108:4336–4337, 129:5011.

11. Ch'ien Ta-hsin, *Shih-chia-chai yang-hsin lu,* 18:426; *HNYL,* 1660; Winston Lo, *The Life and Thought of Yeh Shih,* 212–215.

12. Sun Yin-shih, *Chu-hu lu,* 6:3–4; *SYHA,* 14:14, 14:62; Yang Shih, *Yang Kuei-shan,* 2:7.

13. *SYHA,* 12:86, 38:55.

14. A late Sung figure critical of the Chu Hsi school was Chou Mi (1232–1298); see his *Ch'i-tung,* 11:7–8 and *Chih-ya-t'ang,* 1:36–38. Two well-known anthologies quote Chou: P'an Yung-yin, ed., *Sung-pai,* 6:34–35; Ting Ch'üan-ching, ed., *Sung-jen i-shih,* 878, 891. See also *SYHAPI,* preface, 65.

15. Chu Hsi, *Chu-tzu yü-lei,* 116:4505; *SYHA,* 8:85.

16. Li Hsin-ch'uan, *Tao ming lu,* 2:3–7; *SYHA,* 8:60, 8:85, 11:54–55, 11:107, 12:79–80.

17. Chu Hsi and Lü Tsu-chien, comps., *Reflections,* tr. Wing-tsit Chan.

18. *SYHA,* 8:90, 9:25, 9:126, 11:51, 11:98.

19. *SYHA,* preface: 5–6, 8:21, 8:28, 8:44, 8:79, 9:8, 9:44, 11:86, 16:20, 16:27; Yeh Hung-sa, "Shih-lun Sung-tai shu-yuan chih-tu."

20. *SS,* ch. 430, 438; *SYHA,* 8:21–22, 8:60, 11:99.

21. Chang Po-heng, *Hsu chin-ssu lu,* 9:171; *SYHA,* 8:91, 9:77, 70:899.

22. *SYHA,* 8:13, 9:126.

23. *SYHA,* 11:120.

24. Chu Hsi, *Chu-tzu yü-lei,* 107:4313–4314; *SYHA,* 8:19.

25. *SYHA,* 12:79, 16:48; Terada Gō, *Sōdai kyoikushi.*

26. *SS,* ch. 428–429; *SYHA,* 8:2, 8:64.

27. *SYHA*, 11:72.

28. *SYHA*, 8:57, 15:86.

29. *SYHA*, 8:60, 11:12.

30. Ku Yen-wu, *Jih chih lu*, 16:390, 19:450; *SYHA*, 8:79.

31. Ch'ien Chung-shu, *Sung-shih*, 172–173.

32. Ku Yen-wu, *Jih chih lu*, 17:392, 26:590; *SYHA*, 8:13–14.

33. Chu Hsi, *Chu-tzu yü-lei*, 109:4343.

34. Chu Hsi, *Chu-tzu yü-lei*, 109:4355–4359; *SYHA*, 8:33.

35. See Ma Tuan-lin, *Wen-hsien t'ung-k'ao*, 32:299–305.

36. Wang Ying-lin, *K'un hsueh*, 15:1211.

37. Schirokauer, "Chu Hsi's Political Career."

38. *Sung hui-yao chi-kao*, "Chih-kuan" segment, 72:48; *HTC*, 3803.

39. Wang Fu-chih, *Sung lun*, 13:202–204.

40. Chu Hsi, *Chu-tzu yü-lei*, 107:4310–4311; see also Chu Hsi, *I-Lo yuan-yuan lu*, 4:20–22; 9:9.

41. *SYHA*, 15:36.

42. Ma Tsung-huo, *Chung-kuo Ching-hsueh-shih*, 112–114.

43. Chu Hsi, *Chu-tzu yü-lei*, 114:4456.

44. *SYHA*, 15:38.

45. Ching, "Truth and Ideology: The Confucian Way"; Schirokauer, "Neo-Confucianism under Attack"; *SSCSPM*, 867–898; *SYHA*, 24:25–28; Li Hsin-ch'uan, *Tao ming lu*, 6:7–8.

46. *HTC*, 4281–4282, 4316, 4387.

47. *HTC*, 4422–4424, 4455, 4567, 4585; Sun Yin-shih, *Chu-hu lu*, 8:3–5.

48. *HTC*, 4458, 4464, 4545, 4554, 4587; *SS*, ch. 422.

49. Li Hsin-ch'uan, *Tao ming lu*, ch. 8–10; *TMTY*, 1847.

50. *HTC*, 4562; *SS*, ch. 417, 421.

51. *HTC*, 4605, 4613–4615.

52. *Sung-shih ch'uan-wen hsu tzu-chih t'ung-chien*, 2529.

53. *Ibid.*, 2490–2491, 2533, 2554.

54. *HTC*, 4547, 4622–4630, 4836.

55. *HTC*, 4630, 4849.

56. T'o-t'o *et al.*, eds. *Yuan shih*, ch. 69; Jao Tsung-i, "San Chiao lun."

57. Wang Fu-chi, *Sung lun: Chiu hsiao-shuo, wu* section, 1:4, 1:10, 1:22, 2:142, 2:144.

58. James T. C. Liu and Tu, eds., *Traditional China*, 10–23.

EPILOGUE

1. James T. C. Liu, *Reform.*

2. F. S. C. Northrop, *The Meeting of East and West.*

3. Ch'ien Mu, *Chu-tzu hsin hsueh-an.*

4. Chan, "Neo-Confucianism."

5. Winston Lo, *The Life and Thought of Yeh Shih;* Tillman, *Utilitarian Confucianism;* Wu Yü, *Wu Yü wen-lu,* 10; Yanagida Setsuko, "Sōdai chishusei to koken-ryoku."

6. Li T'ao, *Hsu tzu-chih t'ung-chien ch'ang pien,* 221:3–4.

7. James T. C. Liu, "Liu Tsai: His Philanthropy"; Liu Tzu-chien, "Liu Tsai"; Wang Te-i, *Sung-tai tsai-huang ti chiu-chi cheng-ts'e.*

8. Liu Po-chi, *Cheng-chiu shih.*

9. James T. C. Liu and Tu, eds., *Traditional China,* 10–23; James T. C. Liu, ed., *Political Institutions,* "Introduction."

Abbreviations Used in the Bibliography

SYC: *Sung-shih yen-chiu chi*, Sung-shih tso-t'an-hui, ed.
SYL: *Sung-shih yen-chiu lun-wen-chi*

Glossary of Asian Journal Titles Appearing in the Bibliography

Cheng-chih ta-hsueh hsueh-pao 政治大學學報
Chi-lin shih-ta hsueh-pao 吉林師大學報
Chung-hua wen-shih lun-ts'ung 中華文史論叢
Chung-kuo chiao-t'ung shih (*Zhongguo jiaotong shi*)
        中國交通史
Chung-kuo wen-hua yen-chiu hui-k'an 中國文化研究彙刊
Chung-kuo hsueh-jen 中國學人
Hang-chou ta-hsueh hsueh-pao (*Hangzhou daxue xuebao*)
        杭州大學學報

Hiroshima Daigaku Bungaku bu kiyō 廣島大學文學部紀要
Hokudai shigaku 北大史學
Hsin-ya hsueh-pao 新亞學報
Hsin-ya hsueh-shu nien-k'an 新亞學術年刊
Hsin-ya shu-yuan li-shih-hsi hsi-k'an 新亞書院歷史系系刊
Hsueh-lin man-lu (*Xuelin manlu*) 學林漫錄

Hua-kang hsueh-pao 華岡學報
Hua-nan shih-yuan hsueh-pao (Huanan Shiyuan xuebao)
　　　華南師院學報
Jinbun kenkyū 人文研究
Kagakushi kenkyū 科學史研究
Li-shih chiao-hsueh (Lishi jiaoxue) 歷史教學
Li-shih-hsueh (Lishixue) 歷史學
Li-shih yen-chiu (Lishi yanjiu) 歷史研究
Li-shih Yü-yen Yen-chiu-so chi-k'an 歷史語言研究所集刊
Peking Ta-hsueh hsueh-pao (Beijing Daxue xuebao)
　　　北京大學學報

Rekishi hyōron 歷史評論
Rekishi kyōiku 歷史教育
Rekishigaku kenkyū 歷史學研究
Sekaishi kenkyū 世界史研究
She-hui k'o-hsueh chan-hsien (Shehui kexue zhanxian)
　　　社會科學戰線

Shichō 史潮
Shien 史淵
Shigaku zasshi 史學雜誌
Shih-hsueh hui-k'an 史學彙刊
Shih-hsueh yen-chiu 史學研究
Shih-huo 食貨
Shirin 史林
Shisō 史艸
Shukan Tōyōgaku 集刊東洋學
Ta-lu tsa-chih 大陸雜誌
Tōhō gakuhō 東方學報
Tōhōgaku 東方學
Tōyō bunka 東洋文化
Tōyō gakuhō 東洋學報
Tōyōshi kenkyū 東洋史研究
Tse-shan pan-yueh k'an 責善半月刊
Tsing-hua hsueh-pao 清華學報
Tung-hsi wen-hua 東西文化
Wen shih che 文史哲
Wen-shih tsa-chih 文史雜誌
Yen-ching hsueh-pao 燕京學報
Yu-shih yueh-k'an 幼獅月刊

Bibliography

The bibliography is in the main a list of diverse readings examined during the preparation of this book in order to gain a spectrum of perspectives from various approaches, though many of them have not been cited in the notes. However, interested scholars who are bound to compile bibliographies of their own may find it helpful to consult first the survey of tools and other references that appear in the following introductory paragraphs; full citations are given in the bibliography proper.

On primary sources of the Sung period, nothing in either the Chinese or Japanese language can match the monumental work edited by Yves Hervouet, *A Sung Bibliography*, which resulted from a project of international cooperation led by the late Etienne Balazs.

For the use of a few important primary sources, convenient indices help greatly. See, for example, Umehara Kaoru's index of personal names in the *Chien-Yen i-lai hsi-nien yao-lu* and Kinugawa Tsuyoshi's index of personal names in the *Sung Yuan hsueh-an* and its supplement.

Difficulties with the proper names and the technical terms of the Sung period may be readily overcome by consulting a recent encyclopedic compilation edited by Teng Kuang-ming and Ch'eng Ying-liu, *Chung-kuo li-shih ta-t'zu-ti-an Sung-shih*.

For secondary sources in Chinese, the field is much indebted to Sung Hsi (or Sung Shee) for his *Bibliography of Chinese Articles and Books on Sung History*. Admirably, it includes as much as feasible the publications in the People's Republic of China.

There have been collections of Chinese research articles in recent years in Taiwan and lately also on the mainland. The two leading publications are *SYC* and *SYL* respectively. Detailed citations are given in the bibliography proper.

On the books devoted to Sung history—standard works and text books—no comment seems necessary. One work, however, should be mentioned because it is quite informative on the subject matter under discussion here. The book is Liu Po-chi, *Sung-tai cheng-chiao shih*.

For secondary sources by Japanese scholars, an invaluable compilation was cooperatively produced by the Japanese Committee for the Sung Project, under the chief editorship of the late Aoyama Sadao and entitled *Sōdai kenkyū bunken teiyō*. After two supplements, no further effort has been made. However, one can gather information on more recent publications by checking the May issue of *Shigaku zasshi* every year as well as the annual volume of the *Tōyōgaku bunken ruimoku*.

Secondary sources in Western languages are listed in the bibliographies compiled by Michael C. McGrath, first in 1971 and again in 1980, in the former *Sung Studies Newsletter* now renamed the *Bulletin of Sung Yüan Studies*. It is believed that the compiler will bring forth a third installment.

Of biographical dictionaries, there have been several. They include a quick reference to the dates of key figures, compiled by T'ung-wen Weng (*Repertoires des dates des hommes célèbres de Song*); the 1939 pioneering index to collections of individual Sung biographies in the Harvard-Yenching Sinological Index Series (*Ssu-shih-ch'ih chung Sung-tai ch'uan-chi tsung-he yin-te*); and a more recent one by the Japanese Committee for the Sung Project (*Sōjin denki sakuin*); and for readers familiar with Western languages the four-volume *Sung Biographies*, of rather uneven quality, edited by Herbert Franke. By far the most informative reference, however, is the six-volume Chinese index to biographical materials on Sung figures, edited by Ch'ang Pi-te, Wang Te-i, et al. (*Sung-jen chuan-chi tzu-liao so-yin*), which largely supersedes the earlier ones.

The Japanese Committee for the Sung Project, made yet another notable contribution: a chronology of major events, one volume on the Northern Sung and the other on the Southern Sung.

Tools are indispensable. In concluding, one shining example should be mentioned. Of modest size but tremendous help is Hope Wright, *Geographic Names in Sung China*.

A. WORKS IN ENGLISH AND OTHER WESTERN LANGUAGES

Balazs, Etienne. "Une carte des centres commercial de la Chine à la fin du XIe siècle," in Francoise Aubin, ed., *Etudes Song in Memoriam de Etienne Balazs*, ser. 1, vol. 3. Paris, Ecole Pratique des Hautes Etudes, 1976.

———— and Collette Patte. *Table des matières: Song Houei-yao, Sections economique, administrative, juridique, geographique*. Paris, Ecole Practique des Hautes Etudes, 1958.

Bol, Peter K. "Culture and the Way in Eleventh Century China," Princeton University Ph.D. dissertation, 1982.

Bulletin of Sung-Yüan Studies, formerly *Sung Studies Newsletter* (current Editor: John Chaffe, Department of History, State University of New York at Binghamton, Binghamton, NY, 13901).

Bush, Susan. *The Chinese Literati on Painting: Su Shih (1037–1101) to Tung Ch'i-ch'ang (1555–1636)*. Cambridge, Harvard University Press, 1971.

Chaffee, John. *The Thorny Gates of Learning in Sung China: A Social History of Examinations.* Cambridge, Cambridge University Press, 1985.

Chan, Wing-tsit, tr. *A Source Book in Chinese Philosophy.* Princeton, Princeton University Press, 1963.

————. "Neo-Confucianism as an Integrative Force in Chinese Thought" in Laurence G. Thompson, ed., *Studia Asiatica: Essays in Asian Studies in Felicitation of the Seventy-fifth Birthday of Professor Ch'en Shou-yi.* San Francisco, Chinese Materials Center, 1975.

Chang, Fu-jui. *Les Fonctionnaires des Song: Index des Titres.* Paris, Ecole Pratique des Hautes Etudes, 1964.

Chang, K'ang-i Sun. *The Evolution of Chinese Tz'u Poetry: From Late Tang to Northern Sung.* Princeton, Princeton University Press, 1980.

Ch'en, Kenneth K. S. "The Sale of Monk Certificates during the Sung dynasty: A factor in the decline of Buddhism in China," *Harvard Theological Review,* 49.4: 307–327 (1956).

————. *Buddhism in China: A Historical Survey.* Princeton, Princeton University Press, 1964.

————. *The Chinese Transformation of Buddhism.* Princeton, Princeton University Press, 1973.

Chi Ch'ao-t'ing. *Key Economic Areas in Chinese History.* London, Allen and Unwin, 1936.

Ching, Julia. "Truth and Ideology: The Confucian Way (*Tao*) and Its Transmission (*Tao-t'ung*)," *Journal of the History of Ideas,* 35.3:371–388 (1974).

Chu Hsi, *The Great Learning:* See Legge; Gardner.

Chu Hsi and Lü Tzu-ch'ien, comps. *Reflections on Things at Hand,* tr. Wing-tsit Chan. New York, Columbia University Press, 1967.

d'Argencé, René Yvon Lefebvre. "Ecological Atlas of Southern Sung–Hang-chou," *Sung Studies Newsletter* 4:7–10 (1971).

Dawson, Raymond S., ed. *The Legacy of China.* Oxford, Clarendon Press, 1964.

————. *The Chinese Chameleon: An Analysis of European Conceptions of Chinese Civilization.* New York, Oxford University Press, 1967.

de Bary, William Theodore, Wing-tsit Chan, and Burton Watson, eds. *Sources of Chinese Tradition.* New York, Columbia University Press, 1960.

———— and Irene Bloom, eds. *Principle and Practicality: Essays in Neo-Confucianism and Practical Learning.* New York, Columbia University Press, 1979.

Eichhorn, Werner. "Some Notes on Population Control during the Sung Dynasty," in Yves Hervouet, ed. *Etudes d'histoire et de littérature Chinoises offertes au professeur Jaroslave Průšek.* Paris, Bibliotheque de l'Institut des Hautes Etudes Chinoises, 1976.

Elvin, Mark. *The Pattern of the Chinese Past.* Stanford, Stanford University Press, 1973.

Fairbank, John King, ed. *Chinese Thought and Institutions.* Chicago, University Press, 1957.

Ferenczy, Mary. "On State Regulation of Money Circulation in Sung China," *Acta Orientalia Academiae Scientiarum Hungaricae* 28.3:351–358 (1974).

Feuerwerker, Albert, ed. *History in Communist China.* Cambridge, M.I.T. Press, 1968.

—— and Sally Cheng. *Chinese Communist Studies of Modern Chinese History.* Cambridge, Harvard University Press, 1961.

Finegan, Michael Herald. "Urbanism in Sung China." University of Chicago Ph.D. dissertation, 1976.

Franke, Herbert. "Treaties between Sung and Chin," in Francoise Aubin, ed., *Etudes Song in Memoriam de Etienne Balazs,* ser. 1, vol. 1. Paris, Ecole Pratique des Hautes Etudes, 1970.

—— ed. *Sung Biographies.* 4 Vols. Wiesbaden, Franz Steiner Verlag GMBH, 1976.

Freeman, Michael. "Lo-yang and the Opposition to Wang An-shih: The Rise of Confucian Conservatism 1068–1086." Yale University Ph.D. dissertation, 1973.

Fu, Shen Chun-yueh. "Huang Ting-chien's Calligraphy and His Scroll for Chang Ta-t'ung: A Masterpiece Written in Exile." Princeton University Ph.D. dissertation, 1976.

Fung, Yu-lan. *A Short History of Chinese Philosophy,* ed. Derk Bodde. New York, MacMillan, 1948.

Gardner, Daniel K. *Chu Hsi and the "Ta Hsueh": Neo-Confucian Reflection on the Confucian Canon.* Cambridge, Council on East Asian Studies, Harvard University, 1986.

Gernet, Jacques. *Daily Life in China on the Eve of the Mongol Invasion,* tr. H. M. Wright. Stanford, Stanford University Press, 1962.

Gong, Wei Ai. "The Participation of Censorial Officials in Politics during the Northern Sung Dynasty (960–1126 A.D.)," *Chinese Culture* 15.2:30–41 (1974).

——. "The Usurpation of Power by Ch'in Kuei through the Censorial Organ (1138–1155 A.D.)," *Chinese Culture* 15.3:25–42 (1974).

——. "The Role of Censorial Officials in the Power Struggle during the Last Years of the Southern Sung dynasty (1208–1278)," *Chinese Culture* 17.3:93–112 (1976).

Haeger, John Winthrop, ed. *Crisis and Prosperity in Sung China.* Tucson, University of Arizona Press, 1975.

Hartwell, Robert. "A Revolution in the Chinese Iron and Coal Industries During the Northern Sung, 960–1126 A.D.," *Journal of Asian History* 21:153–162 (1962).

——. "A Cycle of Economic Change in Imperial China: Coal and Iron in Northeast China, 750–1350," *Journal of the Economic and Social History of the Orient,* 10.1:102–159 (1967).

——. "The Evolution of the Early Northern Sung Monetary System, 960–1025," *Journal of the American Oriental Society* 87.3:280–289 (1967).

——. "Classical Chinese Monetary Analysis and Economic Policy in T'ang-

Northern Sung China," *Transactions of the International Conference of Orientalists in Japan* 13:70–81 (1968).

Hervouet, Ives, ed. *A Sung Bibliography,* initiated by Etienne Balazs. Hong Kong, Chinese University of Hong Kong Press, 1978.

Ho, Ping-ti. "Early-ripening Rice in Chinese History," *Economic History Review* 9.2: 200–218 (1956).

———. "An Estimate of the Total Population of Sung-Chin China," in Françoise Aubin ed., *Etudes Song in Memoriam de Etienne Balazs,* ser. 1, vol. 1. Paris, Ecole Pratique des Hautes Etudes, 1970.

Hsiao, Kung-ch'üan. *A History of Chinese Political Thought,* vol. 1, tr. by Frederick W. Mote. Princeton, Princeton University Press, 1979; vol. 2, forthcoming.

Jan, Yun-hua. "Buddhist historiography in Sung China," *Zeistschrift der Deutschen Morgenlandschen Gesellschaft* 114.2:360–382 (1964).

Jeffcott, Colin. "Sung Hang-chou: Its Growth and its Governmental Institutions," Australian National University Ph.D. dissertation, 1970.

Kracke, E. A., Jr. *Civil Service in Early Sung China, 960–1067: With Particular Emphasis on the Development of Controlled Sponsorship to Foster Administrative Responsibility.* Cambridge, Harvard-Yenching Institute Monographs, 1953.

———. *Translations of Sung Civil Service Titles.* Paris, Ecole Pratique des Hautes Etudes, 1957.

———. "The Chinese and the Art of Government," in Raymond S. Dawson, ed., *The Legacy of China.* Oxford, Clarendon Press, 1964.

———. "Sung K'ai-feng: Pragmatic Metropolis and Formalistic Capital," in John W. Haeger, ed., *Crisis and Prosperity in Sung China.* Tucson, University of Arizona Press, 1975.

Lam, Lay Yong. *A Critical Study of the "Yang Hui Suan Fa": A Thirteenth Century Mathematical Treatise.* Singapore, University of Singapore Press, 1977.

Lee, Thomas Hung-chi. *Government and Examination in Sung China.* Hong Kong, Chinese University of Hong Kong Press, 1985.

———. "Life in the Schools of Sung China," *Journal of Asian Studies* 37.1:45–60 (1977).

Legge, James, tr. *The Chinese Classics.* 5 vols. Hong Kong, Hong Kong University Press, 1960.

Libbrecht, Ulrich. *Chinese Mathematics in the Thirteenth Century: The "Shū-shu chiu-chang" of Ch'in Chiu-shao.* Cambridge, M.I.T. Press, 1973.

Lin, Shuen-fu. *The Transformation of the Chinese Lyrical Tradition: Chiang K'uei and Southern Sung Tz'u Poetry.* Princeton, Princeton University Press, 1978.

Lin, Yutang. *The Gay Genius: The Life and Times of Su Tungpo.* New York, John Day, 1947.

Liu, Hui-chen Wang. *The Traditional Chinese Clan Rules.* Association for Asian Studies Monograph, Locust Valley N.Y., J. I. Augustine, 1969.

———. "An Analysis of Chinese Clan Rules," in David S. Nivison and Arthur F.

Wright, eds., *Confucianism in Action.* Stanford, Stanford University Press, 1959. Also in Arthur F. Wright, ed., *Confucianism and Chinese Civilization.* New York, Atheneum, 1964.

Liu, James J. Y. *Major Lyricists of the Northern Sung: 960–1126.* Princeton, Princeton University Press, 1974.

Liu, James T. C. "An Early Sung Reformer: Fan Chung-yen," in John K. Fairbank, ed., *Chinese Thought and Institutions.* Chicago, University of Chicago Press, 1957.

———. *Reform in Sung China: Wang An-shih (1021–1086) and his New Policies.* Cambridge, Harvard University Press, 1959.

———. "The Neo-traditional Period (ca 800–1900) in Chinese History," *Journal of Asian Studies,* 24.1:105–107 (1964).

———. *Ou-yang Hsiu: An Eleventh-century Neo-Confucianist.* Stanford, Stanford University Press, 1967. For the complete version, see Liu Tzu-chien, *Ou-yang Hsiu* in Section C.

———. "The Sung Views on the Control of Government Clerks," *Journal of the Economic and Social History of the Orient,* 10.2–3:317–344 (1967).

———. "Yueh Fei (1103–1141) and China's Heritage of Loyalty," *Journal of Asian Studies* 31.2:291–297 (1972).

———. "How Did a Neo-Confucian School Become the State Orthodoxy?" *Philosophy East and West* 23:4:483–505 (1973).

———. "Liu Tsai His Philanthropy and Neo-Confucian Limitations," *Oriens Extremis,* 25:1–29 (1978).

———, ed. *Political Institutions in Traditional China: Major Issues.* New York, John Wiley, 1974.

——— and Peter J. Golas, eds. *Change in Sung China: Innovation or Renovation?* Boston, D. C. Heath, 1969.

——— and Tu Wei-ming, eds. *Traditional China.* Englewood Cliffs NJ, Prentice-Hall, 1970.

Lo, Irving Yu-cheng. *Hsin Ch'i-chi.* New York, Twayne Publishers, 1971.

Lo, Winston Wan. *The Life and Thought of Yeh Shih.* Gainesville, University Presses of Florida, 1974.

———. "Fiscao Intendants in Southern Sung China," *Journal of Asian History* 9.2: 28–154 (1975).

Ma, Laurence J. C. *Commercial Development and Urban Change in Sung China (960–1279).* Ann Arbor, Geography Department, University of Michigan, 1976.

McGrath, Michael C. "A Bibliography of Western Language Sources on the Sung," *Sung Studies Newsletter,* 3:39–49 (1971).

———. "A Bibliography of Western Language Sources, 1971–1977, on the Five Dynasties, Liao, Sung, Hsi-Hsia, Chin, and Yüan Periods," *Bulletin of Sung Yüan Studies* 15:54–81 (1980).

———. "Military and Regional Administration in Northern Sung China," Princeton University Ph.D. dissertation, 1982.

McKnight, Brian E. *Village and Bureaucracy in Southern Sung China.* Chicago, University of Chicago Press, 1971.

Malmqvist, Gövan. "On the Lyrical Poetry of Hsin Ch'i-chi," *Bulletin of the Museum of Far Eastern Antiquity* 46:29–63 (1974).

Maspero, Henri and Etienne Balazs. *Histoire et Institutions de la Chine Ancienne des Origines au XII Siècle après J.C.* Paris, Presses Universitaires de France, 1967.

Meskill, John, ed. *Wang An-shih: Practical Reformer?* Boston, D.C. Heath, 1963.

Mumford, Lewis. *The City in History: Its Origins, Its Transformations, and Its Prospects.* New York, Harcourt Brace and World, 1961.

Nakayama, Shigeru and Nathan Sivin. *Chinese Science: Explorations of an Ancient Tradition.* Cambridge, M.I.T. Press, 1963.

Needham, Joseph. *Science and Civilization in China.* Multiple volumes, various collaborators. Cambridge, Cambridge University Press, 1954–.

Nivison, David S. and Arthur F. Wright, eds. *Confucianism in Action.* Stanford, Stanford University Press, 1959.

Northrop, F. S. C. *The Meeting of East and West: An Inquiry Concerning World Philosophy.* New York, MacMillan, 1946.

Prüšek, Jaroslav. *Chinese History and Literature.* Dordrecht, Netherlands, Reidel, 1970.

Reischauer, Edwin O. and John K. Fairbank. *East Asia: The Great Tradition.* Boston, Houghton Mifflin, 1960.

Sariti, Anthony W. "Monarchy, Bureaucracy, and Absolutism in the Political Thought of Ssu-ma Kuang," *Journal of Asian Studies* 32.1:53–76 (1972).

Schirokauer, Conrad. "Chu Hsi's Political Career," in Arthur F. Wright and Denis Twitchett, eds., *Confucian Personalities.* Stanford, Stanford University Press, 1962.

———. "Neo-Confucianism under Attack: The Condemnation of *Wei-hsueh*," in John W. Haeger, ed., *Crisis and Prosperity in Sung China.* Tucson, University of Arizona Press, 1975.

Shiba, Yoshinobu. *Commerce and Society in Sung China,* abridged translation by Mark Elvin. Ann Arbor, Center for Chinese Studies, University of Michigan, 1970. For the complete version, see Shiba Yoshinobu in Section C.

Sivin, Nathan. "Shen Kua," in Charles Coulston Gillispie, ed., *Dictionary of Scientific Biography,* vol. 12. New York, Charles Scribner's, 1975. Also reprinted in *Sung Studies Newsletter* 13:31–55 (1977).

Sung Studies Newsletter. See *Bulletin of Sung-Yüan Studies.*

Tao, Jing-shen. *The Jurchen in Twelfth-Century China: A Study in Sinicization.* Seattle, University of Washington Press, 1976.

Tillman, Hoyt Cleveland. *Utilitarian Confucianism: Ch'en Liang's Challenge to Chu Hsi.* Cambridge, Council on East Asian Studies, Harvard University, 1982.

Twitchett, Denis. *Land Tenure and Social Order in T'ang and Sung China.* London, School of Oriental and African Studies, 1962.

Weng, T'ung-wen. *Repertoire des dates des hommes célebres des Song.* Paris, Ecole Pratique des Hautes Etudes, 1962.

Whitfield, Roderick. "Chang Tse-tuan's *Ch'ing-ming shang-ho t'u,*" Princeton University Ph.D. dissertation, 1965.

Williamson, H. R. *Wang An-shih: Chinese Statesman and Educationist of the Sung Dynasty.* 2 vols. London, A. Probsthain, 1935–1937.

Wong, Hon-chiu. "Government Expenditure in Northern Sung China," University of Pennsylvania Ph.D. dissertation, 1975.

Worthy, Edmund. "The Founding of Sung China, 950–1000: Integrative Changes in Military and Political Institutions," Princeton University Ph.D. dissertation, 1976.

Wright, Arthur F., ed. *The Confucian Persuasion.* Stanford, Stanford University Press, 1960.

———— and Denis Twitchett, eds. *Confucian Personalities.* Stanford, Stanford University Press, 1962.

Wright, Hope, *Geographic Names in Sung China.* Paris, Ecole Pratique des Hautes Etudes, 1956.

Yanagida, Setsuko, "Eastern History, China, Five Dynasties, Sung, Yüan," in Japanese National Committee of Historical Sciences, ed. *Japan at the XIIth International Congress of Historical Science in Vienna.* Tokyo, Nihon Gakujitsu Shinkōkai, 1965.

Yoshikawa, Kōjirō. *An Introduction to Sung Poetry.* Cambridge, Harvard University Press, 1967.

B. SOURCES FROM THE SUNG TO THE CH'ING PERIOD

Chang Po-heng 張伯珩. *Hsu chin-su lu* 續近思錄 (Sequel to *Reflections on things at hand*). Taipei, Shih-chieh Shu-chü, 1962.

Chang Shih-nan 張世南. *Yu-huan chi-wen* 游宦紀聞 (Notes from various posts). Peking, Chung-hua punctuated ed., 1981.

Chao Ting 趙鼎. *Chung-cheng Te-wen chi* 忠正德文集 (Collected works of the Honorable Chao Ting). Ssu-k'u chen-pen ed.

Ch'en Pang-chan 陳邦瞻. *Sung-shih Chi-shih pen-mo* 宋史紀事本末 (Topical summaries of the Sung dynastic history). Peking, Chung-hua punctuated ed., 1977.

Ch'en Yuan. 陳淵 *Mo-t'ang chi* 默堂集 (Works of the Silent Hall). Ssu-k'u chen-pen ed.

Ch'i Yün 紀昀 *Ssu-k'u-ch'üan-shu tsung-mu t'i-yao.* 四庫全書總目提要 (Abstract of the catalogue of the Four Treasuries Collectanea). Kuo-hsueh chi-pen ts'ung-shu ed. Revised ed. Taipei, Commercial Press, 1971.

Ch'ieh fen hsü-lu 竊憤續錄 (Record of secret resentment: a sequel). Hsueh-hai lei-pien ed. 學海類編

Ch'ien Shih-sheng 錢士升 . *Nan-Sung shu* 南宋書 (History of the Southern Sung). 1797 ed.

Ch'ien Ta-hsin 錢大昕 . *Shih-chia-chai yang-hsin lu* 十駕齋養新錄 (Notes on cultivation of new knowledge). Kuo-hsueh Chi-pen ts'ung-shu ed. .

Chin-shih chi-shih pen-mo 金史紀事本末 (Topical summaries of the Chin Jurchen dynastic history). Tsui Wen-yin 崔文印 , ed. Peking, Chung-hua, 1980.

Ching-kang pai-shih 靖康稗史 (Informal history of the Ching-kang era). Shanghai, private ed., 1936.

Chiu hsiao-shuo 舊小說 (Old tales). Shanghai, Commercial Press, 1920.

Chou Mi 周密 . *Ch'i-t'ung yeh-yü* 齊東野語 (Back country accounts). Han-fen-lou ed.

——— . *Chih-ya-t'ang tsa-ch'ao* 志雅堂雜抄 (Miscellaneous notes of Chih-ya Studio). Yueh-ya-t'ang ts'ung shu ed.

Chuang Cho 莊綽 . *Chi-le pien* 雞肋篇 (Chicken rib notebook). Peking, Chung-hua punctuated ed., 1983.

Chu Hsi 朱熹 . *I-Lo yuan-yuan lu* 伊洛淵源錄 (Neo-Confucian origins since the Northern Sung). With parts added 新增 by Hsieh To 謝鐸 . Kyoto, Chung-wen ch'u-pan-she, 1972.

——— . *Chu-tzu yü-lei* 朱子語類 . (Classified quotations of Chu Hsi). Compiled by Li Ching-te 黎靖德 . Photolithograph of 1473 edition. Taipei, Cheng-chung, 1962.

Hsu Meng-hsin 徐夢莘 . *San-ch'ao pei-meng hui-pien* 三朝北盟會編 (Consolidated records of Northern relations under the three emperors). Taipei, Wen-hai, 1962.

Huang Huai 黄淮 and Yang Shih-ch'i 楊士奇 , comps. *Li-tai ming-ch'en tsou-i* 歷代名臣奏議 (Anthology of memorials by famous statesmen through successive dynasties). Taipei, Hsueh-sheng, 1964.

Huang-Sung chung-hsing liang-ch'ao sheng-cheng 皇宋中興兩朝聖政 (Sagacious statecraft of the two restoration reigns of the Imperial Sung). Official compilation, author unknown. Taipei, Wen-hai, 1967.

Huang Tsung-hsi 黄宗羲 and Ch'üan Tsu-wang 全祖望 . *Sung-Yuan hsueh-an* 宋元學案 (Sung and Yuan Confucian schools). Wan-yu-wen-k'u ed.

Hung Mai 洪邁 . *Yung-tsai sui-pi* 容齋隨筆 (Random notes of Yung Studio). Kuo-hsueh chih-pen ts'ung-shu ed.

Ku Yen-wu 顧炎武 . *Jih chih lu* 日知錄 (Notes of daily knowledge), ed. by Huang Ju-nan 黄汝南 . Taipei, Shih-chieh Shu-chü, 1962.

Li Hsin-ch'uan 李心傳 . *Chien-yen i-lai hsi-nien yao-lu* 建炎以来繫年要錄 (Chronology of key events since the Chien-yen reign at the beginning of the Southern Sung). Kuo-hsueh chih-pen ts'ung-shu ed.

——— . *Chiu-wen cheng-wu* 舊聞證誤 (Correction of mistakes in old accounts). Peking, Chung-hua, 1983.

————. *Tao ming lu* 道命錄 (Record of the Confucianist experience). Pei-pu ts'ung-shu ed.

Li T'ao 李燾. *Hsu tzu-chih t'ung-chien ch'ang-pien* 續資治通鑑長編 (Draft sequel to the *Comprehensive Mirror for aid in government*). Taipei, Shih-chieh Shu-chü, 1961. (The production of a punctuated edition is currently in progress at Chung-hua in Peking).

Lü Pen-chung 呂本中. *Shih-yu tsa-chi* 師友雜記 (Miscellaneous notes on teachers and companions). Ts'ung-shu chi-ch'eng ed.

Lü Tsu-ch'ien 呂祖謙, ed. *Sung-wen chien* 宋文鑑 (Model compositions of the Sung period). Ssu-pu ts'ung-k'an ed.

Ma Tuan-lin 馬端臨. *Wen-hsien t'ung-k'ao* 文獻通考 (Encyclopedia of institutions with critical examination). Shanghai, Commercial Press, 1936.

Meng Yuan-lao 孟元老. *Tung-ching meng-hua lu* 東京夢華錄 (Record of the splendor in the Eastern Capital of [K'ai-feng]). With four accounts of Hang-chou appended. Peking, Chung-hua punctuated ed., 1956.

Nan-chin chi-wen lu 南燼紀聞錄 (Reports of the ashes in the South). Author unknown. Hsueh-hai lei-pien ed.

P'an Yung-yin 潘永因. *Sung-pai lei-ch'ao* 宋稗類鈔 Classified anthology of the Sung anecdotes). 1669 ed.

Pi Yuan 畢沅. *Hsu tzu-chih t'ung-chien* 續資治通鑑 (Sequel to the *Comprehensive Mirror for aid in government*). Peking, Chung-hua punctuated ed., 1959.

Shao Po 邵博. *Shao-shih wen-chien hou-lu* 邵氏聞見後錄 (The subsequent record of what I heard and saw). Peking, Chung-hua punctuated ed., 1983.

Sun Yin-shih 孫應時. *Chu-hu chi* 燭湖集 (Torch lake record). 1803 ed.

Sung hui-yao chi-kao 宋會要輯稿 (Draft collection of essential Sung government records). Peking, Chung-hua, 1957 photo reproduction of 1936 ed. Another version, reportedly a recent discovery, may be published before long.

Sung Lien 宋濂 ed. *Yuan shih* 元史 (Yuan [Mongol] dynastic history). Peking, Chung-hua punctuated ed., 1977.

Sung-shih ch'uan-wen hsu tzu-chih t'ung-chien 宋史全文續資治通鑑 (Draft history of the Sung as a sequel to the *Comprehensive Mirror for aid in government*). Taipei, Wen-hai, 1969.

T'ang Keng 唐庚. *Mei-shan chi* 眉山集 (Collected works of a native of Mei-shan). Ssu-k'u chen-pen ed.

Ting Ch'üan-ching 丁傳靖, ed. *Sung-jen i-shih hui-pien* 宋人軼事彙編 (Consolidated anthology of Sung anecdotes). Shanghai, Commercial Press, 1935.

T'o-t'o et al. 脫脫, eds., *Chin shih* 金史 (Chin [Jurchen] dynastic history.) Peking, Chung-hua punctuated ed., 1975.

————. *Sung shih* 宋史 (Sung dynastic history). Peking, Chung-hua punctuated ed., 1977.

Ts'ai T'iao 蔡條. *Tieh-wei-shan ts'ung-t'an* 鐵圍山叢談 (Miscellanea at

Iron-clad Mount). The name of this mount had its origin in Sanscrit known as *Cakvavâda parvada.* Peking, Chung-hua punctuated ed., 1983.

Wang Ch'eng 王偁. *Tung-tu shih lueh* 東都事略 (Summarized events at the Eastern Capital [K'ai-feng]). Taipei, Wen-hai, 1969.

Wang Fu-chih 王夫之. *Sung lun* 宋論 (Critical essays on the Sung). Kuo-hsueh chi-pen ts'ung shu ed.

Wang Hsiang 王相 comp. *Ch'ien-chia shih* 千家詩 (Poetry for thousands of families). Many popular editions.

Wang Ming-ch'ing 王明清. *Hui chu lu* 揮塵錄 (Record during duster-fanning). Peking, Chung-hua punctuated ed., itemized by number, 1961.

Wang Tzu-ts'ai 王梓材 and Feng Yuan-hao 馮雲濠. *Sung-Yuan hsueh-an pu-i* 宋元學案補遺 (Supplement to the *Sung and Yuan Confucian schools*). Taipei, Shih-chieh Shu-chü, 1962.

Wang Ying-lin 王應麟. *K'un-hsueh chi-wen* 困學紀聞 (Notes of hard study). Kuo-hsueh chi-pen ts'ung-shu ed.

Yang Shih 楊時. *Yang Kuei-shan wen-chi* 楊龜山文集 (Collected works of Yang Shih). Ssu-pu ts'ung-k'an ed.

Yang Yao-pi 楊堯弼. *Wei Ch'i-lu* 偽齊錄 (Record of the bogus Ch'i regime). Ou-hsiang ling-shih ed.

Yueh K'o 岳珂. *T'ing shih* 桯史 (Side-table history). Peking, Chung-hua punctuated ed., 1981.

C. MODERN WORKS IN CHINESE AND JAPANESE

Amaho Motonosuke 天野元之助. "Chin Fu no *Nōsho* to suitōsaku gijutsu no tenkai" 陳敷の農書と水稲作技術の展開 (Ch'en Fu's *Farming Book* and the spreading techniques of irrigated rice), *Tōhō gakuhō* 19:23–64; 21:37–133. (Kyoto, 1950 and 1952).

———. "Sōdai no nōgyō to sono shakai kōzō" 宋代の農業とその社會構造 (Sung agriculture and its social structure), *Jinbum kenkyū* 14.6:1–42 (1963).

———. "Chūgoku ni okeru nōgu no hattatsu" 中國にすける農具の發達 (The developoment of farming implements in China), *Tōyō gakuhō* 47.4:57–84 (Kyoto, 1965).

———. *Chūgoku nōgyōshi kenkyū: zōhoban* 中國農業史研究：增補版 (Studies in Chinese agricultural history). Kyoto, Tōyōshi Kenkyū-kai, 1979.

Aoki Masaru 青木正兒. *Shina bungaku shisō shi* 支那文學思想史 (A history of Chinese literature and thought). Tokyo, Iwanami Shoten, 1943.

Aoyama Festschrift, see Tōyō Bunko.

Aoyama Sadao 青山定雄. "Tō sō Benga kō" 唐宋汴河考 (The Pien River in T'ang and Sung times), *Tōhō gakuhō* 2:1–49 (Tokyo, 1931).

——. "Hokusō no sōunho ni tsuite" 北宋の漕運法について (The Northern Sung river transport of tributes), in *Ichimura Hakushi koko kinen tōyōshi ronsō* 市村博士古稀紀念東洋史論叢 (Festschrift in Chinese history in honor of Dr. Ichimura). Tokyo, Fuzanbō, 1933.

——. "Sōdai no yūhō" 宋代の郵舗 (The Sung post stations), *Tōhō gakuhō* 6:217–260 (Tokyo, 1936).

——. "Sō Gen no chihōshi ni mieru shakai keizai shiryō" 宋元の地方誌に見る社會經濟史料 (Socio-economic information in Sung-Yuan period local gazetteers), *Tōyō gakuhō* 25.2:281–297 (Tokyo, 1938).

——. "Sōdai no chizu to sono tokushoku" 宋代の地圖とその特色 (Sung maps and their characteristics), *Tōyō gakuhō* 11.2:1–44 (Tokyo, 1940).

——. "Godai Sō ni okeru Kōsei no shinkō kenryō 五代宋における江西の新興官僚 (Emerging officials from Kiangsi in the Five Dynasties and the Sung), in *Wada Hakushi kanreki kinen tōyōshi ronsō* 和田博士還暦紀念東洋史論叢 (Festschrift in Chinese history in honor of Dr. Wada). Tokyo, Kōdansha, 1951.

——. *Tō Sō jidai no kōtsū to chishi chizu no kenkyū* 唐宋時代の交通と地誌地圖の研究 (Transportation, local gazetteers, and maps in T'ang and Sung times). Tokyo, Yoshikawa Kōbunkan, 1963.

——. *"Sokaiyō" kenkyū biyō* 宋會要研究備要 (Guide to the *Sung hui-yo*). Tokyo, Tōyō Bunko, 1970.

——. "Hokusō o chūshin to suru shitaifu no kika to seikatsu rinri" 北宋を中心とする士大夫の起家と生活倫理 (The emergence of scholar-official families and their ethics with a focus on the Northern Sung). *Tōyō gakuhō* 57.1–2:35–63 (Tokyo, 1976).

——, ed. *See* Sōshi teiyō Hensan Kyōryoku Iinkei.

Araki Toshikazu 荒木敏一. *Sōdai kakyo seido kenkyū* 宋代科舉制度研究 (The Sung civil service examination system). Kyoto, Tōyōshi Kenkyūkai, 1969.

Chang Chia-chü 張家駒. "Sung-shih nan-tu hou ti nan-fang tu-shih 宋室南渡後的南方都市 (The southern cities after the Sung court moved south), *Shih-huo* 1.10:36–43 (1935).

——. "Chung-kuo she-hui chung-hsin chih chuan-i" 中國社會中心之轉移 (The shift of the center in Chinese society), *Shih-huo* 2.11:20–35 (1935).

——. "Ch'ing-k'ang chih luan yü pei-fang jen-kou ti nan-ch'ien" 靖康之亂與北方人口的南遷 (The fall of the Northern Sung and the southward migration), *Wen-shih tsa-chih* 11.3:21–28 (1942).

——. *Liang-Sung ching-chi chung-hin ti nan-i* 兩宋經濟重心的南移 (The southward shift of the economic center during the Northern and the Southern Sung). Wu-han Hu-pei jen-min ch'u-pan-she, 1957.

——. *Shen Kua* 沈括 (Biography of Shen Kua). Shanghai, Shanghai jen-min ch'u-pan-she, 1962.

Chang Chien 張健. *Sung Chin ssu-chia wen-hsueh p'i-p'ing yen-chiu* 宋金四家文學批評研究 (Literary criticisms of four Sung and Chin masters). Taipei, Lien-ching, 1975.

Chang Meng-lun 張孟倫. *Sung-tai hsing-wang shih* 宋代興亡史 (The rise and fall of the Sung). Shanghai, Commercial Press, 1948.

Chang Yin-lin 張蔭麟. "Shen Kua pien-nien shih-chi" 沈括編年事輯 (Annalistic account of Shen Kua), *Tsing-hua hsueh-pao* 11.2:323–358 (1936).

Ch'ang Pi-te, Wang Te-i, et al. 昌彼德，王德毅等. *Sung-jen chuan-chi tzu-liao so-yin* 宋人傳記資料索引 (Index to biographical materials of Sung figures). 6 vols. Taipei, Ting-wen, 1974–1976.

Chao Kang 趙岡. "Sung Yuan i-lai mien-hua chung-chih chih tui-kuang" 宋元以來棉花種植之推廣 (Promotion of cotton planting since the Sung and Yuan period). *Yu-shih yueh-k'an* 45.11:25–29 (1977).

Chao Li-sheng 趙儷生. "Shih-lun liang-Sung t'u-ti kuan-hsi ti t'e-tien" 試論兩宋土地關係的特點 (The characteristics of land relationship during the Sung period), *Chi-lin Shih-ta hsueh-pao* 1:36–47 (1979).

Ch'en I-p'ing 陳一萍. "Pei-Sung ti hu-kou" 北宋的戶口 (Population in the Northern Sung), *Shih-huo* n.s. 6.7:21–34 (1976).

Ch'en Kao-hua and Wu T'ai 陳高華-吳泰. *Sung Yuan shih-ch'i ti hai-wai mao-i* 宋元時期的海外貿易 (Foreign trade during the Sung-Yuan period). Tientsin, Jen-min ch'u-pan-she, 1981.

Ch'en Lo-su 陳樂素. "San-ch'ao Pei-meng hui-pien k'ao" 三朝北盟會編考 (A textual study of the "Consolidated records of Northern relations under the three emperors") *Li-shih Yü-yen Yen-chiu so chi-k'an* 6.2:197–279 and 6.3:281–341 (1936).

Chi Tzu-yai 季子涯. "Sung-tai shou-kung-yeh chien-k'uang" 宋代手工業簡況 (A survey of Sung handicraft industries), *Li-shih chiao-hsueh* 5:10–14 (1955).

Ch'i Chueh-sheng 齊覺生. "Nan-Sung hsien-ling chih-tu chih yen-chiu 南宋縣令制度之研究 (The Southern Sung system of magistrates), *Cheng-chih ta-hsueh hsueh-pao* 政治大學學報 19:309–370 (Taipei, 1969).

Ch'i Hsia 漆俠. *Wang An-shih pien-fa* 王安石變法 (Wang An-shih's reform). Rev. ed. Shanghai, Jen-min ch'u-pan-she, 1979).

Chia Ta-ch'üan 賈大泉. "Lun Pei-Sung ti ping-pien" 論北宋的兵變 (The Northern Sung army mutinies), in *SYL*, 453–465.

Chiang Fu-ts'ung 蔣復璁. *Sung-shih hsin-t'an* 宋史新探 (New exploration in Sung history). Taipei, Cheng-chung, 1966.

Ch'ien Chung-shu 錢鍾書. *Sung-shih hsuan-chu* 宋詩選註 (Annotated anthology of Sung poetry). Peking, Jen-min wen-hsueh ch'u-pan-she, 1958.

Ch'ien Mu 錢穆. "Lun Sung-tai hsiang-ch'üan" 論宋代相權 (The power of the Sung councilors), *Chung-kuo wen-hua yen-chiu hui-k'an* 2:145–150 (1942).

——. *Kuo-shih ta-kang* 國史大綱 (Outline of Chinese history). 2 vols. Shanghai, Commercial Press, 1947.

——. *Sung Ming li-hsueh kai-shu* 宋明理學概述 (Survey of Sung and Ming Neo-Confucianism). Taipei, Chung-hua wen-hua, 1953.

——. *Chu-tzu hsin hsueh-an* 朱子新學案 (A new case book on Chu Hsi's learning). Taipei, San-min, 1971.

Ch'ien Pao-tsung, ed. 錢寶琮 *Sung Yuan shu-hsueh-shih tsung-shu* 宋元數學史綜述 (A combined review of Sung and Yuan period history of mathematics). Peking, K'o-hsueh ch'u-pan-she, 1966.

Ch'ien Tung-fu 錢冬父. *T'ang Sung ku-wen yun-tung* 唐宋古文運動 (The ancient-style prose movement during the Tang-Sung period). Shanghai, Chung-hua, 1962).

Ch'ih Ching-te 遲景德 "Sung-tai tsai shu fen-li chih-tu chih yen-pien" 宋代宰樞分立制度之演變 (Evolution of the division of power between the Sung chancellors and military commissions), in *SYC* 15:35–62 (1983).

Chikusa Masaaki 竺沙雅章. *Chūgoku Bukyō shakaishi kenkyū* 中國佛教社會史研究 (Studies of Chinese Buddhism and social history). Kyoto, Dōbunsha, 1982.

Chin Ching-fang 金景芳. "Chung-kuo ku-tai-shih fen-ch'i shang-chueh" 中國古代史分期商榷 (Discussion on the periodization of ancient Chinese history), *Li-shih yen-chiu* 歷史研究 2:48–57; 3:50–63 (1979).

Chin Chung-shu 金中樞. "Pei-Sung k'o-chü chih-tu yen-chiu" 北宋科舉制度研究 (The Northern Sung examination system), *Hsin-ya hsueh-pao* 6.1: 205–281 and 6.2:163–242 (1964).

——. "Lun Pei-Sung mo-nien chih ch'ung-shang Tao-chiao" 論北宋末年之崇尚道教 (The veneration of the Taoist religion in late Northern Sung), *Hsin-ya hsueh-pao* 7.2:75–85 and 8.1:187–257 (1966–1967).

——. "Sung-tai chi-chung she-hui fu-li chih-tu" 宋代幾種社會福利制度 (Several Sung social welfare systems), *Hsin-ya hsueh-shu nien-k'an* 10:127–269 (1968).

——. "Sung-tai san-sheng chang-kuan chih-fei chih yen-chiu" 宋代三省長官置廢之研究 (The sung institution and abolition of the head of the three ministries), *Hsin-ya hsueh-pao* 11.1:89–149 (1974).

——. "Sung-tai ku-wen yun-tung chih fa-chan yen-chiu" 宋代古文運動之發展研究 (The development of the Sung ancient-style movement), in *SYC* 10:145–216 (1978).

Chin Yü-fu 金毓黻. *Sung Liao Chin shih* 宋遼金史 (A history of Sung, Khitan, and Jurchen empires). Shanghai, Commercial Press, 1946.

Chou Tao-chi 周道濟. "Sung-tai tsai-hsiang ming-ch'eng yü ch'i shih-ch'üan chih yen-chiu" 宋代宰相名稱與其實權之研究 (Nominal titles and real power of the Sung chief councilors), in *SYC* 3:248–264 (1966).

Chu Ch'i 朱偰. "Sung Chin i-ho chih hsin-fen-hsi" 宋金議和之新分析

(A New analysis of the Sung-Chin peace negotiations), in *SYC* 12:147–168 (1980).

Chu Chia-yuan 朱家源. "Tan-tan Sung-tai ti hsiang-ts'un chung-hu" 談談 宋代的鄉村中戶 (The medium households in rural Sung), in *SYL*, 57–75.

Chu Hsi-tsu 朱希祖. *Wei-Ch'u-lu chi-pu* 偽楚錄輯補 (Amended "Record of the bogus Ch'u regime"). Taipei, Cheng-chung, 1955.

Chu Shih-chia 朱士嘉. *Sung Yuan fang-chih chuan-chi so-yin* 宋元方志傳 記索引 (Biographical index to Sung and Yuan local gazetteers). Shanghai, Chung-hua, 1963.

Chü Ch'ing-yuan 鞠清遠. "Nan-Sung kuan-li yü kung-shang-yeh" 南宋官吏 與工商業 (The Southern Sung officials' involvement with handicraft and trade), *Shih-huo* 2.8:37–39 (1935).

Ch'üan Han-sheng 全漢昇. "Sung-tai Tung-ching tui-yü Hang-chou tu-shih wen-ming ti ying-hsiang" 宋代東京對於杭州都市文明的影響 (The Influence of Sung Eastern Capital [K'ai-feng] upon the urban civilization in Hang-chou), *Shih-huo* 2.3:31–34 (1935).

———. "Sung-tai kuan-li chih su-ying shang-yeh" 宋代官吏之私營商業 (The private trade activities of Sung officials), *Li-shih Yü-yen Yen-chiu-so chi-k'an* 歷史語言研究所集刊 7.1:91–119 (1936).

———. "Sung-tai Kwang-chou ti kuo nei wai mao-i" 宋代廣州的國內外 貿易 (The Canton domestic and foreign trade in Sung times), *Li-shih Yü-yen Yen-chiu-so chi-k'an* 8.3:303–356 (1939).

———. "Sung Chin chien ti tsou-shih mao-i" 宋金間的走私貿易 (Smuggle trade between the Sung and the Jurchen), *Li-shih Yü-yen Yen-chiu-so chi-k'an* 11:425–447 (1943).

———. "T'ang Sung cheng-fu shui-ju yü shui-ju yü huo-pi ching-chi ti kuan-hsi" 唐宋政府歲入與貨幣經濟的關係 (The relationship between the T'ang and the Sung annual revenues and commodity economy), *Li-shih Yü-yen Yen-chiu-so chi-k'an* 20:189–221 (1948).

Fan Wu 范午. "Sung Liao Chin Yuan Tao-chiao nien-piao" 宋遼金元道教 年表 (Chronology of the Taoist religion from Sung to Mongol times), *Tse-shan pan-yueh k'an* 2:6–10 (1941).

Fang Hao 方豪. *Sung shih* 宋史 (Sung history). Taipei, Chung-hua wen-hua, 1954.

———. "Sung-tai jen-kou k'ao-shih" 宋代人口考實 (A realistic estimate of the Sung population), in his *Fang Hao liu-shih tzu-ting kao* 方豪六十自 定稿 (Articles of Fang Hao selected by himself at sixty). Taipei, private ed., 1969.

———. "Sung-tai ti k'o-hsueh" 宋代的科學 (Science during the Sung), in *Chung-hua hsueh-shu yü hsien-tai wen-hua ts'ung-shu* vol. 3, *Shih-hsueh lun-chi* 史學論集 Taipei, Hua-kang ch'u-pan yu-hsien kung-ssu, 1983.

Fujita Toyohachi 藤田豐八. *Tōzai kōshōshi no kenkyū: Nankai hen* 東西交渉史の研究:南海篇 (A history of East-West contacts: the South Seas). Tokyo, Oka Shoin, 1932.

Fumoto Yasutaka 麓保孝. *Hokusō ni okeru Jugaku no tenkai* 北宋における儒學の展開 (The expansion of Northern Sung Confucianism). Tokyo, Shoseki Bunbutsu Ryūtsūkai, 1967.

Harvard-Yenching Institute. *Ssu-shih-ch'i chung Sung-tai chuan-chi tsung-ho yin-te* 四十七種宋代傳記綜合引得 (Combined indices to forty-seven collections of Sung biographical accounts). William Hung et al., eds. Peking, Harvard-Yenching Institute, 1939.

Hibino Takeo 日比野丈夫. "Sō no Rinan ni tsuite no oboegaki" 宋の臨安について覺え書 (Notes on the Southern Sung capital), *Rekishi kyōiku* 14.6: 21–26 (1966).

Hino Kaisaburō 日野開三郎. "Hokusō jidai ni okeru dō tetsu no sanshutsugaku ni tsuite" 北宋時代における銅鉄の産出額について (On the volume of copper and iron production in the Northern Sung), *Tōyō gakuhō* 22.1:100–159 (Kyoto, 1934).

———. "Sōdai tōsaku taikyūshu oyobi fushu hogaku kō" 宋代稻作貸給種及佈種畝額考 (On the cultivated rice acreage and the cultivation through loaned seeds in the Northern Sung), *Shien* 40:69–108 (1949).

Hisatomi Hisashi 久富壽. "Nansō no zaisei to keisōshisen" 南宋の財政と經總制錢 (The Southern Sung finance and the revenues known as Ching-tsung-chih-ch'ien), *Hokudai shigaku* 9:32–54 (1914).

Ho Hsiang-fei 何湘妃. "Nan-Sung Kao-tsung Hsiao-tsung liang-ch'ao Wang An-shih p'ing-cha ti pien-ch'ien kuo-ch'eng yü fen-hsi" 南宋高孝兩朝王安石評價的變遷過程與分析 (The reappraisal of Wang An-shih in the early Southern Sung: its changing course and analysis). Taiwan University M.A. thesis, 1984.

Hori Toshikazu 堀敏一. "Sengo Nihon no Chūgokushi kenkyū ni okeru jidai kubun mondai no gendankai" 戰後日本の中國史研究における時代區分問題の現段階 (Current discussion on periodization in postwar Japanese studies of Chinese history), *Rekishi hyōron* 101:32–43; 102:48–59; 103:48–54 (1984).

Hsia Ch'eng-t'ao 夏承燾. *T'ang Sung tz'u lun-ts'ung* 唐宋詞論叢 (Discourses on T'ang and Sung *tz'u* poetry). Shanghai, Ku-tien-wen-hsueh ch'u-pan-she, 1956.

———. *Lung-ch'uan tz'u chiao-chien* 龍川詞校箋 (The *tz'u* poetry of Ch'en Liang with annotations). Shanghai, Chung-hua, 1961.

Hsia Chün-yü 夏君虞. *Sung-hsueh kai-yao* 宋學概要 (Essence of Sung learning). Shanghai, Commerical Press, 1937.

Hsiao Kung-ch'üan 蕭公權. *Chung-kuo cheng-chih ssu-hsiang-shih* 中國政治

思想史 (A history of Chinese political thought). Chungking, Commercial Press, 1945.

Hsü Kuei and Chou Meng-chiang 徐規．周夢江 . "Sung-tai liang-Che ti hai-wai mao-i" 宋代兩浙的海外貿易 (Chekiang's foreign trade during the Sung), *Hang-chou ta-hsueh hsueh-pao* 1:137–146 (1979).

Hsu Ping-yü 徐秉愉 ."Sung Kao-tsung chih tui Chin cheng-ts'e" 宋高宗之對金政策 (Emperor Sung Kao-tsung's policy toward the Jurchen). Taiwan University M.A. thesis, 1984.

Hu Tao-ching 胡道靜 . "Shen Kua ti k'e-hsueh ch'eng-chiu ti li-shih huan-ching chi ch'i cheng-chih ch'ing-hsiang" 沈括的科學成就的歷史環境及其政治傾向 (Shen Kua's scientific attainment: his historical environment and political inclination), *Wen shih che* 42:50–56 (1956).

———. *Meng-ch'i pi-tan pu-ch'eng* 夢溪筆談補正 (Supplement and annotations to the *Notes of Meng-Ch'i* by Shen Kua), *Chung-hua wen-shih lun-ts'ung* 8: 111–135 (1979).

Hu Yun-i 胡雲翼 . *Sung-shih yen-chiu* 宋詩研究 (Studies of Sung poetry). Shanghai, Commercial Press, 1933.

———. *Chung-kuo tz'u-shih* 中國詞史 (A History of Chinese *tz'u* poetry). Taipei reprint, Ch'i-ming, 1958.

Huang Min-chih 黃敏枝 . "Sung-tai ssu-kuan yü chuang-yuan chih yen-chiu" 宋代寺觀與莊園之研究 (Sung temples and land estates), *Ta-lu tsa-chih* 46.4:26–37 (1973).

Hung Huan-chun 洪煥春 "Shih chi shih-san shih-chi Chung-kuo k'o-hsueh ti chu-yao ch'eng-chiu" 十至十三世紀中國科學的主要成就 (Major achievements of Chinese science in the tenth to the thirteenth centuries), *Li-shih yen-chiu* 3:27–51 (1959).

———. "Sung-tai ti sheng-chan chi-shu" 宋代的生產技術 (The Sung technology of production), *Li-shih chiao-hsueh* 5:8–12 (1960).

Hung, William, *see* Harvard-Yenching.

Hung Yeh 洪業 (William Hung). "Chao Pu i pan-pu *Lun-yü* chjih t'ien-hsia k'ao" 趙普以半部論語治天下考 (A myth of Chao Pu: using half the *Analects* to govern the country), *Tsing-hua hsueh-pao* n.s., 8.1–2:306–336 (1970).

Imabori Seiji 今堀誠二 . "Sōdai no ōki shitsugyōsha kyūgo jigyō ni tsuite" 宋代の冬季失業者救護事業について (Winter relief for the unemployed in Sung times), *Tōyō gakuhō* 39.3:228–257 (Tokyo, 1956).

Iriya Yoshitaka 入矢義高 . "*Tokei mukaroku no bunshō*" 東京夢華錄の文章 (*Tung-ching meng-hua lu* [Record of the splendor in the Eastern Capital] viewed as literature), *Tōhō gakuhō* 20:135–152 (Kyoto, 1951).

Ishida Mikinosuke 石田幹之助 . *Nankai ni kansuru Shina shiryō* 南海に關する支那史料 (Chinese sources relating to the South Seas). Tokyo, Seikatsusha, 1945.

Jao Tsung-i 饒宗頤 . "San-chiao-lun yü Sung Chin hsueh-shu" 三教論與

宋金學術 (The theory of three teachings and the Sung and the Jurchen scholarship), *Tung-hsi wen-hua* 11:24–32 (1968).

Jen-min ta-hsueh 人民大學. *Chung-kuo tzu-pen chu-i meng-ya wen-t'i t'ao-lun chi* 中國資本主義萌芽問題討論集 (Symposium on the problem of sprouts of capitalism in China). Peking, Jen-min ta-hsueh ch'u-pan-she, 1957. *See also* Nan-ching ta-hsueh.

Katō Shigeshi 加藤繁. *Tō Sō jidai ni okeru kingin no kenkyū* 唐宋時代に おける金銀の研究 (Gold and silver in T'ang and Sung times). 2 vols. Tokyo, Tōyō Bunko, 1925–1926.

———. *Shina keizaishi kōshō* 支那經濟史考證 (Studies in Chinese economic history). 2 vols. Tokyo, Tōyō Bunko, 1952–1953.

Kawakami Kōichi 河上光一. *Sōdai no keizai seikatsu* 宋代の經濟生 活 (Sung economic life). Tokyo, Yoshikawa Kōbunkan, 1966.

Kida Tomoo 本田知生. "Hokusō jidai no Rakyuō to shijintachi" 北宋 時代の洛陽と士人達 (Lo-yang and scholar-officials during the Northern Sung), *Tōyōshi kenkyū* 38.1:51–85 (1939).

Kinugawa Tsuyoshi 衣川強. "Sōdai saishō kō" 宋代宰相考 (On Sung chief councilors), *Tōyōshi kenkyū* 29.4:36–76 (1966).

———. "Sōdai no hōkyū ni tsuite" 宋代の俸給について (Emoluments of Sung officials), *Tōhō gakuhō* 41:415–466 (Kyoto, 1970).

———. "Shin Kai no kōwa seisaku o megutte" 秦檜の講和政策をめぐって (Concerning Ch'in Kuei's peace policy), *Tōhō gakuhō* 45:245–294 (Kyoto, 1973).

——— . *Sō Gen gakuen, Sō Gen Gakuen hoi jinmei jigo betsumei sakuin* 宋元學 案、宋元學案補遺人名字號別名索引 (Index to individuals in the *Sung Yuan hsueh-an* and its supplement). Kyoto, Jimbun Kagaku Kenkyūjo, 1979.

K'o Ch'ang-chi 柯昌基. "Sung-tai ku-yung kuan-hsi ti ch'u-pu t'an-so" 宋代 僱傭關係的初步探索 (Preliminary study of labor employment relationships during the Sung), *Li-shih yen-chiu* 2:23–48 (1957).

K'o tun-po 柯敦伯. *Sung-tai wen-hsueh-shih* 宋代文學史 (History of Sung literature). Shanghai, Commercial Press, 1934.

Koiwai Hiromitsu 小岩井弘光. "Nansō shoki gunsei ni tsuite" 南宋 初期軍制について (The military system in the early Southern Sung), *Shukan Tōyōgaku* 28:105–130 (1972).

Ku Chi-kuang 谷霽光. "Wang An-shih pien-fa yü shang-p'in ching-chi" 王安石 變法與商品經濟 (Wang An-shih's reform and commodity economy), *Chung-hua wen-shih lu-ts'ung* 7:71–106 (1978).

Kuan Lü-ch'ing 關履卿. "Lun Pei-Sung ch'u-nien ti chi-ch'üan t'ung-i" 論北宋 初年的集權統一 (Concentration of power and unification in early Northern Sung), *Hua-nan shih-yuan hsueh-pao* 4:102–107 (1980).

Kubo Noritada 窪德忠. "Sōdai no shin Dōkyō kyōdan" 宋代の新道教 教團 (New Taoist groups in Sung times), *Rekishi kyōiku* 12.8:53–59 (1964).

———. *Chūgoku no shūkyō kaikaku: Zenshinkyō no seiritsu* 中國の宗教改革：全真教の成立 (Religious reform in China: the establishment of the Ch'üan-chen cult). Tokyo, Hōzōkan, 1967.

Kuo P'eng 郭朋. *Sung Yuan Fo-chiao* 宋元佛教 (Buddhism in Sung and Yuan times). Fu-chou, Jen-min ch'u-pan-she, 1981.

Kusano Yasushi 草野靖. "Nansō Kōzai kaishi no hatten" 南宋行在會子の發展 (The development of paper currency at the Southern Sung capital), *Tōyō gakuhō* 49.1:1–41 and 49.2:39–75 (Tokyo, 1966).

———. "Sōdai minden no densaku keitai" 宋代民田の佃作形態 (Situation of tenant farming on private land during the Sung), *Shisō* 10:72–112 (1969).

———. "Sōdaishi o dō miruka?" 宋代史をどう見るか ? (What to look for in Sung history?), *Shisō* 14:16–112 (1973).

Li An 李安. "Sung Kao-tsung tz'u Yueh Fei ssu yü Ta-li-ssu k'ao-cheng" 宋高宗賜岳飛死於大理寺考證 (The death of Yueh Fei at the Court of Judicial Review as ordered by Emperor Kao-tsung), *SYC* 4:501–510 (1969).

———. "Yueh Fei tsai Nan-sung tang-shih ti sheng-wang he li-shih ti-wei" 岳飛在南宋當時的聲望和歷史地位 (Yueh Fei's reputation at the time of the Southern Sung and his historical standing), *SYC* 6:117–126 (1973).

Li Chieh 黎傑. *Sung Shih* 宋史 (Sung history). Taipei, Ta-hsin, 1964.

Li Chien-nung 李劍農. *Sung Yuan Ming ching-chi-shih kao* 宋元明經濟史稿 (Draft economic history from the Sung through the Ming times). Peking, San-lien, 1957.

Li ch'un-p'u 李春圃. "Sung-tai feng-chien tsu-t'ien-chih ti chiu-chung hsing-shih" 宋代封建租佃制的九種形式 (Nine types in the Sung feudal tenancy system), *SYL*, 139–150.

Li Hung-ch'i 李弘祺. *Sung-tai chiao-yü san-lun* 宋代教育散論 (Essays on Sung education). Taipei, Tung-sheng, 1980.

Li T'ang 李唐. *Sung Hui-tsung* 宋徽宗 (Emperor Hui-tsung). Hong Kong, Hung-yeh, 1964.

———. *Sung Kao-tsung* 宋高宗 (Emperor Kao-tsung). Hong Kong, Hung-yeh, 1964.

Liang Keng-yao 梁庚堯. *Nan-Sung ti nung-ts'un ching-chi* 南宋的農村經濟 (Rural economy of the Southern Sung). Taipei, Lien-ching, 1984.

———. "Nan-Sung ch'eng-shih ti fa-chan" 南宋城市的發展 (Urban development in the Southern Sung), *Shih-huo* n.s. 10.10:4–27 and 10.11:21–36 (1981).

Liang Kun 梁崑. *Sung-shih p'ai-pieh lun* 宋詩派別論 (Sung schools of poetry). Shanghai, Commercial Press, 1938.

Liang T'ien-hsi 梁天錫. "Sung-tai chih ssu-lu chih-tu" 宋代之祠祿制度

(The pension system of the Sung government), *Ta-lu tsa-chih* 29.2:14–26 (1964).

——. "Pei-Sung t'ai-chien chih-tu chih chuan-pien" 北宋台諫制度之轉 變 (Evolving changes of the Northern Sung censorial system) *Hsin-ya hsueh-shu nien-k'an* 8:147–193 (1966).

——. "Lun Sung tsai-fu hu-chien chih-tu" 論宋宰輔互兼制度 (The Sung system of concurrent appointments of various councilors), *Hsin-ya hsueh-pao* 8.2: 289–320 (1968).

——. "Nan-Sung Chien-yen yü-ying-ssu chih-tu" 南宋建炎御營司制度 (The system of Imperial Headquarters at the beginning of the Southern Sung), *SYC* 5:479–491 (1971).

——. "Nan-Sung chih tu-fu chih-tu" 南宋之督府制度 (The Southern Sung system of regional military commissions), *SYC* 10:229–244 (1978).

Lin Cheng-ch'iu 林正秋. "Nan-Sung shih-ch'i Hang-chou ti ching-chi yü wen-hua" 南宋時期杭州的經濟與文化 (Hang-chou's economy and culture during the Southern Sung), *Li-shih yen-chiu* 12:42–52 (1979).

——. "Nan-Sung tu-ch'eng Lin-an jen-kou-shu k'o-cha" 南宋都城臨安人 口數考察 (An examination of the population figures at Li-nan the Southern Sung capital), *Hang-chou ta-hsueh hsueh-pao* 1:147–149 (1979).

Lin Jui-han 林瑞翰. "Shao-hsing shih-erh-nien i-chien Nan-Sung kuo-ch'ing chih yen-chiu" 紹興十二年以前南宋國情之研究 (The state of the Southern Sung before the peace of 1142), *SYC* 3:215–244 (1966).

Lin K'o-t'ang 林科棠. *Sung-ju yü Fo-chiao* 宋儒與佛教 (Sung Confucians and Buddhism). Shanghai, Commercial Press, 1928.

Lin T'ien-wei 林天蔚. *Sung-shih shih-hsi* 宋史試析 (Analyses of Sung history). Taipei, Commercial Press, 1978.

Liu O-kung 劉鄂公. *Shuo Nan-Sung* 說南宋 (Talking about the Southern Sung). Taipei, P'ing-yuan, 1965.

Liu Po-chi 劉伯驥. *Sung-tai cheng-chiao shih* 宋代政教史 (The political and educational history of the Sung). 2 vols. Taipei, Chung-hua, 1971.

Liu Tzu-chien (James T. C. Liu) 劉子健 "Wang An-shih Tseng Pu yü Pei-Sung wan-ch'i kuan-liao ti lei-hsing." 王安石、曾布與北宋晚期官僚 的類型 (Wang An-shih, Tseng Pu, and the types of bureaucrats in the late Northern Sung), *Tsing-hua hsueh-pao* n.s. 2.1:100–127 (1960).

——. "Jukyō kokka no jūsōteki seikaku ni tsuite" 儒教國家の雙層 的性格 (The dual nature of the Confucian state), *Tōhōgaku* 20:1–7 (1961).

——. *Ou-yang Hsiu ti chih-hsueh yü ts'ung-cheng* 歐陽修的治學與從政 (Ou-yang Hsiu's scholarship and political career). Hong Kong, Hsin-ya Yen-chiu-so, 1963.

——. "Lueh-lun Sung-tai ti-fang kuan-hsueh yü ssu-hsueh ti hsiao-chang" 略論 宋代地方官學與私學的消長 (The rise and fall of the local official schools and private schools during Sung times), *Li-shi Yü-yen Yen-chiu-so chi-k'an* 36:237–248 (1965).

———. "Sung-tai k'ao-ch'ang pi-tuan" 宋代考場弊端 (Cheating in the Sung examination halls), in *Ch'ing-chu Li Chi hsien-sheng ch'i-shih-sui lun-wen-chi* 慶祝李濟先生七十歲論文集 (Festschrift in honor of Dr. Li Chi). Taipei, Li-shih Yü-yen Yen-chiu-so, 1967.

———. "Nan-Sung chün-chu yü yen-kuan" 南宋君主與言官 (The Southern Sung emperors and opinion officials), *Tsing-hua hsueh-pao* n.s. 8.1–2: 340–349 (1970).

———. "Pei-hai li-kuo yü pan-pi shan-ho" 背海立國與半壁山河 (The Southern Sung: back toward the sea while ruling over half of the country), *Chung-kuo hsueh-jen* 4:1–4. (New Asia College, Hong Kong, 1972).

———. "Pao-jung cheng-chih ti te-tien" 包容政治的特點 (Characteristics of accommodative politics), *Chung-kuo hsueh-jen* (1973) 5:1–28.

———. "Lueh-lun Sung-tai wu-kuan ch'ün" 略論宋代武官群 (The Sung military officers), in *Aoyama hakushi koki kinen Sōdaishi ronso* 青山博士古稀紀念宋代史論叢 (Festschrift in honor of Dr. Aoyama). Tokyo, Seishin Shobo, 1974.

———. "Liu Tsai he chen-chi" 劉宰和賑饑 (Liu Tsai and famine relief), *Peking ta-hsueh hsueh-pao* 3:53–61; 4:41–55 (1979).

Lo Chiu-ch'ing 羅球慶. "Pei-Sung ping-chih yen-chiu" 北宋兵制研究 (The Northern Sung military system), *Hsin-ya hsueh-pao* 3.1:167–270 (1957).

Ma Tsung-huo 馬宗霍. *Chung-kuo ching-hsueh-shih* 中國經學史 (A history of studies on the Chinese Classics). Shanghai, Commercial Press, 1937.

Makino Tatsumi 牧野巽. *Kinsei Chūgoku sōzoku kenkyū* 近世中國宗族研究 (Common descent groups in early modern China). Tokyo, Ochinomizu Shobō, 1980.

Mikami Tsugio 三次上男. *Kinshi kenkyū* 金史研究 (Studies in Jurchen history). 3 vols. Tokyo, Chūō Kōron Bijutsu Shuppan, 1970–1973.

Miyazaki Ichisada 宮崎市定. *Godai Sōsho no tsūska mondai* 五代宋初の通貨問題 (The currency problem in the Five Dynasties and early Sung). Kyoto, Hoshino Shoten, 1943.

———. *Tōyō no kinsei* 東洋の近世 (Early modern East Asia). Osaka, Kyōiku Taimususha, 1950.

———. "Sōdai igo no tochi shoyū keitai" 宋代以後の土地所有形態 (Landholding types after the Sung period), *Tōyōshi kenkyū* 12.2:1–34 (1952).

———. *Ajiashi kenkyū* アジア史研究 (Studies in Asian history). 5 vols. Kyoto, Tōyōshi Kenkyūkai, 1957–1978.

———. "Sodai kansei josetsu" 宋代官制序説 (A preface to the Sung civil service system). Preface to Saeki Tomi, *Sōshi shokkanshi sakuin.* Kyoto, Tōyōshi Kenkyūkai, 1963.

————. *Ajiashi ronko* アジア史論考 (Research in Asian history). 3 vols. Tokyo, Asahi Shimbunsha, 1976.

Mori Katsumi 森克巳. "Nissō bōeki no senkai" 日宋貿易の旋回 (The turning of trade between Japan and the Sung), *Tōyō gakuhō* 23.4:522–544 and 24.1:70–99 (Tokyo, 1936).

Mou Jun-sun 牟潤孫. "Ts'ung Chung-kuo ti ching-hsueh k'an shih-hsueh" 從中國的經學看史學 (The discipline of history from the standpoint of the discipline of Chinese Classics). *Hsin-ya shu-yuan li-shih-hsi hsi-k'an* 2:1–5 (1972).

Naitō Shigenobu 内藤戊申. "Chūgokushi no jidai kubunron tenbō" 中國史の時代區分論展望 (Prospect of periodization in Chinese history), *Shirin* 41.1:64–74 (1958).

Naitō Torajio 内藤虎次郎. *Chūgoku kinseishi* 中國近世史 (History of early modern China). Tokyo, Kōbundo, 1947.

Nan-ching ta-hsueh 南京大學. *Chung-kuo tzu-pen-chu-i meng-ya wen-ti t'ao-lun chi: hsu-chi* 中國資本主義萌芽問題討論集：續集 (A sequel to the symposium on the problem of sprouts of capitalism in China). Peking, Jen-min ch'u-pan-she, 1960. *See also* Jen-min ta-hsueh.

Nieh Ch'ung-ch'i 聶崇岐. "Lun Sung T'ai-tsu shou ping-ch'üan 論宋太祖收兵權 (The gathering of military power by the Sung founding emperor), *Yen-ching hsueh-pao* 36:85–106 (1948).

————. *Sung-shih ts'ung-k'ao* 宋史叢考 (Studies in Sung history). Peking, Chung-hua, 1980.

Niida Noboru 仁井田陞. *Tō Sō hōritsu bunsho no kenkyū* 唐宋法律文書の研究 (A study of legal materials of the Tang and Sung dynasties). Tokyo, Tōhō bunka Gakuin, 1937.

Ning K'o 宵可. "Sung-tai chung-wen ch'ing-wu feng-ch'i ti hsing-ch'eng" 宋代重文輕武風氣的形成 (The established Sung custom of civilian superiority over military officers), *Hsueh-lin man-lu* 3:59–66 (1981).

Nogami Sunjo 野上俊靜. *Ryō Kin no Bukkyō* 遼金の佛教 (Khitan and Jurchen Buddhism). Kyoto, Heirakuji Shoten, 1953.

Pai Shou-i 白壽彝. "Sui T'ang Sung shih-tai chih chiao-t'ung" 隋唐宋時代の交通 (Transportation from the Sui through the T'ang to the Sung period), *Chung-kuo chiao-t'ung shih* 3:107–157 (1965).

P'eng Ying-t'ien 彭瀛添. "Liang-Sung ti yu-i chih-tu" 兩宋的郵驛制度 (The Sung postal system), *Shih-hsueh hui-k'an* 8:111–220 (1977).

Saeki Tomi 佐伯富. *Sōshi shokkanshi sakuin* 宋史職官志索引 (Index to the "Monograph of functional officials" in the Sung dynastic history). Kyoto, Tōyōshi Kenkyūkai, 1963.

————. "Kinsei Chūgoku no toshi to nōson" 近世中國の都市と農村 (Cities and villages in early modern China), *Rekishi kyōiku* 14.12:66–72 (1966).

————. *Sō no shin bunka* 宋の新文化 (New culture of the Sung). Tokyo, Jinbutsu ōlaisha, 1967.

————. et al. *Iwanami kōza sekai rekishi* 岩波講座世界歴史 (Iwanami series of world history), vol. 9. Tokyo, Iwanami, 1970.

————. *Chūgokushi kenkyū* 中國史研究 (Studies in Chinese history). 2 vols. Kyoto, Tōyōshi Kenkyūkai, 1969–1977.

Shen Ch'en-nung 沈忱農. "Sung-tai wei-tsu-chih chih shih-mo" 宋代偽組織之始末 (The beginning and the end of the bogus regimes of Sung times), *SYC* 2:235–244 (1964).

Shen Ch'i-wei 沈起煒. *Sung Chin chan-cheng shih-lueh* 宋金戰争史略 (Outline history of the wars between the Sung and the Jurchen). Wuhan, Hubei, Jen-min ch'u-pan-she, 1958.

Shiba Yoshinobu 斯波義信. "Sōdai shōgyōshi kenkyū no tame no oboegaki" 宋代商業史研究のための覺書 (A memorandum for the study of Sung commercial history), *Shigaku zasshi* 72.6:49–69 (1963).

————. "10–13 seiki ni okeru Chūgoku toshi no tenkan" 10～13世紀にすける中國都市の轉換 (Transformation of Chinese cities in the tenth through thirteenth centuries), *Sekaishi kenkyū* 42:22–37 (1966).

————. *Sōdai shōgyōshi kenkyū* 宋代商業史研究 (Studies in Sung commercial history). Tokyo, Kazama Shobō, 1968. *See also* Shiba Yoshinobu, *Commerce and Society in Sung China*, in Section A of the Bibliography for an abridged version in English.

————. "Sōdai no Kōshu ni okeru chinshi no hatten" 宋代の湖州にすける鎮市の發展 (The development of market towns in Hu-chou during Sung times), in *Enoki hakushi senreki kinen Tōyōshi ronsō* 榎博士還暦紀念東洋史論叢 (Festschrift in honor of Dr. Enoki). Tokyo, Yamakawa Shuppansha, 1975.

Shimada Masao 島田正郎. *Ryō shi* 遼史 (History of the Khitan). Tokyo, Meitoku Shuppansha, 1975.

Sogabe Shizuo 曾我部靜雄. *Kaihō to Kōshu* 開封と杭州 (Kai-feng and Hang-chou). Tokyo, Fuzanbō, 1940.

————. *Sōdai zaiseishi* 宋代財政史 (Financial history of the Sung). Rev. ed. Tokyo, Seikatsusha, 1966.

————. *Nichi Sō Kin kahei kōryūshi* 日宋金貨幣交流史 (The circulation of currencies among Japan, the Sung, and the Jurchen). Tokyo, Hōbunkan, 1949.

————. *Sōdai seikeishi no kenkyū* 宋代政經史研究 (Studies in Sung political and economic history). Tokyo, Yoshikawa Kōbunkan, 1974.

————. *Chūgoku shakai keizaishi no kenkyū* 中國社會經濟史の研究 (Studies in Chinese social and economic history). Tokyo, Yoshikawa Kōbunkan, 1976.

Sōshi teiyō Hensan Kyōryoku Iinkei 宋史提要編纂協力委員會 (Japanese Committee for the Sung Project). *Sōdai kenkyū bunken teiyō* 宋代

研究文獻提要   (Abstracts of Japanese books and articles concerning the Sung), plus two supplements. Aoyama Sadao, ed. Tokyo, Tōyō Bunko, 1961–1970.

———. *Sōdaishi nenpyō* 宋代史年表   (Chronology of Sung history). 2 vols. Tokyo, Tōyō Bunko, 1967–1974.

———. *Sōjin denki sakuin* 宋人傳記索引   (Index to Sung biographical accounts). Tokyo, Tōyō Bunko, 1968.

Su Chin-yuan 蘇金源. "Lun Sung-tai k'e-hu ti jen-shen i-fu kuan-hsi" 論宋代客户的人身依附關係 (The personal subordination of tenant households in Sung times), *SYL* 76–88.

——— and Li Ch'un-fu 李春圃. *Sung-tai san-tz'u nung-min ch'i-i shih-liao hui-pien* 宋代三次農民起義史料彙編 (Consolidated sources on the three major peasant uprisings in Sung times). Peking, Chung-hua, 1963.

Sūdo Yoshiyuki 周籐吉之. *Sōdai kanryōsei to daitochi shoyū* 宋代官僚制と大土地所有 (The Sung bureaucratic system and large-scale land ownership). Tokyo, Nihon Hyōronsha, 1950.

———. *Chūgoku tochi seidoshi kenkyū* 中國土地制度史研究   (Studies in the history of the Chinese land system). Tokyo, Tōyō Bunka Kenkyūjo, 1954.

———. *Sōdai keizaishi kenkyū* 宋代經濟史研究 (Studies of Sung economic history). Tokyo, Tōkyō Daigaku Shuppansha, 1962.

———. *To Sō shakei keizaishi kenkyū* 唐宋社會經濟史研究 (Studies of T'ang and Sung socio-economic history). Tokyo, Tōkyō Daigaku Shuppansha, 1965.

———. *Sōdaishi kenkyū* 宋代史研究 (Studies in Sung history). Tokyo, Tōyō Bunko, 1969.

Sun K'e-k'uan 孫克寬. *Sung Yuan Tao-chiao chih fa-chan* 宋元道教之發展 (The development of Taoism during Sung and Yuan times). Tai-chung, Tung-hai Ta-hsueh 東海大學, 1965–1968.

Sun Kuo-tung 孫國棟. *T'ang Sung shih lun ts'ung* 唐宋史論叢 (Essays in T'ang and Sung history). Hong Kong, Lung-men, 1980.

Sun Pao 孫葆. *T'ang Sung Yuan hai-shang shang-yeh cheng-ts'e* 唐宋元海上商業政策 (Sea trade policies from the T'ang through the Sung to Yuan times). Taipei, Cheng-chung, 1969.

Sung Shee [Sung Hsi] 宋晞. "Sung-shang tsai Sung-Li mao-i chung ti kung-hsien" 宋商在宋麗貿易中的貢獻 (Contributions of Sung merchants through trade with Korea), *Shih-hsueh hui-k'an* 8:83–109 (1977).

———. *Sung-shih yen-chiu lun-ts'ung* 宋史研究論叢 (Studies in Sung history). Taipei, Chung-kuo wen-hua yen-chiu-so, 1979, 1980.

———. *Sung-shih yen-chiu lun-wen yü shu-chi mu-lu* 宋史研究論文與書籍目錄 (Bibliography of Chinese articles and books on Sung history). Taipei, Chung-kuo wen-hua ta-hsueh, 1983.

Sung-shih lun-chi 宋史論集 (Collected articles on Sung history). Chuang Chao

莊昭 , ed. Ho-nan Province, Chung-chou shu-hua-she, 1983.

Sung-shih yen-chiu chi 宋史研究集 (Collection of research articles in Sung history). Sung-shih Tso-t'an-hui 宋史座談會 , ed. Sung Shee [Sung Hsi], editor-in-chief. Taipei, Chung-hua Ts'ung-shu Wei-yuan-hui, 1968–.

Sung-shih yen-chiu-chi 宋史研究集 . (Collection of articles in Sung history). Ho-nan shih-ta Sung-shih yen-chiu-shih 河南師大宋史研究室 , ed. K'ai-feng, Ho-nan shih-ta hsueh-pao, 1984.

Sung-shih yen-chiu lun-wen-chi 宋史研究論文集 . (Symposium articles on Sung history). Teng Kuang-ming (Deng Guangming) and Cheng Ying-liu 程應鏐 , eds., for Sung-shih Yen-chiu-hui. Shanghai, Shanghai Ku-chi ch'u-pan-she, 1982.

Tai Ching-hua 戴靜華 . "Sung-tai shang-shui chih-tu chien-shu" 宋代商稅制度簡述 (Outline of Sung commercial taxes), *SYL*, 165–203.

Tai I-hsuan 戴裔煊 . *Sung-tai ch'ao-yen chih-tu yen-chiu* 宋代鈔鹽制度研究 (A Study of the Sung salt certificate system). Shanghai, Commercial Press, 1957.

Takahashi Yoshiro 高橋芳郎 . "Sōdai denko no shinfun mondai" 宋代佃戶の身分問題 (The personal status of Sung period tenants), *Tōyōshi kenkyū* 37.3:64–91 (1978).

Takao Giken 高雄義堅 . *Sōdai Bukkyōshi no kenkyū* 宋代佛教史の研究 (Studies in Sung Buddhism). Tokyo, Hyakkaen, 1975.

T'ang Kuei-chang 唐奎章 . *Sung tz'u san-pai shou chien-chu* 宋詞三百首箋註 . *Sung tz'u san-pai shou chien-chu* (Three hundred Sung *tz'u* annotated). Shanghai, Shen-chou Kuo-kuang-she, 1947.

T'ao Chin-sheng [Jing-shen] 陶晉生 . *Pien-chiang-shih yen-chiu-chi: Sung Chin shih-chi* 邊疆史研究集：宋金時期 (Studies in frontier history: the period of Sung and Chin). Taipei, Commercial Press, 1961.

———. *Chin Hai-ling-ti ti fa Sung yü Ts'ai-shih chan-i ti k'ao-shih* 金海陵帝的伐宋與采石戰役的考實 (The invasion of the Sung by Emperor Hai-ling of the Chin and the battle of Ts'ai-shih). Taipei, Taiwan University, 1963.

T'ao Hsi-sheng 陶希聖 . "Pei-Sung ch'u-ch'i ti ching-chi ts'ai-cheng chu wen-ti" 北宋初期的經濟財政諸問題 (Various economic and financial problems in the early Sung), *Shih-huo* 2.2:29–36 (1935).

Teng Kuang-ming 鄧廣銘 . *Wang An-shih: Chung-kuo shih-i-shih-chi ti kai-ko-chia* 王安石中國十一世紀的改革家 (Wang An-shih: China's eleventh century reformer). Rev. ed. Shanghai, Chung-hua, 1981.

———. *Yueh Fei chuan* 岳飛傳 (Biography of Yueh Fei). Peking, Jen-min ch'u-pan-she, 1983.

———, Ch'eng Ying-liu 程應鏐 , et al. *Chung-kuo li-shih ta-t'zu-ti-an Sung-shih* 中國歷史大辭典：宋史 (Encyclopedia of Chinese history: Sung history). Shanghai, Tz'u-shu ch'u-pan-she, 1984.

Terada Gō 寺田剛 . *Sōdai kyōikushi gaisetsu* 宋代教育史概説 (Outline history of Sung education). Tokyo, Hakubansha, 1965.

Teraji Jun 寺地遵 . "Shin Kai go no seiji katei ni kansuru jakkan no kōsatsu" 秦檜後の政治過程に關する若干の考察 (Some observations on the political process after Chin Kuei), *Tōyōshi kenkyū* 35.3:87–113 (1976).

———. "Kenen, Shōkō nenkan no seiji katei ni kansuru jakkan no kōsatsu" 建炎、紹興年間の政治過程に關する若干の考察 (Some observations on the political process during the first two reign periods of the Southern Sung), *Hiroshima Daigaku Bungaku Bu kiyō* 38.2:52–74 (1978).

Tokiwa Daijō 常盤大定 . *Shina ni okeru Bukkyō to Jukyō Dōkyō* 支那における佛教儒教と道教 (The relationship of Buddhism to Confucianism and Taoism in China). Tokyo, Tōyō Bunko, 1930.

———. *Shina Bukkyō no kenkyū* 支那佛教の研究 (Studies of Chinese Buddhism). Tokyo, Shunjūsha, 1943.

Tonami Mamoru 礪波護 . "Sōdai shitaifu no seiritsu" 宋代士大夫の成立 (The maturity of Sung scholar-officials), in Oguta Yoshihiko, ed. *Chūgoku bunka sōsho* 中國文化叢書 , vol. 8. Tokyo, Tashukan Shoten, 1968.

Tōyō Bunko 東洋文庫 , ed. *Aoyama hakushi koki kinen Sōdaishi ronso* 青山博士古稀紀念宋代史論叢 (Festschrift in honor of Dr. Aoyama). Tokyo, Tōyō Bunko, 1974.

Tsukamoto Zenryu 塚本善隆 . "Sō no zaiseinan to Bukkyō" 宋の財政難と佛教 (Sung financial difficulties and Buddhism), in *Kuwabara hakushi kanreki kinen Tōyōshi ronsō* 桑原博士還曆紀念東洋史論叢 (Festschrift in honor of Dr. Kuwabara). Tokyo, Kōbundō, 1931.

Ts'un-ts'ui Hsueh-she, ed. 存粹學社 . *Sung Liao Chin shih lun-chi* 宋遼金史論集 (Collected articles on Sung, Khitan, and Jurchen history). Hong Kong, Ts'ung-wen, 1971.

Umehara Kaoru 梅原郁 . *Kenen irai keinen yōroku jinmei sakuin* 建炎以來繫年要錄人名索引 (Index of personal names in *Chien-yen i-lai hsi-nien yao-lu* [*HYNL*]). Kyōto, Dōbōsha, 1983.

———. "Sōdai chihō shōtoshi no ichimen: Shin no hensen ō chūshin to shite" 宋代地方小都市の一面：鎮の變遷を中心として (One dimension of small regional cities in the Sung: Focusing on the changes of "chen"), *Shirin* 41.6:35–51 (1958).

———. "Sōdai no chihō toshi" 宋代の地方都市 (The Sung regional cities), *Rekishi kyōiku* 14.12:52–58 (1966).

———. "Sōdai toshi no zeifu" 宋代都市の税賦 (Taxation in Sung cities), *Tōyōshi kenkyū* 28.4:42–74 (1970).

———. "Sōdai no naizō to sozō" 宋代の内藏と左藏 (The Sung Inner Treasury and Left Treasury), *Tōhō gakuhō* 42:127–175 (Kyoto, 1971).

Wang Chi王繼 . *"Hsu Tzu-chih t'ung-chien* chüan-hsiu k'an-k'e k'ao-lueh" 續資治通鑑纂修刊刻考略 (The editing and printing of the *Sequel to the Mirror for aid in government*), *Shih-hsueh yen-chiu* 2:56–67 (1982).

Wang Chih-jui 王志瑞 . *Sung Yuan ching-chi shih* 宋元經濟史 (Economic history of the Sung and Yuan period). Taipei reprint, Commercial Press, 1964.

Wang Fang-chung王方中 . "Sung-tai min-ying shou-kung-yeh ti she-hui ching-chi hsing-chih" 宋代民營手工業的社會經濟性質 (The socio-economic nature of private handicraft trade in Sung times), *Li-shih yen-chiu* 2:39–57 (1959).

Wang Huai-ling 王槐齡 . "Yu-kuan Sung-tai ch'ai-i ti chi-ke wen-t'i" 有關宋代差役的幾個問題 (Several problems of the requisitioned service in Sung times). *SYL*, 151–203.

Wang Min-hsin 王民信 . "Liao Sung san-yuan meng-yueh t'i-chieh ti pei-ching" 遼宋澶淵盟約締結的背景 (The background of the 1004 peace treaty between the Sung and the Khitan), *Shu-mu chi-k'an* 書目季刊 9.2:34–49; 9.3.45–56; 9.4:53–64 (1957–1976).

Wang Ming-sun 王明蓀 . "Chin-ch'u ti kung-ch'en chi-t'uan chi ch'i tui Chin Sung kuan-hsi ti ying-hsiang" 金初的功臣集團及其對宋金關係的影響 (Meritorious officials in the early Jurchen and their influence on the Jurchen-Sung relations), *SYC* 15:199–226 (1983).

Wang Te-i (or Teh-yi)王德毅 . *Sung-shih yen-chiu lun-chi* 宋史研究論集 (Collected research articles in Sung history). Vol. 1: Taipei, Commercial Press, 1968. Vol. 2: Taipei, Ting-wen, 1972.

———. *Sung-tai tsai-huang ti chiu-chi cheng-ts'e* 宋代災荒的救濟政策 (The Sung famine relief measures). Taipei, Commercial Press, 1970.

———. "Hsu Meng-hsin nien-p'u 徐夢莘年譜 (Hsu Meng-hsin's annalistic biography), *SYC* 8:505–532 (1976).

———. "Li Hsin-ch'uan nien-p'u" 李心傳年譜 (Li Hsin-ch'uan's annalistic biography), *SYC* 9:513–574 (1977).

Wang Tseng-yü 王曾瑜 . "Sung-ch'ao ti chai-i ho hsing-shih-hu" 宋朝的差役和形勢戶 (The Sung requisitioned service and the prestigious households), *Li-shih-hsueh* 1.64–73 (1979).

———. "Sung-ch'ao chieh-chi chieh-kou kai-shu" 宋朝階級結構概述 (Outline of the Sung class structure), *She-hui k'o-hsueh chan-hsien* 4:128–136 (1979).

———. *Sung-ch'ao ping-chih chu-t'an* 宋朝兵制初探 (Exploration of the Sung military system). Peking, Chung-hua, 1983.

———. *Yueh Fei hsin-chuan* 岳飛新傳 (A new biography of Yueh Fei). Shanghai, Jen-min ch'u-pan-she, 1984.

Wang T'ung-ling 王桐齡 . "Sung Liao chih kuan-hsi" 宋遼之關係 (The Sung-Khitan relations), *Tsing-hua hsueh-pao* 4.2:1343–1351 (1929).

Wu T'ien-ying 吳天穎 . "Lun Sung-tai Ssu-ch'uan chih-yen-yeh chung ti sheng-ch'an kuan-hsi" 論宋代四川製鹽業中的生產關係 (The productive relationship in the salt industry of Szechuan during the Sung), *Wen shih che* 1.73–79 (1964).

Wu Yü 吳虞. *Wu Yü wen-lu* 吳虞文錄 (The writings of Wu Yü). Shanghai, Ya-tung, 1921.

Yabuuchi (or Yabuti) Kiyoshi 藪內清. "Kenryō seiji to Chōgoku chūsei no kagaku" 官僚政治と中國中世の科學 (Bureaucratic politics and science in medieval China) *Kagakushi kenkyū* 59:1–7 (1961).

——— ed. *Chūgoku chūsei kagaku gijutsushi no kenkyū* 中國中世科學技術史の研究 (Studies of history of science and technology in medieval China). Tokyo, Kadokawa Shoten, 1963.

———. *Sō Gen jidai no kagaku gijutsushi* 宋元時代の科學技術史 (History of science and technology in Sung and Mongol times), Kyoto, Jimbun Kagaku Kenkyūjo, 1967.

———. *Chūgoku no tenmon rekiho* 中國の天文曆法 (Chinese astronomy and calendar-making). Tokyo Heibonsha, 1969.

———. *Chūgoku no kagaku bunmei* 中國の科學文明 (Chinese science and civilization). Tokyo, Iwanami Shoten, 1970.

———. *Chūgoku no sūgaku* 中國の數學 (Chinese mathematics). Tokyo, Iwanami Shoten, 1974.

Yamauchi Masahiro 山內正博. "Chō Shun no Fuhei shuppeisaku" 張浚の富平出兵策 (Chang Ch'ün's strategy of offense at Fu-p'ing), *Tōyōshi kenkyū* 19.1:37–56 (1960).

———. "Nansō no Shisen ni okeru Chō Shun to Go Kai" 南宋の四川にすける張浚と吳玠 (Chang Ch'ün and Wu Chieh in Szechuan during the early Southern Sung), *Shirin* 44.1:98–124 (1961).

Yanagida Setsuko 柳田節子. "Sōdai Chūō shukenteki no bunshin kanryō shihai no seiritsu ō meguite" 宋代中央集權の文臣官僚支配の成立をめぐって (The establishment of the Sung practice of concentrating power at the center with civilian supremacy), *Rekishigaku kenkyū* 26:2–5 (1964).

———. "Sōdai denkosei no seikentō" 宋代佃戶制の再檢討 (Reappraisal of the Sung tenancy system) *Rekishigaku kenkyū* 35:24–33 (1973).

———. "Sōdai chishusei to kokenryoku" 宋代地主制と公權力 (The Sung landowning system and public authority), *Tōyō bunka* 55:15–36 (1975).

Yang Lien-sheng 楊聯陞. "Hsi-hu-lao-jen *Fan-sheng-lu* chiao-cheng" 西湖老人繁勝錄校証 (Emendation of *Fan-sheng-lu*, a record of Hang-chou), *Hua-kang hsueh-pao* 1:113–122 (1965).

Yang Shu-fan 楊樹藩. "Sung-tai tsai-hsiang chih-tu" 宋代宰相制度 (The Sung system of chief councilors), *SYC* 15:1–34 (1983).

Yao Ts'ung-wu 姚從吾. *Tung-pei-shih lun-ts'ung* 東北史論叢 (Collected research articles on northeastern history). Taipei, Cheng-chung, 1959.

———. *Liao-Chin-Yuan-shih lun-wen* 遼金元史論文 (Research articles on the histories of the Khitans, Jurchens, and Mongols). Taipei, Cheng-chung, 1981.

Yeh Hung-sa 葉鴻灑. "Shih-lun Sung-tai shu-yuan chih-tu chih ch'an-sheng chi ch'i ying-hsing" 試論宋代,書院制度之產生及其影響 (The rise and influence of private academies as a Sung institution), *SYC* 9:417–474 (1977).

Yoshida Tora 吉田寅. "Sōdai no kaieki ni tsuite" 宋代の回易について (Round-trip trade in Sung times), *Shichō* 52:23–32 (1954).

Yoshikawa Kōjiro 吉川幸次郎. "Sōjin no rekishi ishiki" 宋人の歴史意識 (The historical consciousness of the Sung people), *Tōyōshi kenkyū* 24.4: 1–15 (1966).

Yü Chia-hsi 余嘉錫. *Yü Chia-hsi lun-hsueh tsa-chu* 余嘉錫論學雜著 (Collected writings of Yü Chia-hsi). Peking, Chung-hua, 1963.

Yuan Chen 袁震. "Sung-tai hu-kou" 宋代戶口 (The Sung population), *Li-shih yen-chiu* 3:9–46 (1957).

Glossary-Index

Chinese characters are provided for names of persons and places, titles of books, and terms when they are needed for precise identification. They are omitted for well-known place names like Szechuan, authors and titles that occur in the Bibliography, titles of the Classics like *Mencius,* and familier terms like *yin* and *yang.*

Harvard East Asian Monographs

46. W. P. J. Hall, *A Bibliographical Guide to Japanese Research on the Chinese Economy, 1958–1970*

47. Jack J. Gerson, *Horatio Nelson Lay and Sino-British Relations, 1854–1864*

48. Paul Richard Bohr, *Famine and the Missionary: Timothy Richard as Relief Administrator and Advocate of National Reform*

49. Endymion Wilkinson, *The History of Imperial China: A Research Guide*

50. Britten Dean, *China and Great Britain: The Diplomacy of Commerical Relations, 1860–1864*

51. Ellsworth C. Carlson, *The Foochow Missionaries, 1847–1880*

52. Yeh-chien Wang, *An Estimate of the Land-Tax Collection in China, 1753 and 1908*

53. Richard M. Pfeffer, *Understanding Business Contracts in China, 1949–1963*

54. Han-sheng Chuan and Richard Kraus, *Mid-Ch'ing Rice Markets and Trade, An Essay in Price History*

55. Ranbir Vohra, *Lao She and the Chinese Revolution*

56. Liang-lin Hsiao, *China's Foreign Trade Statistics, 1864–1949*

57. Lee-hsia Hsu Ting, *Government Control of the Press in Modern China, 1900–1949*

58. Edward W. Wagner, *The Literati Purges: Political Conflict in Early Yi Korea*

59. Joungwon A. Kim, *Divided Korea: The Politics of Development, 1945–1972*

60. Noriko Kamachi, John K. Fairbank, and Chūzō Ichiko, *Japanese Studies of Modern China Since 1953: A Bibliographical Guide to Historical and Social-Science Research on the Nineteenth and Twentieth Centuries, Supplementary Volume for 1953–1969*

61. Donald A. Gibbs and Yun-chen Li, *A Bibliography of Studies and Translations of Modern Chinese Literature, 1918–1942*

62. Robert H. Silin, *Leadership and Values: The Organization of Large-Scale Taiwanese Enterprises*

63. David Pong, *A Critical Guide to the Kwangtung Provincial Archives Deposited at the Public Record Office of London*

64. Fred W. Drake, *China Charts the World: Hsu Chi-yü and His Geography of 1848*

65. William A. Brown and Urgunge Onon, translators and annotators, *History of the Mongolian People's Republic*

66. Edward L. Farmer, *Early Ming Government: The Evolution of Dual Capitals*

67. Ralph C. Croizier, *Koxinga and Chinese Nationalism: History, Myth, and the Hero*

68. William J. Tyler, tr., *The Psychological World of Natsume Sōseki*, by Doi Takeo

STUDIES IN THE MODERNIZATION OF THE REPUBLIC OF KOREA: 1945–1975